ISBN: 9781290004022

Published by:
HardPress Publishing
8345 NW 66TH ST #2561
MIAMI FL 33166-2626

Email: info@hardpress.net
Web: http://www.hardpress.net

LETTERS

OF

JOHN HAY

AND

EXTRACTS FROM DIARY

VOLUME I

WASHINGTON
1908

PRINTED BUT NOT PUBLISHED

Custom, amounting to rule, requires the building of some memorial for men of note at their death,—the carving of some statue,—the painting of some portrait,—suited to their careers; not to instruct the public but to please and satisfy their friends. As these memorials multiply and become a large branch of art and literature, both writers and readers show preference for figures that stand free, and for workmanship that places no artificial medium between the man and the public. Especially the men of many sides,—artists, poets, wits, men-of-the-world,—reject flattery, tolerate no artifice, want to be viewed in no strange light, and shame the literary workman who is so bold as to risk the chances of a comparison between his own powers and the subject he is trying to adorn or exhibit.

The method is sometimes hard in manner and always fragmentary, but is less annoying to the reader than the obtrusion of a third person; and it has been adopted in trying to collect material intended not to give John Hay his place in history, but to preserve the features and figure of the man as he moved or talked or showed himself to his friends and to society. To make this method of biography clearer, the responses should also be given, but this would require a group of figures, and would change the whole object of the art. As the portrait stands, it is meant to represent him alone, and if the lights are somewhat abrupt or broken, they are at least meant only to show a single form.

Therefore no comment or connection has been added to the text of these extracts, except an occasional note where some allusion seemed to need a name or date; but even the most intimate friend could not follow intelligently so long a story without an occasional reminder of a society which is fading from sight or has actually disappeared. These memoranda can be condensed into a small space and are not hard to remember. They begin with the conditions which explain how men like Hay came to exist in the western country.

All the Hays seem to have had a Scotch origin, but this American branch sprang from a soldier in the service of the Elector Palatine between 1700 and 1750 or thereabouts, who may have come to America with the swarm of emigrants from the Palatinate who invaded Pennsylvania in those days, but who was evidently a man of education and standing. One of his four sons, John, the eldest, settled in York, Pennsylvania, where he took a rather prominent position; while another, Adam, went a little further West, to Berkeley County at the bottom of the Shenandoah Valley in Virginia, bordering the Potomac River, where he settled.

iii

Tradition failed to tell whether Adam had a share in the Campaign of Braddock who passed up to Cumberland with his army in May, 1755; but he certainly shared in some part of Washington's career, for his son John, born February 13, 1775, remembered being patted on the head by Washington; and, since Washington's last visit to the neighborhood seems to have been in 1784, the boy was nine years old.

This son John is said to have found his father so strict a master that, before the boy came of age, he emigrated to Kentucky. Like Henry Clay and many other Virginians at the same time, he helped to build up the town of Lexington which claimed to be a center of western cultivation. There John Hay married Jemima Coulter and brought up a family of fourteen children; and there he stayed until 1830.

John Hay shared many of the views of Henry Clay; among the rest, his antipathy to General Jackson, and his want of sympathy with slavery. These two opinions defined social position in the West. They explain his removal in 1830 to free territory. At fifty-five years old he abandoned Kentucky and wandered away to the remote Sangamon County in Illinois where he helped to strengthen the town of Springfield. In the same year Abraham Lincoln, born in Kentucky in 1809, emigrated to Sangamon County. To this chance, possibly, the Third Chapter of the *Life of Lincoln* owes some of its sympathetic interest.

Old John Hay lived to be one of Lincoln's friends and supporters,—outlived him, in fact, a few days, just long enough to watch Lincoln's funeral pass his windows,—and died May 20, 1865, ninety years old, a monument of the past, leaving, among the other thirteen children, one son, Milton, at the head of the Bar, enjoying a professional and social position to be kept in mind as decisive on the career of his nephew the future Secretary of State.

Meanwhile another son, Charles, born in Kentucky, February 7, 1807, had been educated at Lexington, where classical training held its own, and had taken a degree as Doctor of Medicine at the Medical College there. He, too, shared in his father's antipathies, and also moved his residence across the Ohio River in 1830, but not so far as Springfield. He stopped at Salem in Indiana, only about thirty-five miles from Louisville on the Ohio River. By a curious coincidence, the leading lawyer of the place was named John Hay Farnham; he had married Evelyn Maria Leonard; and both Farnhams and Leonards were purest New England stock. The Farnhams were last from Newburyport, the Leonards from Middleboro, Massachusetts; and their connections covered the country. With the Farnhams, in Indiana, lived at that time Mrs. Farnham's sister, Helen Leonard, born not far from New Bedford and Fall River, at Assonet, February 7, 1809,—two years, to a day, younger than Charles Hay. They were married, October 12, 1831, and lived to great age, in great affection, respected far beyond the common by the society about them.

They had six children, all born at Salem in Indiana except the youngest. As all are mentioned in these letters, the names and dates of birth are best given in one note :—

Leonard, born December 3, 1834; enlisted as private soldier in the Fifth U. S. Infantry, 18 June, 1864; commissioned as Second Lieutenant in the Ninth U. S. Infantry, July 2, and First Lieutenant, September 29, of the same year. He remained in the service and became Captain in the same Regiment March 11, 1878.

Mary, born December 17, 1836, married October 8, 1863, Captain Woolfolk of the regular Army, who resigned after the war, and became Circuit Judge, dying at Denver in 1880. John, the future Secretary of State, born October 8, 1838. Charles, born March 23, 1841, Second Lieutenant in the Third U. S. Cavalry and Aide on General Hunter's staff during the Civil War. He resigned at the peace, and settled at Springfield, where he married May 10, 1865, Mary Ridgeley, also of Springfield, to whom the early letters constantly allude. Charles Hay became repeatedly Mayor of Springfield, and his brother's letters often refer to him.

All these children were born at Salem in Indiana. The youngest, Helen, was born September 13, 1844, in Warsaw, Illinois, where she was married in 1870 to

Harwood O. Whitney; and died June 19, 1873, as is told in the course of the story.

Nearly all the allusions in these letters, as far as they relate to the family, refer to Springfield. None of the young John Hay's letters to his father and mother, or to his family at Warsaw, have been found. He thought them too intimate to be kept. The gap is impossible to fill, for his relations with his father and mother were affectionate and confidential. The little aid that is at hand to fill the gaps of the correspondence can be given in the mere note that Dr. Charles Hay moved his residence to Warsaw, Illinois, in 1841. The town of Warsaw, on the Mississippi River, about eighty miles west of Springfield, happened to be then the newest hope of western ambition. There the boy John, at three years old, began life in surroundings very like those of a New England town. His father soon got a large practice, and rode far and wide about the neighborhood on horseback visiting his patients. His profession was a liberal one; his education was classical; his social position was that of a Whig and Virginian of the federalist school, relics of General Washington and John Marshall; and his wife belonged as little as himself to the Jacksonian democracy of the backwoods. They set their children a standard rather higher than they might have found in the East, where the young generation clung less closely to the ideals of the past. The greater world that lay outside of their Warsaw life would widen the children's education to their wants, but they would need to undo nothing that their parents had done; and, in the case of the boy John, as though they foresaw his easy contact with a multifarious life, they sent him in 1855 to Brown University in Rhode Island, where the Leonards felt most at home. There he took his degree in June, 1858.

When he quitted the University he saw his life before him in a path so plainly marked that he could scarcely miss it. Even as a young man he was very like himself, never greatly changing with years, and one of his last letters to Nicolay recalls the unity of his ambitions and achievements, marking how regularly his life had moved from phase to phase, from first to last, finding each phase easy. In 1858, he saw his uncle, Milton Hay, at Springfield, with a large law practice and a high social position, ready to receive him as a student in the office, and he knew that at Springfield law and politics went hand in hand. The law-office of Milton Hay opened into that of Abraham Lincoln. Mr. Lincoln was then immersed in the famous Lincoln-Douglas campaign and his political career was already certain to be in the front rank. No young man with tastes such as those of John Hay could have rejected such a chance. He went to Springfield to study law, and his first letters show him there, studying not law but French. The rest was simple. Like all, or nearly all, the old anti-slavery leaders, Mr. Lincoln was serious by nature, and more than most he tended to melancholy. Past fifty years of age, he was older than his years, and he found relief in the humor and cheeriness of those about him. With them, as John Hay himself told in his "Life in the White House" he was "the Lincoln of the Eighth Circuit, the cheeriest of talkers, the riskiest of story tellers"; but to the young man he was at the same time an object of great deference, as the extracts of diary show. At no time of his life could Hay's own manners have been called familiar, for, with all his gaiety he was a man of the world and knew how to be lively or serious with his surroundings, but this faculty may have seemed valuable at that moment to a man of Mr. Lincoln's nature; while, as the political situation took shape, Hay inevitably felt himself drawn towards its central figure, the most sympathetic among all Americans, living or dead.

To this natural affinity, chance added the accident that, among the very few men at Springfield with whom Hay could be intimate, the most obvious was John G. Nicolay, six years older than himself, German by origin and as intensely serious as he was thorough and exact. When Mr. Lincoln, on his election as President, decided to take Nicolay with him to Washington as Private Secretary, it was natural that both of them should have seen in Hay the aid they most needed to smooth their path, or to relieve their weariness, in the many-sided, exhausting and sometimes fretful personal relations of the White House.

Hay naturally and gladly came, perhaps hoping to make of the temporary station only a short step to some permanent career; but the series of extracts taken from his note books show how he was quickly caught and swept along by the outbreak of war, and their sequence is close enough to need no commentary, except an occasional reference to the *Life of Lincoln* where most of his material was used.

Neither do the two episodes in the winters of 1863 and 1864 need much comment. They tell their own story except so far as they leave to be inferred that Hay felt restless in the White House and wanted to be nearer the field of war. Evidently informed that the reconstruction of Florida would be a work of as much delicacy as importance, he sought a mission there, and devoted a winter to the task. He found the difficulties greater than he could overcome, and after much effort, gave up the scheme.

With the last extracts from the note books made in the White House, the story of this experience as Private Secretary abruptly ends; but these show that, before the assassination, Hay had asked and obtained the promise of an appointment abroad. Mr. Seward gladly took him into the service of the State Department on March 22, 1865. An ambitious young man had little or nothing to gain by remaining in a subordinate place in the White House, while before the new post abroad could be taken, the murder of Mr. Lincoln had already put an end to any chance of further usefulness at home. The letters and diary contain no allusion to the death of Mr. Lincoln and the account given in the History (Vol. x, pp. 300–301) is all that is known to have been written by Hay on the subject.

Equally little has been found in regard to his residence in Paris for the next two years. There he had John Bigelow as chief, and Napoleon III, to study. He took the experience as a necessary part of his education, but he never showed much interest in it, or much sympathy for France, and he expressed energetic antipathy for the Emperor. Very early in his residence, in August, 1865, only a few weeks after his arrival in Paris, he wrote the poem "Sunrise in the Place de la Concorde," which is the best record of his first diplomatic attitude and atmosphere. Readers of his life will be most struck by noticing that, almost in spite of himself, his imagination was filled much less by the "lurking jail-bird" that stole the treasure ot liberty, than by—

"The tremulous shafts of dawning
As they shoot on the Tuileries early,
Strike Luxor's cold gray spire ;
And wild in the light of the morning
With their marble manes on fire
Ramp the white Horses of Marly."

These were things which few Secretaries of Legation could see, and which were not on the line of preferment ; but nothing shows that Hay cared much for preferment at that time. After the strain of the Civil War, he felt, like most of the young men who were in it, a reaction and fatigue which took most naturally the form of poetry, although he settled readily into the routine of office-work and study of the language. This gained, after two years in Paris, he resigned and came home.

The letters begin here with the interesting series addressed to Nicolay who was then Consul in Paris. The situation at home was discouraging, but the quarrels of Andrew Johnson's administration happened at that moment to drive Mr. Motley from the Vienna mission, and Mr. Seward, with whom young Hay was always a favorite, invited him to go out as *chargé* till a new minister could be agreed upon. The letters at this point are full enough of his acts and thoughts to need no comment. They tell how, as soon as the new minister, Henry M. Watts, was confirmed, Hay resigned and came home. He had acquired only a certain knowledge of German and a large field of diplomacy.

Once more, in the following year, when President Grant's administration came into office and sent General Sickles to Spain as minister, the post of Secretary was offered to Hay, and he went to Madrid for a year. He seems then to have considered his diplomatic education complete, or sufficient, and returned to America, in the autumn of 1870, to seek his fortune in the press.

His letters first allude to an attempt to help Nicolay in managing the *Republican* at Chicago, which broke down for financial reasons; but they say little of his own literary doings; and although his *Castilian Days* and *Pike*

County Ballads gave him at this time, in 1871, a sudden popularity, he was always inclined to treat them as occasional trifles, and to think that they hurt, rather than helped, his career. For himself, he looked for more serious work, even to the law as profession, but he could not escape the field of the press for which he had fitted himself with extraordinary completeness; so that when Whitelaw Reid invited him into the office of the *New York Tribune,* he found himself at once so much at ease, and so pleasantly established, that he conquered even the prejudices of Horace Greeley, who remembered acutely the negotiations at Niagara described in the extracts of diary for July, 1864, but who soon appreciated the value of the young man in the new character of ally. The letters tell something, though not much, about the newspaper life of the years after 1871, which greatly colored and controlled the course of Hay's career. The *New York Tribune,* the only consistent and thorough Republican newspaper in New York, was itself a school, and stamped its character on all its staff. Seldom quite in harmony with the machinery of the party in the State, it had at times an energy and influence that rose against the machinery and broke down the men who controlled it. As an organ, the *New York Tribune* had hardly a rival, and as an ally, its value was great—perhaps decisive.

From this period, the letters show the steps of Hay's career so plainly as to need very little commentary. He had been no long time on the *Tribune* before he met and became engaged to Clara, daughter of Amasa Stone, of Cleveland, Ohio, which led to their marriage, February 4, 1874, and presently to his going to live in Cleveland. The change drew him away from the newspaper press, and allowed him to take up, with Nicolay, the long-intended *Life of Lincoln*. Of these years, 1874–1879, little, except the literary record, remains; but constant allusions to his children seem to need the note, that, of the four, the oldest, Helen, married in 1902, Payne Whitney. The second, Adelbert, born November 1, 1876, went as Consul to the Transvaal during the Boer War, and died tragically at New Haven in 1901; Alice, married James W. Wadsworth, Jr., of Geneseo, in 1902; lastly, Clarence, born December 19, 1884.

At last in 1879, after some hesitation, described in a remarkable letter from Whitelaw Reid, Mr. Evarts decided to invite Hay to reënter the service of the State Department; and, after an equal hesitation, Hay consented to serve as Assistant Secretary of State for two years while Mr. Evarts remained at the head of the Department. This renewal of activity in politics led to the very interesting series of letters to Whitelaw Reid in 1880 and 1881.

The story is more nearly consecutive than any other part of the life. After the difficult and delicate situation which followed the defeat of Grant at Chicago in 1880 and the nomination and election of Garfield, Secretary Blaine who succeeded Evarts in the Department of State would have been glad to keep Hay in office; but President Garfield would have liked still better to restore him to the White House, and actually proposed to raise the office of Private Secretary to a sort of position that would induce Hay to accept it. The letters on this subject are printed as far as they have been found.

Hay declined to return to duties which were never very much to his taste, and still less suitable to his position; but for the moment, he was called to other duties which he could not reject. The marriage of Whitelaw Reid and his wedding vacation in Europe imposed on some one the task of editing the *Tribune* in his absence, and Mr. Reid asked Hay to do him this favor, which, at the moment, seemed not very serious. Scarcely had Hay taken charge of the office than the feud with Roscoe Conkling broke out, followed by the assassination of Garfield, events in which the *Tribune* was deeply involved.

The letters show that at about this time, Hay had fancied himself ambitious to enter Congress, and was surprised to find, when the object came within his grasp, that he had deceived himself; that he had already seen enough of practical politics. He turned back, very willingly, to literature, and between 1882 and 1890, completed with Nicolay the *Lincoln*, which was laboriously edited in the *Century* and afterwards published in ten volumes. The letters on this subject are mostly casual, brief and strictly critical; only a few have been selected, merely to show their character and fill the series.

The years between 1890 and 1897 offer no great public interest in Hay's correspondence. He took no active part in politics under the administrations of Cleveland and Harrison. His personal relations were with the Ohio candidates, Garfield, John Sherman and William McKinley, or with Mr. Blaine, and such letters as he wrote to them are lost, or of little interest. With Mr. McKinley whose candidacy grew slowly in dimensions, relations became closer than with the others, but seem never to have led to correspondence. The election of McKinley as President in November, 1896,—an election in which Hay had taken an active though not very public part,—brought upon him the question of office. Never eager for prominence, Hay inclined to put forward Whitelaw Reid as the proper representative of the *Tribune* influence to which the election of McKinley was largely due; but Mr. McKinley decided the question for himself by appointing Hay as Ambassador in London. The choice was personal rather than political, and showed regard for the fitness of the public service rather than reward for service in the party.

Few letters of a private kind were written during the year or eighteen months of his residence as Ambassador, of which two months were passed in a trip to Egypt.

The Spanish war threw on him some unexpected cares in the summer of 1898, but the most serious consequence to him was its indirect effect in breaking down the strength of Secretary John Sherman, which caused President McKinley to summon Hay to Washington as soon as possible, in September, 1898. Then began his service in the State Department, rivalling that of James Madison, John Quincy Adams, William Henry Seward, and Hamilton Fish in length, and surpassing all rivalry in the volume of work accomplished.

The letters selected to carry on the story during these seven years have been chosen only for their personal, not at all for their public interest. None have been admitted that are supposed to have official value or even diplomatic bearing on any part of the actual interests of the country. These matters belong to history and to the administration of President McKinley as a whole; the records are in the Department of State; and the interests are still more or less open to dispute. The State Department itself would not assist, and might not permit, the story of its long and laborious efforts, involving complicated conditions, in widely separated parts of the world to be laid bare,—or still worse, mangled in telling,—while the same interests in the same, or similar forms are still active. The story cannot be treated as the personal property of a government official, even in the expressions of private correspondence; but, in order to explain the allusions that occur in such letters as are admitted, the succession of business needs to be noted as it occurred.

Hay assumed charge of the office in October, 1898, and found a number of important matters, some of them pending since fifty years, waiting action. The result of the Spanish war and the changes in the balance of power in Europe gave him a hope of settling them, and he began at once with the Clayton-Bulwer Treaty which obstructed the legislative scheme for a Nicaragua Canal. After much negotiation he signed with Sir Julian Pauncefote, on February 5, 1900, a convention that was submitted to the Senate and proved unsatisfactory to that body, which adopted a number of amendments.

The amendments in their turn were unsatisfactory to Hay, who dropped the old convention, and renewed negotiations with Sir Julian Pauncefote, ending in the signature of a new convention, November 18, 1901, which the Senate accepted, December 16, by a vote of 72 to 6. Frequent allusions occur in his private letters to this negotiation which consumed three years of time and severely strained his strength. Its success at last marked the turning point of his career and established his authority, till then much contested.

At the same time and for similar objects he negotiated with Denmark a Treaty for the purchase of St. Thomas, St. John's and Santa Cruz, for $5,000,000 signed January 24, 1902, and promptly ratified by the Senate, February 17, but rejected by the Danish Senate, or upper house, by a tie vote on October 22. This failure seriously impaired the measures necessary for the completion of the Isthmian Canal; but a greater embarrassment was caused by the sudden abandonment of the Nicaragua Route, for which the necessary diplomatic arrangements had been made, and the purchase of the Panama Route from the French company, by an Act approved June 28, 1902, which threw on Hay the task of dealing with the Government of Colombia. For reasons which are not in place here, he failed in his negotiations with Colombia, and the knot was cut by the negotiation of what was called the Bueno-Varilla Treaty, guaranteeing the independence of the Republic of Panama, ratified by the Senate on February 23, 1904, by a vote of 66 to 14.

This series of negotiations, covering six years, carried out a policy desired and affirmed by the United States Government in all its branches, without party distinction, for at least fifty years, and for its creation or principle Hay had no share of responsibility. Likewise in negotiating, with the President's approval, a long series of Reciprocity Treaties, he acted under what the President conceived to be the mandate of the Republican Party Platform adopted at Philadelphia, June 20, 1900. The Republican Senators thought otherwise and admitted no discussion. All these Treaties failed. On the other hand, a number of Treaties aiming at the creation of Courts of Arbitration and peaceful settlement of disputes, met little or no opposition, since they seemed to interfere with no interest.

His arrangement of the Samoan question with Germany by the Treaty of December 22, 1899,—one of his first and most serious measures—was allowed by common and tacit consent, to pass almost unnoticed; but the Alaskan question with Canada gave an infinity of trouble, and the Convention signed at Washington, January 24, 1903, and approved February 11, arranging for a final decision of the Canadian claim, was probably his highest triumph of delicate and difficult manipulation against tripartite reluctance.

Even this hardly gave him so much personal annoyance as was caused by the affairs of Venezuela, to which his letters scarcely refer. His rule in diplomacy was to settle all questions, if possible, by word of mouth, and to write few papers. This practice reversed the old custom of American diplomacy, but reached results more rapidly. His name is attached to no state papers such as fill the records of Jefferson, J. Q. Adams, or Webster and Marcy; it is attached only to the results; yet even the results sometimes fade out of sight when the student tries to fix precisely their nature. This is especially true of the field where he won most fame. The phrases "open door" and "administrative entity" may alone survive as the only literary record of five or six years filled with incessant activity in the affairs of the extreme east; and these phrases, both in what they express and what they avoid expressing, show Hay's method:—a method that he may have learned from Abraham Lincoln. Not averse to the strongest measures when he could see no choice, he relied by instinct on patience and good-temper, but above all on his judgment. The manner in which he dealt with the Chinese and Manchurian problem cannot yet be told in his own words; too many interests and persons are still involved; and a partial or garbled account would be worthless for the portrait; but future text books of American diplomacy will probably use this story as their standard of instruction. Students will be shown how a situation of extreme delicacy, bristling with possible errors, was managed without a mistake, and made to yield an unparalleled reputation at the cost of no display of force. The patience, the persistence, the good-temper with which Hay pursued his object, from the moment of his instructions of September 6, 1899, to the telegraphic confirmation by the Senate, December 18, 1903, of his Treaty with China opening to him the Manchurian trade, with necessary consulates, are instructive enough in themselves, and, as lessons in diplomacy, deserve careful study; but they are much more instructive as a study of Hay himself, his peculiar combination of obstinate persistence with good humored caution,—of perfect self-control with singular, and what a highly competent critic called "delightful audacity." To the student, who alone penetrates these dim paths of international politics, the humor is more evident than the art, but it surprises and puzzles the reader, because it is not the humor of 1900 but rather the freshness of 1860. The hand is the hand of Hay, but the temper, the tone, the wit and genius bear the birthmark of Abraham Lincoln.

The student, noticing the ease and rapid resource with which Hay seemed always to handle these intricate and cumbrous problems, might think that he was favored by circumstances, but the record proves the contrary. His failures were many, and the friction was greater than even the failures reveal. Very slowly he conquered control—in a certain degree—at home, and Congress ceased to regard him as an amateur politician; but, abroad, the circumstances turned decisively in his favor only when his strength was exhausted, and death was a matter of days. The letters, if read attentively, show that his ultimate triumph was one of judgment, not of act, for he could risk no act that Congress could be depended upon to approve; and that he was still carrying the load of affairs, in their fullest strain, when at the close of the Fifty-eighth Congress, March 3, 1905, his strength gave way, and he was obliged to sail, on March 18, for Europe. The letters follow him to Nauheim, Paris and London; where, only at the moment of his return to America he heard, on June 1, the result of the battle of Tsushima. On June 6, he sailed from Liverpool; on June 8, the Tsar accepted mediation. It was too late for him to complete his own work. The President completed it for him, and the letters can only follow him back for a few days to Washington, and thence to his country house at Lake Sunapee in New Hampshire, where he died July 1, 1905.

LETTERS
OF
JOHN HAY

TO MISSES JULIA, ANNIE AND MARY R——.

Springfield, Ill.,
This afternoon,
Six o'clock.

TO THE MISSES R——:[1]

I am lamentably ignorant as to whether Goldsmith is one of your favorite poets, but if he is, you have doubtless admired his beautiful and merciful lines:—

> No Phlox that range the valley free
> To slaughter I condemn;
> Taught by the power that pities me,
> I learn to pity them.

[1] 'Sent with a huge bunch of wild, blue phlox, 1860.'

Please follow the example of the gentle bard and pity the wretched condition of these chaotic flowers, and let your exquisite taste produce a combination that shall do justice to the sentiments with which we gathered and send them.

Yours "Haw"-fully,

JNO. G. NICOLAY.

Yours blue-mingly,

JOHN HAY.

HAY TO MISS MARY R——.

MADEMOISELLE MARIE:[1]

Vous avez, sans doute, entendu les mots sublimes d'un auteur inconnu,

"Si au premier vous ne reussissez pas
Tachez, tachez, une autre fois!"

Croyant en les principes de ces mots memorables, voulez vous, avec votre humble serviteur, prendre votre revanche sur le desappointment de le Jeudi

[1] 'We were all studying French at the time with a Mons. Anglade.' —M. R. H.

dernier, et faire un autre essai pour entendre le discours de M. Herndon ?

Le votre,

JEAN HAY.

´, `, ^ Distribuez les accents pour moi, s'il vous plait.

HAY TO MISS MARY R——.

Springfield, Ill.

MADEMOISELLE MARIE:

Je suis bien heureux que je puis annoncer a vous que M. Lincoln, l'honnête vieux Abe, va faire un discours a la salle du Cuisinier[1] demain au soir. Voulez vous rappeler votre promesse et m'accompagner ? J'espère d'entendre beaucoup de les choses bonnes, qui reposent comme Lazare apres son mort, en "Abraham's Bosom."

Peut-etre il est necessaire que j'explique la raison pourquoi je suis de si bonne heure en urgeant mes pretentions a votre compagnie. Voila la raison ! Il y aura ce soir une "Société à Coudre" et vous rencontrez là beaucoup de vos amis et vos adoreurs.

[1] Cook's Hall.

Est-il possible que vous voulez vous souvenir de votre engagement, sans que je le mentionne a vous? Je pense que je suis "Out of sight, out of mind;" mais, absent ou present, je suis Tout a vous.

HAY TO MISS MARY R——.

Springfield, Ill.

MISS MARY:

I remember having heard, in the innocent days when I went to Sunday School, some advice to the effect that if mine eye offend me I shall pluck it out and cast it from me. I have been strongly tempted to follow the admonition during the last few days in which I have been playing the part of the sullen Cyclops. But now I can adopt in some measure the language of the poet and say:—

"Thee I revisit safe."

I intended that quotation at first to refer to the "Holy Light" referred to by the blind bard, but won't it be neater to read it as it is?

Circumstances over which I had no control,—convenient phrase!—prevented me from sending you last evening the explanation I had written.

I use the first moment of my enfranchisement to beg the privilege of making some other engagement with you to go somewhere to see or hear something or somebody. Prayer-meeting *par example!* R. S. V. P.

All my visual powers have been employed since I last saw you in a diligent and delighted perusal of the columns of the Lincoln Clarion; a paper filled with useful reading, and edited with great decision of character.[1]

Yours of course.

HAY TO MISS MARY R——.

Springfield, Illinois.

MISS MARY:

I think we will at length have an opportunity, this evening, to discover the important principles that underlie the great contest between Symbolicism and Anti-Symbolicism, M. Anglade. If you are interested in this momentous subject, will you go with me this evening to the Lutheran Church, Providence and the weather permitting?

[1] "The *Lincoln Clarion* had published one of my school-girl compositions on "Decision of Character."—M. R. H.

Besides the pleasure to be derived from the orations of the zealous young soldiers of the Church Militant, there is a further inducement in the music that you will ye-aw if you have ye-aws to ye-aw. You will remember the music is very en-*ticin*.

I particularly admire the neat and unobtrusive manner in which that pun is introduced. I flatter myself I can do some things![1]

HAY TO MRS. R——.

Executive Mansion,
March 19, 1861.

MY DEAR MRS. R——:

An enterprising genius has just opened a little collection of Japanese curiosities under Willard's, and everybody goes there and gets unmercifully cheated. I was beguiled into the shop to-day and my eyes fell upon these little mother-of-pearl trinkets. I inquired their possible use and was told they were used in Japanese gambling, but were sold here for counters. I remembered the pleasant whist-parties at your house, and take

[1] "Mrs. Tyson was singing in the Lutheran Church."

the liberty of sending them. There is nothing domestic about them. The box, the wood and the paper are all *d'outre mer*.

Mr. B—— and his *cara sposa* left us to-day. It made me positively homesick. I would give everything for a day or two in Springfield. Not that I love Washington less, but that I love Springfield more. This town will be very pleasant after a while when we have leisure to enjoy it.

With great respect.

HAY TO MISS MARY R——.

Washington, 1861.

MY DEAR FRIEND:

I send you this book[1] because it is new—that is its only recommendation. It sketches with the most miraculous fidelity characters that are not worth sketching. It reminds me of a satiric cartoon of a Dutch painter, representing Art knocking in vain at his door, and the artist within industriously engaged in drawing an old shoe. This woman has wonderful power but is wasting it on unworthy subjects.

[1] George Eliot's *Silas Marner*.

There is something strange, almost startling in this story. There is not one single character in it who is not below mediocrity in mind, morals and manners. Yet these people, so drearily commonplace, in actual life, move us strongly in the book. It is not sympathy with the people; it is sympathy with the success of the portraits.

When women write books they make young people fall in love very foolishly. I want to write a novel on common-sense principles and change all that, some day, when I have grown rich and idle, and have forgotten to-day and yesterday.

We are very jolly here now, on a warfooting. We are hoping for a little brush with the traitors, but are very much afraid they will deprive us of that pleasure.

. . . . I wish I were in Springfield for a little while. I am afraid to leave here just now, lest I should lose some fun in my absence.

Your friend.

DIARY.

April 18, 1861.

The White House is turned into barracks. J. L—— marshalled his Kansas warriors to-day at

Willard's and placed them at the disposal of Major H——, who turned them to-night into the East Room. It is a splendid company, worthy such an armory. Besides the western jayhawkers, it comprises some of the best material of the east. Senator P—— and old Anthony B—— stood shoulder to shoulder in the ranks. J. L—— walked proudly up and down the ranks with a new sword that the Major had given him. The Major has made me his aid, and I labored under some uncertainty as to whether I should speak to privates or not.

. . . . All day the notes of preparation have been heard at the public buildings and the armories. Everybody seems to be expecting a son or brother or "young man" in the coming regiments.

To-night Edward brought me a card from Mrs. Ann S. S—— expressing a wish to see the President on matters concerning his personal safety. As the Ancient was in bed, I volunteered to receive the harrowing communication. Edward took me to the little room adjoining the hall, and I waited. Mrs. S——, who is neither young nor yet fair to any miraculous extent, came in leading a lady, who was a little of both, whom she introduced as Mrs. Col. L——. I was delighted at this chance interview with the Medea, the Julia, the Mona Lisa of my stage-struck days. After many hesitating and bashful trials, Mrs. L—— told the impulse that brought them. Some young Virginian, long-haired, swaggering chivalrous of course, and indiscreet friend, had come into town in great anxiety for a new saddle, and meeting her had said that he, and half a dozen others, including a dare-devil guerilla from Richmond, named F——, would do a thing within forty-eight hours that would ring through the world. Connecting this central fact with a multiplicity of attendant details, she concluded that the President was either to be assassinated or captured. She ended by renewing her protestations of earnest solicitude, mingled with fears of the impropriety of the step. L—— has made her very womanly since he married her. Imagine J. M. D—— a blushing, hesitating wife!

They went away, and I went to the bedside of the Chief *couché*. I told him the yarn; he quietly grinned. Going to my room I met the Captain. He was a little boozy and very eloquent. He dilated on the troubles of the time, and bewailed the existence of a garrison in the White House, "to give eclat to J. L——!"

H. Lamar came in about midnight saying that Cash Clay was drilling a splendid company at Willard's Hall, and that the town was in a general tempest of enthusiastic excitement. Which not being very new, I went to sleep.

Friday, April 19. Early this morning I consulted with Major Hunter as to measures proper to be taken in the matter of guarding the house. He told me that he would fulfil any demand I should make. The forenoon brought us news of the destruction of Government property at Harper's Ferry. It delighted the Major, regarding it as a deadly blow at the prosperity of the recusant Virginia.

I called to see Joe Jefferson, and found him more of a gentleman than I had expected. A very intellectual face, thin and eager, with large, intense blue eyes, the lines firm, and the hair darker than I had thought. I then went to see Mrs. Lander, and made her tell her story all over again "just by way of a slant." Miss Lander the sculptor was there. Coming up, I found the streets full of the bruit of the Baltimore mob,[1] and at the White House was a nervous gentleman who insisted on

[1] *Abraham Lincoln*, IV, 123. The attack on the Sixth Massachusetts Regiment took place in Baltimore towards noon this day.

seeing the President to say that a mortar battery has been planted on the Virginia heights, commanding the town. He separated himself from the information and instantly retired. I had to do some very dexterous lying to calm the awakened fears of Mrs. L—— in regard to the assassination suspicion.

After tea came P—— and P—— from Baltimore. They came to announce that they had taken possession of the Pikesville Arsenal in the name of the Government—to represent the feeling of the Baltimore conservatives in regard to the present imbroglio there, and to assure the President of the entire fidelity of the Governor and the State authorities. The President showed them H—— and B——'s despatch, which (said) "Send no troops here. The authorities here are loyal to the Constitution. Our police force and local militia will be sufficient;" meaning as they all seemed to think, that they wanted no Washington troops to preserve order; but, as S—— insists, that no more troops must be sent through the city. S—— seemed to agree with S——. His answer to a despatch of inquiry was:—"Governor H—— has no authority to prevent troops from passing through Baltimore." S—— interpolated, "no right."

P—— and P—— seemed both loyal and hopeful. They spoke of the danger of the North being roused to fury by the bloodshed of to-day and pouring in an avalanche over the border. The President most solemnly assured them that there was no danger :—"Our people are easily influenced by reason. They have determinded to prosecute this matter with energy, but with the most temperate spirit. You are entirely safe from lawless invasion."

W—— came up to say that young H—— saw a steamer landing troops off Fort Washington. I told the President. S—— immediately drove to S——'s.

About midnight we made a tour of the house. H—— and the Italian exile V—— were quietly asleep on the floor of the East Room, and a young and careless guard loafed around the furnace fires in the basement; good looking and energetic young fellows, too good to be food for gunpowder, —if anything is.

Miss D—— called to-day to offer her services in the hospital branch. She makes the most munificent and generous offers.

April 20, 1861. Colonel Washington called this morning but could not see the President.

It would seem like a happy chance to have a General Washington living and fighting among us at this time.

The streets were full of the talk of Baltimore. It seems to be generally thought that a mere handful of men has raised this storm that now threatens the loyalty of a State.

I went up with N——, P—— and W—— to see the Massachusetts troops quartered in the Capitol. The scene was very novel. The contrast was very painful between the grey-haired dignity that filled the Senate Chamber when I saw it last, and the present throng of bright-looking Yankee boys, the most of them bearing the signs of New England rusticity in voice and manner, scattered over the desks, chairs and galleries, some loafing, many writing letters slowly and with plough-hardened hands, or with rapid-glancing clerkly fingers, while G—— stood patient by the desk and franked for everybody. The Hall of Representatives is as yet empty. Lying on a sofa and looking upward, the magnificence of the barracks made me envy the soldiers who should be quartered there. The wide-spreading sky-lights overarching the vast hall like heaven, blushed and blazed with gold and the heraldic devices of the married States, while, all around it, the eye was rested by the massive simple splendor of the stalagmitic bronze reliefs. The spirit of our institutions seemed visibly present to inspire and nerve the acolyte, sleeping in her temple beside his unfleshed sword . . . .

The town is full to-night of feverish rumors about a meditated assault upon the town, and one, which seems to me more probable, on Fort McHenry. The garrison there, is weak and inadequate, and in spite of the acknowledged bravery of R—— and H——, it must fall if attacked.

E—— telegraphs that his regiment has been raised, accepted, and that he wants them sent to Fort Hamilton for preliminary drill. C—— authorised the answer that the commander there should have orders to that effect. Much is hoped from the gallant Colonel's Bloodtubs. They would be worth their weight in Virginia currency in Fort McHenry to-night.

The Massachusetts men drilled to-night on the Avenue. They afford a happy contrast to the unlicked patriotism that has poured ragged and unarmed out of Pennsylvania. They step together well, and look as if they meant business.

J. L—— wrote a note to the President to-day,

offering to bring any assignable number of northern fighting men over the border at the shortest possible notice. Gen. S—— seems to think that four or five thousand men will be a sufficient garrison to hold this town against any force that may be brought out from Maryland or Virginia woods.

April 21 (Sunday). This morning came a penitent and suppliant crowd of conditional secessionists from Baltimore, who, having sowed the wind, seem to have no particular desire to reap the whirlwind. They begged that no more federal troops should be sent through Baltimore at present; that their mob was thoroughly unmanageable, and that they would give the government all possible assistance in transporting its troops, safely, across the State by any other route. The President, always inclined to give all men credit for fairness and sincerity, consented to this arrangement, contrary to the advice of some of his most prominent counsellors; and afterwards said that this was the last time he was going to interfere in matters of strictly military concernment; that he would leave them hereafter wholly to military men.

I spoke of the intended resignation of Col. M——. The Tycoon was astonished. Three days ago M—— had been in his room making the loudest protestations of undying devotion to the Union. This canker of secession has wonderfully demoralised the army. Capt. F—— is the firmest and soundest man I meet. He seems to combine great honesty of purpose with accurate and industrious business habits and a lively and patriotic soldier's spirit that is better than anything else to-day.

This morning we mounted the battlements of the Executive Mansion, and the Ancient took a long look down the bay. It was a "water-haul."

Any amount of feverish rumors filled the evening. The despatch from M. A——, in regard to 1,500 Massachusetts troops being seen off Annapolis, seemed to please the President very much. Then there was a Fort Monroe rumor and a 7th Regiment rumor, and a Rhode Island rumor; all which, to-morrow will sift.

We passed the evening pleasantly at E——'s, where were the English Legation, and returned to find V—— and his borderers guarding the imperial palace, pacing in belted and revolvered dignity, up and down the wide portico, to give style and tone to the defensive guard, looking, as he said, like gentlemen in feature and dress. We went up and found a despatch stating that no troops had arrived at the Navy Yard. *Tant pis* we said, and slept.

April 22, 1861. . . . . The whining traitors from Baltimore were here again this morning. The President, I think, has done with them. In conversation with Major H—— last night, in reply to the Major's blunt assertion that the troops should have been brought through Baltimore if the town had to be leveled to the earth, he said that that order commanding them to return to Pennsylvania was given at the earnest solicitation of the Maryland conservatives who avowed their powerlessness in Baltimore, but their intention to protect the federal troops elsewhere, granted them as a special extension; as an exhaustion of the means of conciliation and kindness. Hereafter, however, he would interfere with no war measures of the army.

A young lady called to-day from Baltimore, sent by her father, H. P——, Esq., to convey to the Government information as to the state of affairs in the Plug-ugly city. She was very pretty and southern in features and voice, and wonderfully plucky and earnest in the enunciation of her devotion to the Stars and Stripes. She stated that the mails had been stopped at the Baltimore Post-office—arms expected from Virginia—Fort McHenry to be attacked to-night—the scared Commanders here thoroughly traitorous, and other things. I met her again this afternoon and talked three hours. Her quiet courage and dauntless patriotism brought back to me the times of De Montfort and Queen Eleanor, and the girl of Dom Remy. I gained a new idea of the possibilities of true, brave hearts being nourished in Republics. Just as she stepped into her carriage, her friend called her "Lilie," and I knew her name. She seemed so heart whole in her calm devotion to the Union that flirtation died in her presence and better thoughts than politicians often know, stole through the mind of one who listened to the novelty of an American woman, earnest, intelligent, patriotic and pretty.

This afternoon the Pocahontas and the Anacostia came peacefully back from their cruise and folded their wings in the harbor. The Pocahontas has done her duty at Norfolk and is welcome to our bay, with its traitor-haunted shores. She reports no batteries at the White House Point, and makes no record of any hostile demonstration from the banks of Alexandria. The very fact of the Pocahontas coming so quietly in, is a good one.

A telegram intercepted on its way to Baltimore states that our Yankees and New Yorkers have landed at Annapolis. Weary and foot-sore but very welcome, they will probably greet us to-morrow.

. . . . It is amusing to drop in some evening at C——'s Armory. The raw patriots lounge elegantly on the benches, drink coffee in the ante-room, change the boots of unconscious sleepers in the hall, scribble busily in editorial note-books, while the sentries snore at the doors, and the grizzled Captain talks politics on the raised platform, and dreams of border battle and the hot noons of Monterey.

It was melodramatic to see C. C—— come into the President's reception room to-day. He wore, with a sublimely unconscious air, three pistols and an Arkansas tooth pick, and looked like an admirable vignette to 25 cents worth of yellow-covered romance.

Housekeepers here are beginning to dread famine. Flour has made a sudden spring to $18 a barrel, and corn-meal rejoices in the respectable atmosphere of $2.50 a bushel. Willard is preparing for war, furling all sails for the storm. The dinner-table is lorn of *cartes,* and the tea-table reduced to the severe simplicity of pound-cake.

April 23. This morning D. W—— came rushing into the office, looking for S—— with what he called important news. He said that the two ships at the Navy Yard were the Pawnee and the Kingston. They brought marines and naval stores from Norfolk, which place they left after carrying what government property they could not remove. The Premier cursed quietly because the Baltic had not come; told W—— not to contradict the report that the Baltic had come; said the treason of H—— would not surprise him; that the Seventh could cut their way through three thousand rioters; that Baltimore delenda est; and other things,—and strolled back into the audience chamber.

At dinner we sat opposite old Gen. S——, who was fierce and jubilant. No frenzied poet ever predicted the ruin of a hostile house with more energy and fervor than he issued the rescript of destiny against Baltimore. "We've got 'em," he said. "It is our turn now. We keep steadily one week ahead of them, as S—— says. We have burned their hospital and poor-house, Harper's Ferry and the Norfolk Navy Yard. Now let them fight or starve." He was peculiarly disgusted with the impertinence of Delaware. "The contemptible little neighborhood without population enough for a decent country village, gets upon her hind legs and talks about armed neutrality. The only good use for traitors is to hang them. They are worth more, dead than alive." —Thus the old liberty-loving Teuton raged.

A gaunt, tattered, uncombed and unshorn figure appeared at the door and marched solemnly up to the table. He wore a rough, rusty overcoat, a torn shirt, and suspenderless breeches. His thin hair stood fretful-porcupine-quill-wise upon his crown. He sat down and gloomily charged upon his dinner. A couple of young exquisites were eating and chatting opposite him. They were guessing when the road would be open through Baltimore. "Thursday!" growled the grim apparition; "or Baltimore will be laid in ashes."

It was J. L——.

To-night there seems to be reliable news at the State Department that the Seventh Regiment and the Massachusetts troops would start from Annapolis to-night, and through the favoring moonlight march to the Junction, where the Government has possession of the Road. The hostile peasantry can harass them fearfully on the way, from fence-corners and hill-sides, if they are ready and brave. . . . A large and disappointed throng gathered at the Depot this morning hoping to get deliverance. But the hope was futile. They seem doomed to see the rising of the curtain. . . .

April 24. . . . This has been a day of gloom and doubt. Everybody seems filled with a vague distrust and recklessness. The idea seemed to be reached by Lincoln when chatting with the volunteers this morning, he said: "I don't believe there is any North! The Seventh Regiment is a myth! Rhode Island is not known in our geography any longer. You are the only Northern realities." Seward's messengers, sent out by the dozen, do not return. The Seventh and Butler's are probably still at Annapolis. A rumor this evening says the Railroad is in the hands of the Government and the Seventh's sappers and miners are at work repairing it. . . .

April 25. At the request of the Tycoon, who imagined he had seen something significant steaming up the river, I went down to the Navy Yard. Saw D——, who at once impressed me as a man of great coolness and power. The boat was the Mt. Vernon, who reported everything right in the river.

About noon the Seventh Regiment came. I went to the Depot and saw L——, who communicated the intelligence of their peaceful passage, with which I straightway gladdened the heart of the Ancient. C. S—— was with him as I returned. He was just reading a letter from H—— advising the immediate manufacture of rifled cannon from the Chicopee Works. Lincoln seemed to be in a pleasant, hopeful mood, and, in the course of the conversation, partially foreshadowed his present plan. He said: "I intend, at present, always leaving an opportunity for change of mind, to fill Fortress Monroe with men and stores; blockade the ports effectually; provide for the entire safety of the Capital; keep them quietly employed in this way, and then go down to Charleston and pay her the little debt we are owing her."

. . . . General B[utler] has sent an imploring request to the President to be allowed to bag the whole nest of traitorous Maryland legislators and bring them in triumph here. This the Tycoon, wishing to observe every comity even with a recusant State, forbade.

To-day we got a few letters and papers and felt not quite so forlorn. . . .

April 26. Massachusetts and Rhode Island troops in large numbers arrived to-day. . . . I called on S[prague], the Governor of Rhode Island, with N[icolay] A small insignificant youth, who bought his place; but who is certainly all right now. He is very proud of his company, of its wealth and social standing.

C[arl] S[churz] was here to-day. He spoke with wild enthusiasm of his desire to mingle in this war. He has great confidence in his capability of arousing the enthusiasm of the young. He contemplates the career of a great guerilla chief with ardent longing. He objects to the taking of Charleston and advises forays on the interior states. . . .

The Seventh Regiment band played gloriously on the shaven lawn at the south front of the Executive Mansion. The scene was very beautiful. Through the luxuriant grounds, the gaily dressed crowd idly strolled, soldiers loafed on the promenades, the martial music filled the sweet air with vague suggestion of heroism, and C. S—— and the President talked war.

April 28. All this blessed Sunday, free from war's alarms, we have lounged *sans souci*. S—— and his staff called on the President; and the Cabinet dropped in and gave a last word to the new Proclamation, blockading Virginia. . . .

April 29. Going into N——'s room this morning, C. S—— and J. L—— were sitting. J—— was at the window, filling his soul with gall by steady telescopic contemplation of a secession flag impudently flaunting over a roof in Alexandria. "Let me tell you," said he to the elegant Teuton, "we have got to whip these scoundrels like h——l, C. S——. They did a good thing stoning our men at Baltimore and shooting away the flag at Sumter. It has set the great North a howling for blood, and they'll have it."

"I heard," said S——, "you preached a sermon to your men yesterday."

"No, sir! this is no time for preaching. When I went to Mexico there were four preachers in my regiment. In less than a week I issued orders for them all to stop preaching and go to playing cards. In a month or so, they were the biggest devils and best fighters I had."

An hour afterward C. S—— told me he was going home to arm his clansmen for the wars. He has obtained three months' leave of absence from his diplomatic duties, and permission to raise a cavalry regiment. I doubt the propriety of the movement. He will make a wonderful land pirate; bold, quick, brilliant and reckless. He will be hard to control and difficult to direct. Still, we shall see. He is a wonderful man.

April 30. . . . . Three Indians of the Pottawatomies called to-day upon their great father. . . . The President amused them greatly by airing the two or three Indian words he knew. I was amused by his awkward efforts to make himself understood by speaking bad English: *e. g.*— Where live now? When go back Iowa?

Frederick H—— and I dined together. He seems stung by the inaction which his lameness, besides his foreign duties, imposes upon him. He evidently chafes with generous emulation of the coming glories of S—— in the field. He is a delicate-souled and thoughtful genius, but has not the vigor and animal arrogance that help S—— to bully his way through life. H—— will probably indulge his bent for literature in the high solitude of Quito. He intimated a course of articles in the *A*—— and an ultimate book.

Coming home from the theatre I met B——, S—— and F—— coming out of the audience chamber. Going in, I saw the great map of Virginia, newly hung, and fronted by conscious-looking chairs. The air is full of ghastly promises for Maryland and Virginia. Meanwhile the north is growing impatient. Correspondents talk impertinently, and the *N. Y. T*—— advises the immediate resignation of the Cabinet, and warns the President that he will be superseded. . . .

May 1. . . . . There were a half-dozen good-looking members of the Seventh Regiment called upon the Commander-in-Chief of the Armies and Navies this afternoon. He was very frank and cordial with them. He spoke amusedly of the *Times's* proposition of deposing him, and said that the Government had three things to do:—Defend Washington; Blockade the Ports; and retake Government property. All the possible despatch was to be used in these matters, and it would be well if the people would cordially assist in this work before clamoring for more. The proclamation calling out the troops is only two weeks old. No people on earth could have done what we have in that time.

M. Blair came in with the intelligence that our office-holders had been quietly installed at Baltimore under the floating of the constellated banner, and that the police-board had removed the restriction on the sale of flour. He thought the outbreak at the Massachusetts passage was the work of secession officials who were unwilling to lose their lease of plunder. He thoroughly believed in the loyalty of Maryland. The President seemed to think that if quiet was kept in Baltimore, a little longer, Maryland might be considered the first of the redeemed. . . .

May 4. The Maryland disunionists — that branch of them represented by B. McL—— called to-day upon the President. . . . They roared as gently as 'twere any nightingale. The only point they particularly desired to press was that there was no special necessity at present existing for the armed occupation of Maryland. . . . They also implored the President not to act in any spirit of revenge for the murdered soldiers. The President coolly replied that he never acted from any such impulse; and, as to their other views, he should take them into consideration, and should decline giving them any answer at present.

Gen'l S—— gave orders to Gen'l B—— to occupy the Relay House as soon as practicable, and B—— instantly replied that he should hold divine service with his command there to-morrow (Sunday).

May 5. Which he did.

May 7. I went in to give the President some little items of Illinois news, saying among other things that S—— was behaving very badly. He replied with emphasis that S—— was a miracle of meanness; calmly looking out of the window at the smoke of two strange steamers puffing up the way, resting the end of the telescope on his toes sublime.

I spoke of the proposition of B—— to subjugate the South, establish a black republic in lieu of the exterminated whites, and extend a protectorate over them while they raised our cotton. He said: "Some of our northerns seem bewildered and dazzled by the excitement of the hour. D—— seems inclined to think that this war is to result in the entire abolition of slavery. Old Col. H——, a venerable and most respectable gentleman, impresses upon me most earnestly the propriety of enlisting the slaves in our army."

I told him his daily correspondence was thickly interspersed by such suggestions.

"For my own part," he said, "I consider the central idea pervading this struggle is the necessity that is upon us of proving that popular government is not an absurdity. We must settle this question now, whether, in a free government, the minority have the right to break up the government whenever they choose. If we fail, it will go far to prove the incapability of the people to govern themselves. There may be one consideration used in stay of such final judgment, but that is not for us to use in advance: That is, that there exists in our case an instance of a vast and far-reaching disturbing element, which the history of no other free nation will probably ever present. That, however, is not for us to say at present. Taking the government as we found it, we will see if the majority can preserve it."

He is engaged in constant thought upon his Message. It will be an exhaustive review of the questions of the hour and of the future. . . .

May 9. . . . There was a very fine matinee at the Navy Yard given by some musical members of the 12th New York. They sang well, the band played well, and the President listened well. After the programme the President begged for the Marseillaise. The prime gentleman gave the first verse and then generously repeated it, interpolating nonchalantly "Liberty or Death" in place of "Abreuve nos sillons" which he had forgotten.

Then we went down to the Pensacola and observed the shooting of the great Dahlgren gun Plymouth. . . . The President was delighted. . . .

May 10. C. S—— loafed into my room this morning, and we spoke of the slaves and their ominous discontent. He agreed with me that the Commandants at Pickens and Monroe were unnecessarily squeamish in imprisoning and returning to their masters the fugitives who came to their gates begging to be employed. . . . S—— says that thousands of Democrats are declaring that now is the time to remove the cause of all our woes. What we could not have done in many life-times the madness and folly of the South had accomplished for us. Slavery offers itself more vulnerable to our attack than at any point in any century, and the wild malignity of the South is excusing us before God and the world.

So we talked in the morning.

But to-night I saw a letter from Mrs. W—— stating that T. E——, T. W. H——, the essayist of Boston, and young J. B——, were "going to free the slaves." What we were dreaming of came over my mind with horrible distinctness, but I shrank from the apparition. This is not the time nor are these the men to do it. They should wait till the government gives some kind of sanction to the work. . . .

May 11. . . . . This afternoon the Marine Band played on the south lawn, and C. S—— sat with Lincoln on the balcony. After the President had kissed some thousand children, C—— went into the library and developed a new accomplishment. He played with great skill and feeling, sitting in the dusk twilight at the piano until the President came by, and took him down to tea. S—— is a wonderful man. An orator, a soldier, a philosopher, and exiled patriot, a skilled musician! He has every quality of romance and of dramatic picturesqueness. . . .

HAY TO JAMES A. HAMILTON.

Executive Mansion,
Aug. 19, 1861.

MY DEAR SIR:

I am the unluckiest wretch that lives. I did not receive the kind note you sent me until Friday night at Long Branch. As it was horribly dull there, I concluded instantly upon reading your kind invitation, to return to New York and go to you Saturday afternoon. But then I found there was no telegraphic station at Irvington or

Dobb's Ferry, and that I could not apprize you of my coming. I went down town and lunched with Mr. R—— at Exchange Place. Coming back I was thunder-struck to find you had been at my hotel and were gone.

There were only three resources left me:—Suicide, intoxication or profanity. As I never drink and am still living, you can imagine which I chose. I thought my stupidity could only be expiated by a rigorous penance. So I resolved not to return to Long Branch, not to enjoy myself in New York, but to go sulkily back to Washington and stay at my desk until my luck changed.

Some day, before long, I will take my fate by the throat and conquer it. It has become a monomania with me to eat salt with you at Nevis, and it shall be done.

Very gratefully.

HAY TO MRS. E——.

Executive Mansion,
Aug. 21, 1861.

DEAR MRS. E——:

If the events of the last few days were to be

taken as an earnest of the future, I would invest my surplus shekels in a cheap tombstone, write "Miserrimus" on it, and betake myself to Prussic acid glacé. I have been like Poe's Raven's "unhappy master whom unmerciful disaster followed fast and followed faster, till he thought all life a bore." It is not a particularly hilarious chronicle, but here it is.

Finding it hideously dull at Long Branch (the gay and festive Jenkins of the H—— is paid by the line for making the world believe that the place is not ghastly and funereal, the crowd a sort of queer half-baked New Jersey confectionery, with a tendency to stammer when spoken to and to flatten its nose against our windows while we ate), I determined to go up to New York and accept a most kind invitation from Col. Hamilton to come to him Saturday. Arriving there I found there was no telegraph to Irvington or Dobb's Ferry. I could not apprize him of my coming or arrange for him to meet me. I blasphemed at this a little, and went quietly down town and was busy for an hour or two. Coming back I found Mr. Hamilton's card at the Hotel. He had been and gone.

My rage transcended grief. I was so mad at myself that I was uncivil to everyone else. Mr.

D—— came in with brilliant plans for the next day. I mildly but firmly requested him to mobilize himself for an instant trip to the Court of His Most Sulphurous Majesty. I concluded to take a royal revenge on myself by ordering myself back to Washington.

I came and found the air like a damp oven. They are painting the White House, and the painters from their horrid hair (I mean their brushes) shake pestilence and things. The people in the streets are stupid or scared. It is a bad neighborhood.

I can do nothing but wish it were "not me but another man."

Let me tell you a fact which proves me insane or Washington preternaturally dull. Yesterday I went to dinner at Willard's late, and after taking my seat I saw a solitary diner at a distance. I took up my soup and walked. I sat down and ate dinner with

BING.

I was so dull he was almost endurable.

I have not seen Mr. E—— since I returned. I have not felt like proper company for a gentleman and a Christian. I have felt as outlawed as a hasheesh eater.

There is another offshoot of English nobility coming over in a day or two, a son of the Earl of M——, Hon. Robert B——. I hope W—— will find it out, and by way of showing him a delicate attention, take him to the observational settee whence, on clear afternoons is to be seen, windows favoring, the Presidential ensarking and bifurcate dischrysalisizing. In view of his late letter, I would mildly inquire "What next?" Please make your brother and sister remember me, and give my love to F——.

HAY TO NICOLAY.

(Washington) Aug. 21, 1861.

MY DEAR GEORGE:

Nothing new. An immense crowd that boreth ever. Painters, who make God's air foul to the nostril. Rain, which makes a man moist and adhesive. Dust, which unwholesomely penetrates one's lungs. Washington, which makes one swear.

There is not an item. We are waiting for your arrival to make one.

HAY TO NICOLAY.

Washington, Aug. 24 (1861).

DEAR GEORGE:

Yours of the 22d received this morning. I don't wish to hurry you, but write simply to say that Dr. P——'s prediction has been realized. I am flat on my back with bilious fever. I had a gay, old delirium yesterday, but am some better to-day. Doctor thinks I will be round in a day or two. Bob L—— came this morning bringing positive orders from his mother for me to join her at New York for an extension of her trip. Of course I can't go—as things look. There is no necessity whatever for you to return just now. There is no business in the office, and S—— is here all the time. He can do as well as either of us. As soon as I get able I shall leave. The air here is stifling. You had better stay as long as you like, for there is nothing but idleness here. As soon as I get on my pins I shall start. It will be a sort of breach of etiquette, but as Joe Gargery feelingly observes:—"Manners is manners, but your 'elth's your 'elth!"

Don't come till you get ready.

DIARY.

Aug. 22, 1861. A long hiatus! The nights have been too busy for jottings.

.... We went over to S——'s, found him comfortably slippered, and after talking about consular nuisances, went over to McC——'s. Everything seems going right. Discipline is perfecting. The Dry Tortugas have squelched mutiny. The drills and reviews keep the men alive. H—— is soon to go to Illinois as they need a head. At first he wanted to take McD—— but S—— objected. Regiments are constantly coming in, and arms for them. McC——'is growing jolly. S—— is in better humor than I have lately seen him.

Aug. 28. I went West and passed several days in St. Louis. Saw very much of F—— and his wife. He was quiet, earnest, industrious, imperious. She very much like him, though talking more and louder.

Oct. 10. To-night I went over to McC——'s quarters with the President and S——. L—— was with us part of the way. L—— was gasconading a little. He said he would like a good place to die in with a corporal's guard, to set the nation right in the face of the world after the cowardly shame of Bull Run. The President, as L—— walked off, said :—"If he really wanted a job like that, I could give it to him. Let him take his squad and go down behind Manassas and break up their railroad." S—— said he disbelieved in personal courage as a civilised institution. He had always acted on the opposite principle,—admitting you are scared, and assuming that the enemy is. If this matter had been managed on his basis, it would have been arranged satisfactorily before now.

We came to McC——'s quarters and met in the telegraph office a long and awkward youth who spoke in a high-pitched and rapid tone to S—— : —"We are just in from a ride of all day." S—— introduced him to me as Capt. Orleans. He went up-stairs to call McC——, and the President said quietly : "One doesn't like to make a messenger of the King of France, as that youth, the Count of Paris, would be, if his family had kept the throne."

McC—— came hurriedly in and began to talk with the President. They discussed the events of to-day and yesterday. McC—— was much pleased at the conduct of his men—no rowdyism or plundering to-day. He was merely to-day finishing yesterday's work. The rest of this week will be used in the same way. Says the President:—"We have gained a day on our sea expedition. The vessels will leave on the 14th, it is thought, instead of the 15th."

As we left, McC—— said:—"I think we shall have our arrangements made for a strong reconnoissance about Monday, to feel the strength of the army. I intend to be careful and do as well as possible. Don't let them hurry me is all I ask." "You shall have your own way in the matter, I assure you," said the President, and went home.

Oct. 12. To-night the President went to S——'s, I with him. At the door a telegram was handed him from McC—— stating that the enemy was before him in force and would probably attack in the morning. "If they attack," he added, "I shall beat them." We went to S——'s and talked of many things. S—— spoke of L——'s restlessness and griefs at inaction; his offered resignation, and resolve to go West and begin again,—that watching the Potomac was not congenial, and other such. Gen. S—— was already fixing his orders for exactly the work he wanted to do.

Col. S—— came in with despatches from McC——, ordering H——'s Bladensburg Brigade in—one countermanding and one reaffirming. S—— then went out to order transportation for 6,000.

G. V. F—— came in and began to talk about the great expedition that is fitting at Annapolis. He wants, when they have sailed, to have 14,000 more men detached from the Army of the Potomac to be held in readiness awaiting the result of the expedition. If it causes a retreat of the rebels, then this additional force can be easily spared. The fleet will probably sail on Tuesday, and will have some work to do at Fernandina, Pensacola, Mobile. Gen'l S—— told F—— that 3,500 men would be enough to take Mobile, assisted by their ships. F—— himself seemed very confident that the expedition would succeed. His only nervousness was in relation to submarine batteries which modern science has rendered very destructive and entirely feasible.

S—— spoke also of M——'s despatch which seems to contain a most cheering account of honest sympathy existing in the best class of English society towards us. M——'s letter embraced free and cordial conversations with Earl R——, Earl G——, C——, M. L——, Prince A—— and the Queen.

There was much talk of D. W——, in which the financial *sanssoucism* of the great man was strikingly prominent. S—— thought he would not live, nor C——, a tithe as long as J. Q. A——. The President disagreed with him, and thought W—— will be read forever.

Oct. 17. At S——'s to-night we met Capt. S—— who showed very bad taste by alluding to the Chicago Convention and S——. The President told a good yarn.

One day in Springfield shortly after some of the lower counties had held meetings and passed Resolutions eulogistic of Trumbull, John Wentworth sitting near Lincoln at breakfast one morning, said:—"Lincoln, have you seen them Resolutions?" "I have seen what I suppose you refer to."

"Them Trumbull fellers are going to trick you again."

"I don't see any trickery about it, and if there was, there is no way to help the matter."

"I tell you what, Lincoln," said John, with a look of unutterable sagacity; "You must do, like Seward does—get a feller to run you." It was vastly amusing to both the President and Secretary.

The Secretary of State talked about intercepted correspondence, and the double-dealing and lying of our English friends F—— and B——.

Going to McC——'s with B——, they talked about the campaign. McC—— thought the enemy were massing at Manassas. He said he was not such a fool as to buck against that place in the spot designated by the foe. While there the President received a despatch from S—— at Annapolis, asking for the 79th New York, the Highlanders. The President was vexed at this, and at S——'s intimation that the fleet would not sail before Sunday. McC—— was also bored by the request, but S—— strongly seconded it. McC—— said he would sleep on it.

We came away, the President still vexed at S——. At S——'s door he turned suddenly and said:—"I think I will telegraph to S—— that I will not break up McC——'s command, and that I haven't much hope of his expedition anyway."

"No," said S——, "You won't say discouraging things to a man going off with his life in his hands. Send them some hopeful and cheering despatch."

The President came home and this morning telegraphed S——:—"I will not break up Mc——'s army without his consent. I do not think I will come to Annapolis." This was all. I think his petulance very unaccountable.

Oct. 22. This has been a heavy day. Last night Col. B—— was killed at Leesburg at the head of his Brigade. Mc—— and the President talked sadly over it. Mc—— said, "There is many a good fellow that wears the shoulder-straps going under the sod before this thing is over. There is no loss too great to be repaired. If I should get knocked on the head, Mr. President, you will put another man immediately into my shoes." "I want you to take care of yourself," said the President.

McC—— seemed very hopeful and confident—thought he had the enemy, if in force or not. We left him making arrangements for the morrow. (During this evening's conversation, it became painfully evident that he had no plan, nor the slightest idea of what S—— was about).

To-night we went over again. McC—— was at Poolesville. Telegraphs that loss is heavy and that troops behaved well. All right in that quarter.

At S——'s to-night the President talked about Secession, Compromise, and other such. He spoke of a committee of southern pseudo-unionists coming to him before Inauguration for guaranties, etc. He promised to evacuate Sumter if they would break up their Convention, without any row or nonsense. They demurred. Subsequently he renewed proposition to S——, but without any result. The President was most anxious to prevent bloodshed.

I never heard secession made more absurd than by the conversation of to-night; S——, C——, K—— and Bishop McI——.

To-day Deputy-Marshal came and asked what he should do with process to be served on P—— in contempt business. I took him over to S——, and S—— said: "The President instructs you that the Habeas Corpus is suspended in this city at present, and forbids you to serve any process upon any officer here." Turning to me: "That is what the President says, is it not, Mr. Hay?" "Precisely his words," I replied; and the thing was done.

October 26. This evening the Jacobin Club, represented by T——, C—— and W—— came up to worry the administration into a battle. The agitation of the summer is to be renewed. The President defended McC——'s deliberateness. We then went over to the General's Headquarters. We found Col. K—— there. He was talking also about the grand necessity of an immediate battle to clean out the enemy at once. He seemed to think we were ruined if we did not fight. The President asked what McC—— thought about it. K—— answered:—"The General is troubled in his mind. I think he is much embarrassed by the radical difference between his views and those of Gen'l S——."

Here McC—— came in,—K—— went out,—the President began to talk about his wonderful new repeating-battery of rifled guns, shooting 50 balls a minute. The President is delighted with it, and has ordered ten, and asks McC—— to go down and see it, and if proper, detail a corps of men to work it. He further told the General that R. J—— wants the Maryland volunteers in Maryland to vote in November. All right.

They then talked about the Jacobins. McC—— said that W—— preferred an unsuccessful battle to delay. He said a defeat could be easily repaired by the swarming recruits. McC—— answered that "he would rather have a few recruits before a victory, than a good many after a defeat."

The President deprecated this new manifestation of popular impatience, but at the same time said it was a reality, and should be taken into the account:—"At the same time, General, you must not fight till you are ready."

"I have everything at stake," said the General; "if I fail, I will not see you again or anybody."

"I have a notion to go out with you, and stand or fall with the battle" . . . .

Oct. 27. We went over to S——'s to-night and found C—— and W—— there. They had been talking to S—— to get up a battle, saying that one must be fought; saying that defeat was no worse than delay, and a great deal more trash. M—— and S—— then began to growl about their guns. S—— and the President soon dried that up. W—— came in, a strong, healthy, hearty, senator, soldier and man. He was bitter on the Jacobins, saying the safety of the country demanded that the General should have his time. Going up to McC——'s the Leesburg business was discussed; McC—— saying that S——'s report would be in to-morrow; every one forebore comment.

. . . . The night of the 1st November we went over to McC——'s. The General was there and read us his General Order in regard to S——'s resignation and his own assumption of command. The President thanked him for it and said it greatly relieved him. He added:—"I should be perfectly satisfied if I thought that this vast increase of responsibility would not embarrass you." "It is a great relief, Sir! I feel as if several tons were taken from my shoulders, to-day. I am now in contact with you and the Secretary. I am not embarrassed by intervention." "Well," says the President, "draw on me for all the sense I have, and all the information. In addition to your present command, the supreme command of the army will entail a vast labor upon you." "I can do it all," McC—— said quietly.

Going to S——'s he talked long and earnestly about the matter. He had been giving a grave and fatherly lecture to McC—— which was taken in good part; advising him to enlarge the sphere of his thoughts, and feel the weight of the occasion.

Then we went up and talked a little while to the Orleans princes. De Joinville is deaf and says little. The boys talk very well and fluently. . . .

Nov. 8. Here is a cheeky letter just received.

MY DEAR SIR:

Gen'l W—— has resigned. Gen'l F—— must. Gen'l S—— has retired.

I have an ambition, and I trust a laudable one, to be Major-General of the United States Army.

Has anybody done more to deserve it? No one will do more. May I rely upon you, as you may have confidence in me, to take this matter into consideration?

I will not disgrace the position. I may fail in its duties.

Truly yrs.,

The President.

P. S.—I have made the same suggestion to others of my friends.

Nov. 11. To-night B——'s Germans had a torchlight procession in honor of McC——'s promotion. I never saw such a scene of strange and wild magnificence as this night-march was. Afterwards we went over to McC——'s and talked about the southern flurry. The President thought this a good time to feel them. McC—— said: "I have not been unmindful of that. We will feel them to-morrow." The President and the General were both very jolly over the news.

Nov. 13. I wish here to record what I consider a portent of evil to come. The President, Governor S—— and I went over to McC——'s house to-night. The servant at the door said the General was at the wedding of Col. W—— at Gen'l B——'s and would soon return. We went in, and after we had waited about an hour, McC—— came in, and without paying any particular attention to the porter who told him the President was waiting to see him, went up-stairs, passing the door of the room where the President and Secretary of State were seated. They waited about half an hour, and sent once more a servant to tell the General they were there; and the answer came that the General had gone to bed.

I merely record this unparalleled insolence of epaulettes without comment. It is the first indication I have yet seen of the threatened supremacy of the military authorities.

Coming home I spoke to the President about the matter, but he seemed not to have noticed it, specially, saying it was better, at this time, not to be making points of etiquette and personal dignity.

On the 27th of January the President issued his General War Order No. 1, to those whose direction it was to be. He wrote it without any consultation, and read it to the Cabinet, not for their sanction but for their information. From that time he influenced actively the operations of the campaign. He stopped going to McC——'s, and sent for the General to come to him. Everything grew busy and animated after this Order. It was not fully carried out in its details. Some of the Corps anticipated, others delayed action. Fort Henry and Fort Donaldson showed that H—— was doing his share. The Army of the Potomac still was sluggish. His next Order was issued after a consultation with all the Generals of the Potomac Army in which, as S—— told me next morning, "we saw ten Generals afraid to fight." The fighting Generals were McD——;

S——, H—— and K——, and B——. These were placed next day at the head of the Army Corps.

So things began to look vigorous. Sunday morning, the 9th of March, the news of the Merrimac's frolic came here. S—— was fearfully stampeded. He said they would capture our fleet, take Fort Monroe, be in Washington before night. The President thought it was a great bore, but blew less than S——. As the day went on, the news grew better. And at four o'clock the telegraph was completed, and we heard of the splendid performance of the Monitor. That evening we heard also of the evacuation of the Potomac batteries, the luckiest of all possible chances, as the worst thing about the Merrimac's damages was the fact that they would impede the enterprise of taking those batteries. This was McD——'s explanation to me when I told him of it.

At evening came the news of Manassas being evacuated; this came through contrabands. McC—— started instantly over the river. The next day the news was confirmed and the next night Manassas was occupied. People said a great deal about it, and thought a great deal more.

On the evening of the 11th of March, the President requested me to call together the heads of the Departments of War, State and Treasury. S[eward] came first. The President read to him General Order No. 3. He approved it thoroughly. He agreed with the President when the President said that though the duty of relieving Gen'l McC—— was a most painful one, he yet thought he was doing Gen'l McC—— a very great kindness in permitting him to retain command of the Army of the Potomac, and giving him an opportunity to retrieve his errors. S[eward] spoke very bitterly of the imbecility which had characterised the General's operations on the upper Potomac. The Secretary of State urged that the War Order go out in the name of S[tanton]. He said it would strengthen the hands of the Secretary, and he needed public confidence. While he was urging this, S[tanton] came in, and at once insisted that it go in the President's name. He said that a row had grown up between him and McC——'s friends, and he feared it would be thought to spring from personal feeling. The President decided to take the responsibility.

B[lair] was not consulted. The President knew that he would object to the disposition of F[remont], and preferred to have no words about it. B[lair] and the President continued on very good terms in spite of the publication of B——'s letter to F——. B—— came to explain it to the President, but he told him that he was too busy to quarrel with him. If he (B.) didn't show him the letter, he would probably never see it. He retained his old status in Cabinet councils. . . .

HAY TO NICOLAY.

March 31, 1862.

Little M—— sails to-day for down river. He was in last night to see Tycoon. He was much more pleasant and social in manner than formerly. He seems to be anxious for the good opinion of everyone.

HAY TO NICOLAY.

Thursday morning.

McC—— is in danger, not in front but in rear. The President is making up his mind to give him a peremptory order to march. It is disgraceful to think how the little squad at Yorktown keeps him at bay.

HAY TO NICOLAY.

Friday, April 4, 1862.

McC—— is at last in motion. He is now moving on Richmond. The secret is very well kept. Nobody out of the Cabinet knows it in town. Dick W—— is in a great fidget about it. He knows something is in the wind but can't guess what.

HAY TO NICOLAY.

Executive Mansion,
Washington, April 9, 1862.

Glorious news comes borne on every wind but the South Wind. While P—— is crossing the turbid and broad torrent of the Mississippi in the blaze of the enemy's fire, and G—— is fighting the overwhelming legions of B—— at Pittsburg, the little Napoleon sits trembling before the handful of men at Yorktown afraid either to fight or run. S—— feels devilish about it. He would like to remove him if he thought it would do. Things go on here about as usual.

There is no fun at all. . . . I am getting along pretty well. I only work about twenty hours a day. I do all of your work and half of my own now you are away. Don't hurry yourself. We are getting on very well. I talk a little French too now. I have taken a great notion to the G——s. I went to see them the other day. The children were less scared than usual, and they and Madame la Baronne talked long and earnestly of the state of your hygiene, and said "it was good intentions you for to go to the West for small time."

HAY TO NICOLAY.

Executive Mansion,
Washington, August 1, 1862.

MY DEAR JNO. GEORGE:

There is positively nothing of the slightest interest since you left. The abomination of desolation has fallen upon this town. I find that I can put in twenty-four hours out of every day very easily, in the present state of affairs, at the Executive Mansion. The crowd continually increases instead of diminishing. The Tax

Business has begun to grind. C—— is having things very much his own way. He makes out a batch of twenty or thirty commissions at a time, filling in the names, and presenting them to the President to sign.

HAY TO NICOLAY.

Executive Mansion,
Washington, August 11, 1862.

MY DEAR GEORGE:

You will have seen by the papers that P—— has been running his head into a hornet's nest. He fought a desperate battle the other day—or rather B—— did—P—— coming up at the end of it.

He stands now in good position, eager for another fight and confident of licking the enemy. The Tycoon has given orders that he shan't fight unless there is a first-rate chance of cleaning them out. The Tycoon thinks a defeat there would be a greater nuisance than several victories would abate.

There is no further news. It is horribly hot, all but me who have gone to shaking again.

Your infernal south windows always give me the chills. S—— has broken them up, however, and doses me remorselessly to keep them away.

If in the wild woods, you scrouge an Indian damsel, steal her moccasins while she sleeps and bring them to me.

The Tycoon has just received a pair, gorgeously quilled, from an Indian Agent who is accused of stealing. He put them on and grinned. Will he remember them on the day when C—— proposes another to fill the peculating donor's office? I fear not, my boy! I fear not!

Aug. 30. Saturday morning, the 30th of August, I rode out into the country and turned in at the Soldiers' Home. The President's horse was standing by the door, and in a moment the President appeared, and we rode into town together.

We talked about the state of things by Bull Run and P——'s prospect. The President was very outspoken in repard to McC——'s present conduct. He said that it really seemed to him McC—— wanted P—— defeated. He mentioned to me a despatch of McC——'s in which he proposed, as one plan of action, to "leave P—— to get out of his own scrape and devote ourselves to securing Washington." He spoke also of Mc——'s dreadful panic in the matter of Chain Bridge, which he had ordered blown up the night before, but which order had been countermanded; and also of his incomprehensible interference with F——'s Corps which he recalled once, and then, when they had been sent ahead by H——'s order, begged permission to recall them again; and only desisted after H——'s sharp injunction to push them ahead till they whipped something, or got whipped themselves. The President seemed to think him a little crazy. Envy, jealousy and spite are probably a better explanation of his present conduct. He is constantly sending despatches to the President and H—— asking what is his real position and command. He acts as chief alarmist and grand marplot of the army.

The President, on my asking if H—— had any prejudices, rejoined:—"No! H—— is wholly for the service. He does not care who succeeds or who fails, so the service is benefited."

Later in the day we were in H——'s room. H—— was at dinner and S—— came in while we were waiting for him, and carried us off to dinner. A pleasant little dinner and a pretty wife as white and cold and motionless as marble, whose rare smiles seemed to pain her. S——— was loud about the McC——— business. He was unqualifiedly severe upon McC———. He said that after these battles there should be one court-martial, if never any more. He said that nothing but foul play could lose us this battle, and that it rested with McC——— and his friends. S——— seemed to believe very strongly in P———. So did the President, for that matter.

We went back to the Headquarters and found Gen'l H———. He seemed quiet and somewhat confident. He said the greatest battle of the century was now being fought. He said he had sent every man that could go to the field. At the War Department we found that Mr. S——— had sent a vast army of volunteer nurses out to the field, probably utterly useless, over which he gave Gen'l W——— command.

Everything seemed to be going well and hilarious on Saturday, and we went to bed expecting glad tidings at sunrise. But about eight o'clock the President came to my room as I was dressing, and calling me out, said :—" Well, John, we are whipped again, I am afraid. The enemy reinforced on P——— and drove back his left wing, and he has retired to Centreville where he says he will be able to hold his men. I don't like that expression. I don't like to hear him admit that his men need holding."

After awhile, however, things began to look better, and, people's spirits rose as the heavens cleared. The President was in a singularly defiant tone of mind. He often repeated, "We must hurt this enemy before it gets away." And this morning, Monday, (September 1), he said to me, when I made a remark in regard to the bad look of things:—"No, Mr. Hay, we must whip these people now. Pope must fight them; if they are too strong for him he can gradually retire to these fortifications. If this be not so,—if we are really whipped, and to be whipped, we may as well stop fighting."

It is due in great measure to his indomitable will that army movements have been characterized by such energy and celerity for the last few days. There is one man who seems thoroughly to reflect and satisfy him in everything he undertakes. This is Haupt, the Railroad man at Alexandria. He has, as Chase says, a Major General's head on his shoulders. The President is particularly struck with the business-like character of his despatch, telling in the fewest words the information most sought for, which contrasted so strongly with the weak, whining, and incorrect despatches of the whilom General-in-Chief. If heads or shoulder straps could be exchanged, it would be a good thing, in either case, here. A good railroader would be spoiled, but the General gained would compensate. The corps of H—— starting from Alexandria, have acted as pioneers, advance-guard, voltigeurs, and every other light infantry arm of the service.

Sept. 5, 1862. This morning I walked with the President over to the War Department, to ascertain the truth of the report that J—— had crossed the Potomac. We went to the telegraph office and found it true. On the way over, the President said:—" McC—— is working like a beaver. He seems to be aroused to doing something by the sort of snubbing he got last week. I am of opinion that this public feeling against him will make it expedient to take important command from him. The Cabinet yesterday were unanimous against him. They were all ready to denounce me for it, except B——. He has acted badly in this matter, but we must use what tools we have. There is no man in the army who can man these fortifications and lick these troops of ours into shape half as well as he." I spoke of the general feeling against McC—— as evinced by the President's mail. He rejoined:—"Unquestionably he has acted badly toward P——. He wanted him to fail. That is unpardonable. But he is too useful just now to sacrifice." At another time he said: —"If he can't fight himself, he excels in making others ready to fight" . . . .

To-day, going into the Executive Mansion, I met Gov. S—— coming out. I turned back and walked home with him. He said our foreign affiairs are very much confused. He acknowledged himself a little saddened. Walking on, he said: —"Mr. Hay, what is the use of growing old? You learn something of men and things, but never until too late to use it. I have only just now found out what military jealousy is. I have been wishing for some months to go home to my people; but could not while our armies were scattered and in danger. The other day I went down to Alexandria, and found Gen'l McC——'s army landing. I considered our armies united virtually and thought them invincible. I went home, and the first news I received was that each had been attacked, and each, in effect, beaten. It never had occurred to me that any jealousy could prevent these Generals from acting for their common fame and the welfare of the country."

I said it never would have seemed possible to me that one American General should write of another to the President, suggesting that "P—— be allowed to get out of his own scrape his own way."

He answered :—"I don't see why you should have expected it. You are not old. I should have known it." He said this gloomily and sadly.

September 23. The President wrote the Proclamation on Sunday morning carefully. He called the Cabinet together on Monday, Sept. 22, made a little talk to them, and read the momentous document. Mr. B—— and Mr. B—— made objections; otherwise the Cabinet was unanimous. The next day Mr. B——, who had promised to file his objections, sent a note stating that, as his objections were only to the time of the act, he would not file them lest they should be subject to misconstruction.

I told the President of the serenade that was coming, and asked if he would make any remarks. He said, no; but he did say half a dozen words, and said them with great grace and dignity. I spoke to him about the editorials in the leading papers. He said he had studied the matter so long that he knew more about it than they did.

At Gov. C——'s there was some talking after the serenade. C—— and C—— made speeches, and the crowd was in a glorious humor. After the crowd went away, to force Mr. B—— to say something, a few old fogies staid at the Governor's, and drank wine. C—— spoke earnestly of the Proclamation. He said:—"This was a most wonderful history of an insanity of a class that the world had ever seen. If the slaveholders had staid in the Union, they might have kept the life in their institution for many years to come. That what no party and no public feeling in the North could ever have hoped to touch, they had madly placed in the very path of destruction." They all seemed to feel a sort of new and exhilarated life; they breathed freer; the President's Proclamation had freed them as well as the slaves. They gleefully and merrily called each other and themselves abolitionists, and seemed to enjoy the novel accusation of appropriating that horrible name.

Sept. 26. Last night, September 25, the President and I were riding to Soldiers' Home; he said he had heard of an officer who had said they did not mean to gain any decisive victory, but to keep things running on so that they, the army, might manage things to suit themselves. He said he should have the matter examined, and if any such language had been used his head should go off.

I talked a great deal about the McC—— conspiracy, but he would make no answer to anything. He merely said that McC—— was doing nothing to make himself either respected or feared.

HAY TO NICOLAY.

Executive Mansion,
Washington, Aug. 27, 1862.

MY DEAR SIR:

Where is your scalp? If anybody believes you don't wish you were at home, he can get a pretty lively bet out of me. I write this letter firing into the air. If it hits you, well. It will not hurt so much as a Y——'s rifle. If in God's good Providence your long locks adorn the lodge of an aboriginal warrior and the festive tomtom is made of your stretched hide, I will not grudge the time thus spent, for auld lang syne. In fancy's eye I often behold you the centre and ornament of a wildwood circle, delighting the untutored children of the forest with Tuscan melodies. But by the rivers of Babylon you refuse to yield to dalliance—yea, you weep when you remember Washington whose magnificent distances are nevermore for you.

Washington is not at the present speaking an alluring village. Everybody is out of town and nobody cares for nobody that is here. One exception tres charmante which is French for devilish tidy. Miss C—— K—— is here with a pretty cousin from B—— which E—— S—— is quite spooney about her while I am languidly appreciative.

G——'s Theatre re-opens next Saturday and D—— breathes again. Some pretty women are engaged, to whom I am promised introductions. There is also a new Club House established in the city, to which I have sometimes gone to satisfy the ragings of famine. I think you will patronize it extensively when you come back. I ride on horseback mornings. I ride the off horse. He has grown so rampagious by being never driven (I have no time to drive) that no one else whom I can find can ride him. S—— B—— and L—— ride sometimes the near horse.

I am yours,

HAY TO MISS MARY R——.

Executive Mansion,
Washington, Jan. 22, 1863.

MY DEAR MISS MARY:

I suppose you have long before this decided that I was never again to be believed or trusted, it has been so long since you kindly gave me permission to send you these books. But I am not so much to blame as you would think. I have made myself a nuisance at the book-stores asking for them ever since I returned. The demand for them, Mr. P—— informs me, has been so great that the supply was temporarily exhausted and I have been compelled to wait until now for a complete set.

I have just finished reading the entire work. I think nothing approaching it in sustained excellence has been written in our day. It is a great novel, a splendid historical monogram, a brilliant theological disquisition, and a profound treatise of political philosophy. No man in our day has thought it worth while to use the vehicle of fiction for the transmission of such weighty and portentous truths. No philosopher or statesman has had sufficient grace and vigor of imagination to envelope his ideas in a garb so attractive, and no novelist has been gifted with that strength and scope of intellect which would enable him to grasp with so firm a hand the gravest problems of society and progress. In delicacy and fervor of fancy and depth of pathos, in sustained and unflagging power, and in absolute mastery of the machinery of artistic construction, I have read nothing that can even be brought into comparison with it.[1]

Of course there will be many things in it which you will not approve, and many which you will not understand fully until you have finished the book; and even then if you are dissatisfied, it is not with the author but with society and the great social wrongs against which he is a crusader.

I envy you heartily, Miss Mary, the leisure

[1] The French edition of "Les Misérables."

which you are to devote to this wonderful book. I deeply regretted the quiet and "the tranquil mind," with which I should have read it in Springfield a year or two ago.

Very truly your friend as then and there.

HAY TO NICOLAY.

Stone River, S. C.,
Wednesday, April 8, 1863.

MY DEAR NICO:

I arrived here to-night at the General's head-quarters and was very pleasantly received by both him and H——. They are both in fine health and spirits. H—— is looking better than I ever saw him before. They asked after you. On the way down I had for *compagnons de voyage* Gen'ls V—— and G——; G—— on sick leave and V—— to report for duty.

I hear nothing but encouraging accounts of the fight of yesterday in Charleston harbor. Gen'l S——, chief of staff, says we are sure to whip them; much surer than we were before the attack. The monitors behaved splendidly. The Keokuk was sunk and the Patapsco somewhat damaged, but as a whole they encountered the furious and concentrated fire of the enemy in a style for which even our own officers had scarcely dared to hope. The attack will soon be resumed with greater confidence and greater certainty of what they are able to do than before. An expedition is on for the army from which they hope important results. The force of the enemy is much larger than ours, but not so well posted, and as they are entirely ignorant of our plans they are forced to scatter and distribute their strength so as greatly to diminish its efficiency. Our troops are in good order and fine spirits apparently. I think highly of S—— from the way he talks; like a firm, quick and cool-headed man. On the whole, things look well, if not very brilliant.

The General says he is going to announce me to-morrow as a volunteer Aide without rank. I am glad of it as the thing stands. If I had not been published as having accepted, hesitated and rejected such an appointment, I would not now have it. But I want my abolition record clearly defined, and that will do it better than anything else in my mind and the minds of the few dozen people who know me. . . .

I wish you could be down here. You would

enjoy it beyond measure. The air is like June at noon and like May at morning and evening. The scenery is tropical. The sunsets unlike anything I ever saw before. They are not gorgeous like ours, but singularly quiet and solemn. The sun goes down over the pines through a sky like ashes-of-roses, and hangs for an instant on the horizon like a bubble of blood. Then there is twilight such as you dream about. . . .

April 9. Alas for the pleasant prognostications of the military men! The General this morning received the despatches, which you will see before this, confessing that the attack has been a failure. I do not as yet, know all the results of this bitter disappointment. Charleston is not to be ours as yet, and another instance is added to the many, of the President having clearer perceptions of military possibilities than any man in the Cabinet or the field. He thought it would fail.

HAY TO NICOLAY.

Stone River, S. C., April 10.

I have written some particulars of my interview with Admiral D—— which I thought the President should know. Please give it to him, reading it yourself if you care to. I went up into the harbor yesterday. The gray-coated rascals were on both sides, waiting for another attack. A crowd of them were crawling cautiously over the bluff to look at the wreck of the Keokuk which has sunk near the shore. They are very busy throwing up new batteries on Morris Island, and did not fire on us though we were in easy range. While I was gone they published the order making me Voln. A. D. C.

HAY TO PRESIDENT LINCOLN.

Stone River, S. C.,
April 10, 1863.

MY DEAR SIR:

I went yesterday morning to Charleston Harbor to deliver to Admiral D—— the despatches with which the Navy Department had charged me. I found the Admiral on board the "Ironsides," which, with the rest of the Monitor fleet, was lying inside the bar, at the point where they had anchored after the engagement of Tuesday. I delivered my despatches, and, while he was reading them, I had some conversation with Capt.

R——, fleet captain of the S. A. B. Squadron. He said that although the attack had been unsuccessful and the failure would of course produce a most unhappy effect upon the country, which had so far trusted implicitly in the invincibility of the Monitors, all the officers of the Navy, without exception, united in the belief that what they had attempted was impossible, and that we had reason for congratulation that what is merely a failure had not been converted into a terrible disaster. The matter has now been fairly tried. With favoring circumstances, with good officers, with good management, the experiment has completely failed. We sailed into the harbor not sanguine of victory. We fought only about forty minutes, and the unanimous conclusion of the officers of the Navy is that an hour of that fire would have destroyed us. We had reached and touched the obstructions. To have remained there long enough to have removed them would have ensured the destruction of some of the vessels. If the others had gone by the fort they would still have been the target of the encircling batteries. There was no sufficient land force to have taken possession of the city. There was no means of supplying them with ammunition and provision, for no wooden ship could live ten minutes in that fire.

The only issue would have been the capture of the surviving and the raising of the sunken vessels. This would have lost us the command of the coast, an irremediable disaster. So the Admiral took the responsibility of avoiding the greater evil by saving the fleet, and abandoning an enterprise which we think has been fairly proved impossible.

The Admiral, who had been listening and assenting to the latter portion of what R—— had been saying, added :—" And as if we were to have a visible sign that an Almighty hand was over us for our good, the orders you have given me show how vast was the importance of my preserving this fleet, whose power and prestige are still great and valuable, for the work which I agree with the President in thinking most momentous, the opening of the control of the Mississippi River. After a fight of forty minutes we had lost the use of seven guns. I might have pushed some of the vessels past Fort Sumter, but in that case we ran the enormous risk of giving them to the enemy, and thus losing the control of the coast. I could not answer for that to my conscience."

The perfect approval of their own consciences which these officers evidently felt, did not prevent their feeling the deepest grief and sorrow for the unhappy results of the enterprise. Their whole conversation was as solemn as a scene of death. At one time I spoke of the estimation in which they were held by the government and the country, which, in my opinion, rendered it impossible that blame should be attached to them, and their eyes suddenly filled with tears. A first repulse is a terrible thing to brave and conscientious men accustomed only to victory.

I was several times struck by the identity of opinion and sentiment between Admiral D—— and yourself. You had repeatedly uttered, during my last week in Washington, predictions which have become history.

When I left the harbor, they were preparing the torpedo raft for the destruction of the sunken Keokuk.

I have taken the liberty of writing thus at length, as I thought you should know the sentiments of these experienced officers in regard to this unfortunate matter. I hope, however, the news may be received that due honor may be given to those who fought with such bravery and discretion the losing fight.

Yours very respectfully,

HAY TO NICOLAY.

April 14, 1863.

MY DEAR NICO:

Here is one of the cleverest things I have seen since the war began. It is an impromptu order of H——'s on Miss Mary Brooks, a New York lady, who was down here on a visit with Mrs. R——. The "Hay" is, of course, Charlie, not *the Colonel.*

We are living very pleasantly here since the return from Charleston of the K——'s. The General has some fine horses and the rides are pleasant.

Yours truly,

J. H.

HEADQUARTERS, Dept. of the South,
Hilton Head, S. C., March 25, 1863.

SPECIAL ORDERS,
A. No. 1.

I. With her charming looks
And all her graces,
Miss Mary Brooks,
Whose lovely face is
The sweetest thing we have seen down here
On these desolate Islands for more than a year,
Is hereby appointed an extra Aide
On the Staff of the General Commanding,

With a Captain of Cavalry's strap and grade,
And with this most definite understanding.

II. That Captain Mary,
Gay and airy,
At nine each day, until further orders,
To Colonel Halpine shall report
For special duty at these Headquarters :—
And Captain Mary,
(Bless the fairy !)
Shall hold herself, upon all occasions,
Prepared to ride
At the Adjutant's side
And give him of flirting his regular rations ;
And she shan't vamoose
With the younglings loose
Of the junior Staff,—such as Hay and Skinner ;
But, galloping onward, she shall sing,
Like an everlasting lark on the wing—
And she shan't keep the Adjutant late for dinner.

III. The Chief Quartermaster of Department
Will give Captain Mary a riding garment :—
A long, rich skirt of a comely hue,
Shot silk, with just a suspicion of blue,—
A gipsey hat, with an ostrich feather,
A veil to protect her against the weather,
And delicate gauntlets of pale buff leather ;
Her saddle with silver shall all be studded
And her pony,—a sorrel,—it shall be blooded :
Its shoes shall be silver, its bridle all ringing
With bells that shall harmonize well with her singing.
And thus Captain Mary,
Gay, festive and airy,

Each morning shall ride
At the Adjutant's side
And hold herself ready, on all fit occasions,
To give him of flirting his full army rations.

By Command of Maj.-Gen'l D. HUNTER,
ED. W. SMITH,
Assistant Adjutant-General.

Official Copy:
CHAS. G. HALPINE,
Lieut.-Col. and Assistant Adjutant-General,
10th Army Corps, and Department of the South.

HAY TO NICOLAY.

Hilton Head, S. C.,
April 16, 1863.

MY DEAR NICOLAY:

The General and the Admiral this morning received the orders from Washington directing the continuance of operations against Charleston. The contrast was very great in the manner in which they received them. The General was absolutely delighted. He said he felt more encouraged, and was in better heart and hope than before, at this indication of the earnestness of the government to finish this business here. He said, however, that the Admiral seemed in very low spirits about it. He talked despondingly about it, adhering to the same impressions of the desperate character of the enterprise as I reported to the President after my first interview with him. Perhaps having so strongly expressed his belief that the enterprise was impracticable he feels that he is rebuked by an opposite opinion from Washington.

Gen'l H—— is in the best feather about the matter. He believed before we came back that with the help of the gunboats we could take Morris Island and from that point reduce Fort Sumter; and he is well pleased to have another chance at it. Whether the intention of the government be to reduce Charleston now, with adequate men and means, or by powerful demonstrations to retain a large force of the enemy here, he is equally anxious to go to work again.

I write this entirely confidentially for you and for the President to know the ideas prevalent here.

Gen'l S—— has been with you before this, and has given to the government the fullest information relative to military matters here. His arrival, I suppose, will only confirm the resolution already taken. Admiral D——'s despatches by the Flambeau of course put a darker shade on the matter than anything S—— will say, as he was strongly in favor of staying there and fighting it out. . . .

HAY TO NICOLAY.

Hilton Head, S. C.,
April 23, 1863.

MY DEAR NICO:

In yours of the 15th received last night, you say "there was verbal indication of much wrath at the report that D—— intended to withdraw his fleet and abandon his position." I was surprised at this. If you have received my different letters you will see why. He would have obeyed orders had he done so. You say we have gained *points d'appui* for future work. The navy say not. They say they cannot lie off Morris Island to cover the landing of our troops, (or rather the crossing from Folly Island, the only practicable route), without imminent danger of being driven ashore and wrecked by the first northeasterly breeze that comes. It is not for me to say what is, or what is not, possible. My old ideas have been horribly shattered when I have seen two men, each of whom I had formerly considered an oracle on every subject connected with ships, accusing each other of ignorance and charlatanism.

I do not think D—— is either a fool or a coward. I think there is a great deal of truth in his statement that, while the fight in Charleston harbor demonstrated the great defensive properties of the Monitors, it also proved that they could not be relied upon for aggressive operations.

With an adequate force I think H—— could dislodge the enemy from Morris Island, and from that point make a hole in Fort Sumter; but even then little has been done. The General is sanguine. He wants a fight. I hope he may have one before I return.

To-day I start for Florida. . . .

Saturday, the 11th of July, 1863. The President seemed in a specially good humor to-day, as he had pretty good evidence that the enemy were still on the north side of the Potomac, and M—— had announced his intention of attacking them in the morning. The President seemed very happy in the prospect of a brilliant success. He had been rather impatient with Gen'l M——'s slow movements since Gettysburg, but concluded to-day that M—— would yet show sufficient activity to inflict the *coup de grace* upon the flying rebels.

Sunday, 12th July. Rained all the afternoon. Have not yet heard of M——'s expected attack.

Monday, 13th. The President begins to grow anxious and impatient about M——'s silence. I thought and told him there was nothing to prevent the enemy from getting away by the Falling Waters if they were not vigorously attacked. E—— says K—— is up on their rear. Nothing can save them if M—— does his duty. I doubt him. He is an engineer.

14th July. This morning the President seemed depressed by M——'s despatches of last night. They were so cautiously and almost timidly worded,—talking about reconnoitring to find the enemy's weak place, and other such. He said he feared he would do nothing.

About noon came the despatch stating that our worst fears were true. The enemy had gotten away unhurt. The President was deeply grieved. "We had them within our grasp," he said; "we had only to stretch forth our hands and they were ours. And nothing I could say or do could make the army move."

Several days ago he sent a despatch to M—— which must have cut like a scourge, but M——

returned so reasonable and earnest reply that the President concluded he knew best what he was doing, and was reconciled to the apparent inaction which he hoped was merely apparent.

Every day he has watched the progress of the army with agonizing impatience, hope struggling with fear. He has never been easy in his own mind about Gen'l M—— since M——'s General Order in which he called on his troops to drive the invader from our soil. The President says:—"This is a dreadful reminiscence of McC——. The same spirit that moved McC—— to claim a great victory because Pennsylvania and Maryland were safe. The hearts of ten million people sunk within them when McC—— raised that shout last fall. Will our Generals never get that idea out of their heads? The whole country is our soil."

15th July. . . . R——t L—— says the President is grieved silently but deeply about the escape of L——. He said:—"If I had gone up there I could have whipped them myself." I know he had that idea.

16th July. N—— leaves to-day for the Rocky Mountains. Had a little talk with the President about M——. Says H—— thinks S—— never had a military idea and never will learn one. Thinks S—— is somewhat to blame for the Winchester business. President says, however you may doubt or disagree from H——, he is very apt to be right in the end. . . .

Gen'l W—— came in. He said in answer to A——'s question, "Why did L—— escape?" "Because nobody stopped him," rather gruffly.

W—— says that at a council of war of Corps Commanders, held on Sunday the 12th, he was present on account of the sickness of his Corps Commander, he (W——) being temporarily in command of the Corps. On the question of fight or no fight, the weight of authority was against fighting. F——, S——, S—— and ——— strenuously opposed a fight. M—— was in favor of it. So was W——, who did most of the talking on that side, and P—— was very eager for it, as also was W—— himself. The non-fighters thought, or seemed to think, that if we did not attack, the enemy would, and even M—— thought he was in for action, had no idea that the enemy intended to get away at once. H—— had little to say on the subject.

M—— was in favor of attacking in three

columns of 20,000 men each. W—— was in favor of doing as S—— J—— did at Chancellorsville, double up the left, and drive them down on Williamsport. I do not question that either plan would have succeeded. W—— said to H——, who sat beside him:—"General, there are a good many officers of the regular army who have not yet entirely lost the West Point idea of southern superiority. That sometimes accounts for an otherwise unaccountable slowness of attack. . . ."

July 18. To-day we spent six hours deciding on Court Martials, the President, Judge H—— and I. I was amused at the eagerness with which the President caught at any fact which would justify him in saving the life of a condemned soldier. He was only merciless in cases where meanness or cruelty were shown.

Cases of cowardice he was specially averse to punishing with death. He said it would frighten the poor devils too terribly to shoot them. On the case of a soldier who had once deserted and reënlisted, he endorsed:—"Let him fight instead of shooting him!"

One fellow who had deserted, and escaped after

conviction, into Mexico, he sentenced, saying:—"We will condemn him as they used to sell hogs in Indiana, as they run."

He told one good story about U. F. L—— getting a fellow off who had stolen a hog, by advising him to go and get a drink, suggesting that the water was better in Tennessee.

19 July, Sunday. . . . The President was in very good humor; . . . in the afternoon he and I were talking about the position at Williamsport the other day. He said:—"Our army held the war in the hollow of their hand, and they would not close it." Again he said:—"We had gone through all the labor of tilling and planting an enormous crop, and when it was ripe we did not harvest it!" Still he added, "I am very, very grateful to M—— for the great service he did at Gettysburg."

HAY TO NICOLAY.

Executive Mansion,
Washington, August 7, 1863.

MY DEAR NICO:

. . . . B—— and his mother have gone to the

white mountains. (I don't take any special stock in the matter, and write the locality in small letters.) B—— was so shattered by the wedding of the idol of all of us, the bright particular Teutonne, that he rushed madly off to sympathise with nature in her sternest aspects. They will be gone some time. The newspapers say the Tycoon will join them after a while. If so, he does not know it. He may possibly go for a few days to C—— M——, where H—— L—— is now staying, though that is not certain.

This town is as dismal now as a defaced tombstone. Everybody has gone. I am getting apathetic and write blackguardly articles for the *Chronicle* from which W—— extracts the dirt and fun, and publishes the dreary remains. The Tycoon is in fine whack. I have rarely seen him more serene and busy. He is managing this war, the draft, foreign relations, and planning a reconstruction of the Union, all at once. I never knew with what tyrannous authority he rules the Cabinet till now. The most important things he decides, and there is no cavil. I am growing more and more firmly convinced that the good of the country absolutely demands that he should be kept where he is till this thing is over. There is no man in the country so wise, so gentle and so firm. I believe the hand of God placed him where he is.

They are all working against him like braves though,—H—— and that crowd—but don't seem to make anything by it. I believe the people know what they want, and unless politics have gained in power and lost in principle, they will have it. . . . .

DIARY.

Aug. 9. This being Sunday and a fine day I went down with the President to have his picture taken at G——'s. He was in very good spirits. He thinks that the rebel power is at last beginning to disintegrate; that they will break to pieces if we only stand firm now. Referring to the controversy between two factions at Richmond, one of whom believes still in foreign intervention, northern treason, and other chimæras; and the other, the administration party, trusts to nothing but the army, he said:—"D—— is right. His army is his only hope, not only against us, but against his own people. If that were crushed, the people would be ready to swing back to their old bearings."

He is very anxious that Texas should be occupied and firmly held in view of French possibilities. He thinks it just now more important than Mobile. He would prefer that G—— should not throw his army into the Mobile business before the Texas matter is safe. He wrote in that sense, I believe, to G—— to-day. . . .

Aug. 13. Rode to-day with the President and the Secretary of State to the Capitol. Saw the statuary of the east pediment. The President objected to P——'s statue of the Woodchopper, as he did not make a sufficiently clean cut.

Coming home the President told S—— of what F—— B—— said about an interview he had had with P—— in the West. P—— said, "We are gone up; there is no further use of talking!" "How about your institution?" F—— asked. "Gone to the Devil!"

S—— said: "Slavery is dead; the only trouble is that the fools who support it from the outside do not recognise this, and will not, till the thing is over. In our Masonic warfare we made a great fight. The Masons were beaten; they knew and felt it, and retired from the fight. But the Jack Masons, as they were called, kept up their dismal howls of sympathy for the masons, long after they had given up the fight and forgotten all about it. So now, though slavery is dead, the Democratic party insists on devoting itself to guarding the corpse." . . . .

August 19. . . . . This evening and yesterday evening an hour was spent by the President in shooting with S——'s new repeating rifle. A wonderful gun, loading with absolutely contemptible simplicity and ease, with seven balls, and firing the whole, readily and deliberately, in less than half a minute. The President made some pretty good shots. S——, the inventor, a quiet little Yankee who sold himself in relentless slavery to his idea for six weary years before it was perfect, did some splendid shooting. . . . An irrepressible patriot came up and talked about his son John who, when lying on his belly on a hill-top at Gettysburg, feeling the shot fly over him, like to lost his breath—felt himself puffing up like a toad—thought he would bust. Another, seeing the gun recoil slightly, said it wouldn't do; too much powder; a good piece of audience shouldn't rekyle; if it did at all, it should rekyle a little forrid.

22 August. The President to-day said J—— L—— was acting so splendidly now that he absolved him in his own mind for all the wrong he ever did, and all he will do hereafter. . . .

23 August. Last night we went to the Observatory with Mrs. Y——. They were very kind and attentive. The President took a look at the moon and Arcturus. I went with him to the Soldiers' Home, and he read Shakespeare to me, the end of Henry V, and the beginning of Richard III, till my heavy eyelids caught his considerate notice, and he sent me to bed. This morning we ate an egg, and came in very early. He went to the library to write a letter to C——, and I went to pack my trunk for the North. . . . Staid about a week at Long Branch. Fine air—disgusting bathing—pretty women, and everything lovely. No politics, no war, nothing to remind me while there that there was such a thing as government or a soul to save. Count G—— was an undertone of nuisance—that was all.

September 9. Dined with W——. Met H——, B—— and F——. H—— was in fine flow. Before dinner we talked about H—— and his connection with H——'s resignation. He says he was forced to ask to be relieved by repeated acts which proved that he was not to be allowed to manage his army as he thought best, but that it was to be manœuvred from Washington. He instanced Maryland Heights, whose garrison he was forbidden to touch, yet which was ordered to be evacuated by the very mail which brought his (H——'s) relief. And other such many.

At dinner he spoke of our army. He says: "It was the finest on the planet. He would like to see it fighting with foreigners. It gave him an electric feeling to be with it. It was far superior to the Southern army in everything but one. It had more valor, more strength, more endurance, more spirit; the rebels are only superior in vigor of attack. The reason of this is that, in the first place our army came down here capable of everything but ignorant of everything. It fell into evil hands—the hands of a baby, who knew something of drill, little of organisation, and nothing of the morale of the army. It was fashioned by the congenial spirit of this man into a mass of languid inertness destitute of either dash or cohesion. The Prince de Joinville, by far the finest mind I have ever met with in the army, was struck by this singular, and as he said, inexplicable contrast between the character of American soldiers as integers and in mass. The one active, independent, alert, enterprising; the other indolent, easy, wasteful and slothful. It is not in the least singular. You find a ready explanation in the character of its original General. S—— is an instance of the cankerous influence of that staff. I sent him out to destroy the bridges behind L——. He rode 150 miles and came back without seeing the bridges he should have destroyed. He took with him 4,000 men; he returned with 4,500. His purposeless ride had all the result of a defeat. He claimed to have brought in an enormous train of negroes and other cattle. He brought 30 contrabands and not a man or a mule. He is a brave, good man, but he is spoiled by McC——.

"After the battle of Malvern and after the battle of Fair Oaks we could have marched into Richmond without serious resistance, yet the constitutional apathy of this man prevented."

Says B——:—"On the night of the battle of Malvern I saw the red lights of M——'s signal officer, blazing near me, and I went to him to gain information. He told me he had just received a despatch from Gen'l McC—— asking where was Gen'l F. J. P——; he wanted news. I volunteered a despatch:—'We have won a glorious victory, and if we push on and seize our advantage, Richmond is ours.' The day of Gaines' Mills, I had taken my position when P—— ordered me out of it into a hollow where I was compelled to assume a strictly defensive position. I once or twice terribly repulsed the enemy, but my orders peremptorily forbade pursuit. I had to keep up the spirits of the men by starting the rumor that McC—— was in Richmond. I am sure I thought he would be there that day. In the night, going to Gen'l McC——'s head-quarters, he asked me what about our Corps. I told him that with a few strong divisions we could attack and drive the enemy. He said he hadn't a man for us."

He said that the night before the evacuation of Yorktown he staid in McC——'s tent. McC—— said he expected to bag 78,000 of them. "You won't bag one," replied T——. And he didn't.

H—— says:—"M—— sometimes sent important orders which McC—— never saw. On one occasion when I had advanced my pickets very near Richmond I received an order through H——,—"Let Gen'l H—— return from his brilliant reconnoissance. We cannot afford to lose his division." I did not see how my division could be lost, as in that country there was no cutting me off. I started back, however, and soon met McC—— himself who asked me what it meant, my withdrawal. I showed him his own order. He said he had never seen it, and I ordered my men back. I returned over the swamp, and held my position for weeks afterwards."

H—— and B—— both agree as to the terrible defeat the rebels suffered at Malvern and the inefficiency which suffered them to escape without injury. They say there was a Corps, fresh and unharmed, which might have pursued the rebels and entered Richmond in triumph (F——'s).

. . . . H—— drank very little, not more than the rest, who were all abstemious, yet what little he drank made his cheek hot and red, and his eye brighter. I can easily understand how the stories of his drunkenness have grown, if so little affects him as I have seen. He was looking very well to-night. A tall and statuesque form—grand fighting head and grizzled russet hair—red-florid cheeks and bright blue eye, forming a fine contrast with B——, who sat opposite. A small, stout, compact man, with a closely chiselled Greek face and heavy black moustaches, like Eugene Beauharnais. Both very handsome and very different. . . .

September 10. . . . I dined to-night at W——'s with H——, B——, F——, W——, and Col. R—— of P——. . . . H—— says:—"Our war has developed no great cavalry officer. S—— has good points, but does not fulfil his early promise. P—— is splendid, enterprising and brave, but full of mannerisms and weaknesses. B—— is far superior to any others in all the qualities of a great rider. But none of them approach the ideal."

Speaking of L——, he expressed himself slightingly of L——'s abilities. He says he was never much respected in the army. In Mexico he was surpassed by all his lieutenants. In the cavalry he was held in no esteem. He was regarded very highly by Gen'l S——. He was a courtier, and readily recommended himself by his insinuating manner to the General, whose petulant and arrogant temper has driven of late years all officers of spirit and self-respect away from him.

"Look at all his staff-officers! sleek and comfortable and respectable and obsequious: T——, C——, H——, W——, etc."

"The strength of the rebel army rests on the broad shoulders of L——. He is the brain of L——, as S—— J—— was his right arm. Before every battle he has been advised with. After every battle L—— may be found in his tent. He is a weak man and little of a soldier. He naturally rests on L——, who is a soldier, born. . . . . ."

HAY TO NICOLAY.

Executive Mansion,
Washington, September 11, 1863.

MY DEAR NICOLAY:

A week or so ago I got frightened at

> "The brow so haggard, the chin so peaked,
> Fronting me silent in the glass,"

and sending for S—— (who had been giving the northern watering places for the last two months a model of high breeding and unquestionable deportment), I left for a few days at Long Branch and two or three more at Providence. I was at the Commencement at B—— University, and made a small chunk of a talk. I only staid a little over a week, and came back feeling heartier.

I must be in Warsaw early in October on account of family affairs. As I infer from your letter that you cannot return before November, or, as Judge O—— says, before December, I will have to give the reins up for a few days to S—— and H—— again. I hope the daring youth will not reduplicate the fate of Phaeton.

Washington is as dull here as an obsolete almanac. The weather is not so bad as it was. The nights are growing cool. But there is nobody here except us old stagers who can't get away. We have some comfortable dinners and some quiet little orgies on whiskey and cheese in my room. And the time slides away.

We are quietly jolly over the magnificent news from all round the board. R—— won a great and bloodless victory at Chattanooga which he had no business to win. The day that the enemy ran, he sent a mutinous message to H—— complaining of the very things that have secured us the victories, and foreshadowing only danger and defeat.

You may talk as you please of the Abolition Cabal directing affairs from Washington; some well-meaning newspapers advise the President to keep his fingers out of the military pie, and all that sort of thing. The truth is, if he did, the pie would be a sorry mess. The old man sits here and wields like a backwoods Jupiter the bolts of war and the machinery of government with a hand equally steady and equally firm.

His last letter is a great thing. Some hideously bad rhetoric—some indecorums that are infamous,—yet the whole letter takes its solid place in history as a great utterance of a great man. The whole Cabinet could not have tinkered up a letter which could have been compared with it. He can rake a sophism out of its hole better than all the trained logicians of all schools. I do not know whether the nation is worthy of him for another term. I know the people want him. There is no mistaking that fact. But politicians are strong yet, and he is not their "kind of a cat." I hope God won't see fit to scourge us for our sins by any one of the two or three most prominent candidates on the ground.

I hope you are getting well and hearty. Next winter will be the most exciting and laborious of all our lives. It will be worth any other ten.

DIARY.

20 September. Sunday morning, the 20th of September, the President showed me R——'s despatches of the day before, detailing the first day's fighting, and promising a complete victory on the next day. The President was a little uneasy over the promise, and very uneasy that B—— was not within supporting distance.

The next morning he came into my bed-room before I was up, and sitting down on my bed said:—"Well, R—— has been whipped as I feared. I have feared it for several days. I believe I feel trouble in the air before it comes. R—— says we have met with a serious disaster—extent not ascertained. B—— instead of obeying the orders which were given on the 14th, and going to R——, has gone up on a foolish affair to Jonesboro to capture a party of guerillas who are there."

Day by day the news brightens up. T——

held his own magnificently, and virtually whipped the enemy opposed to him. The scattered divisions came together. The enemy halted. R—— established himself again at Chattanooga. The stampede seemed to be over.

On Wednesday night, the 23d, coming home, I found on my table some interesting despatches from the rebel papers which I thought the President would like to read. They contained pretty full accounts of rebel losses in the late battles; among other things chronicling the death of B. H—— H——, Mrs. L——'s brother-in-law, who spent some time with the family here and was made a paymaster by the President. I took them over to the War Department to give them to an orderly to carry to the President. I found there the Secretary of War who was just starting to the Soldiers' Home to request the President to come to the Department to attend a council to be held there that night, rendered expedient, as he said, by recent despatches from Chattanooga.

While I was in the room they were endeavoring to decipher an intricate message from R—— giving reasons for the failure of the battle. The Secretary says: "I know the reasons well enough. R—— ran away from his fighting men and did not stop for thirteen miles." A moment after, he broke in :—"No, they need not shuffle it off on McC——. He is not much of a soldier. I never was in favor of him for a Major-General. But he is not accountable for this business. He and C—— both made pretty good time away from the fight to Chattanooga, but R—— beat them both."

I went out to the Soldiers' Home through a splendid moonlight, and found the President abed. I delivered my message to him as he dressed himself, and he was considerably disturbed. I assured him as far as I could that it meant nothing serious, but he thought otherwise, as it was the first time S—— had ever sent for him. When we got in, however, we found a despatch from R—— stating that he could hold Chattanooga against double his number; could not be taken until after a great battle; his stampede evidently over.

They came together to discuss the practicability of reinforcing R—— from M——. Present: A. Lincoln, H——, S——, S——, C——, W—— and H——, and for a while McC——. It was resolved to do it. The 11th and 12th Corps were selected for the purpose, H—— to be placed in command of both. Finished the evening by a supper with S——, where few ate.

On the morning of the 26th Gen'l H——, 11th Corps, came in as he was passing through town. A fine, handsome, thoughtful looking New Englander; and G—— came at the same time, an exchanged prisoner whom the rebs captured at Gettysburg; later in the evening came S——, 12th Corps. He said he would call in the morning. He did so, Sunday morning, accompanied by Governor S——. The result of the visit, a request by the President to General R—— urging him to take S—— from H——'s force and give H—— some corresponding force. S—— does not seem to me a very large man. He seems peevish, irritable, fretful. H—— says he is all that on account of his digestive apparatus being out of repair. H—— does not speak unkindly of him while he never mentions H—— but to attack him.

To-night (Sept. 27) drove out to the Soldiers' Home with H——. The President who had been spending the evening at the War Department, arranging some plan by which B—— may be allowed to continue his occupation and protection of East Tennessee, went out at nine o'clock, and H——, who wanted to take leave, went out afterwards, picking me up on the street. He does not specially approve of the campaign down there. He thinks we might force them to fight at disadvantage, instead of allowing them to continually choose the battle-ground. Does not think much can be made by lengthening R——'s line indefinitely into Georgia. Atlanta is a good thing on account of the railroads and storehouses and factories. But a long line weakens an army by constant details, while the enemy, falling back gradually, keeps his army intact till the itinerary equalises the opposing forces. H—— goes in the morning. I hope they will give him a fair show. S——'s hostility is very regrettable. H—— is a fine fellow. The President says:—"Whenever trouble arises I can always rely upon H——'s magnanimity." The President this morning asked him to write to him. I told him if he did not wish to write to the President, he might write to me. I wish I were able to go with him. But N—— is in the mountains getting beef on his bones, and I am a prisoner here. With R——, S——, B—— and H——, they will have a magnificent army there in a few days and some great fighting if B—— does not run. Deserters say R. P. H—— is coming. I don't believe that.

October 18, 1863. Sunday. I arrived in Washington to-day after an absence of a little more than two weeks.

On presenting myself to the President this morning . . . . I gave him my impression of the conduct of Mr. C—— in trying to cut under in the way he is doing, instancing what D—— of New York had related. He said "it was very bad taste, but that he had determined to shut his eyes to all these performances; that C—— made a good Secretary, and that he would keep him where he is:—if he becomes President, all right! I hope we may never have a worse man. I have all along clearly seen his plan of strengthening himself. Whenever he sees that an important matter is troubling me, if I am compelled to decide it in a way to give offence to a man of some influence, he always ranges himself in opposition to me, and persuades the victim that he (C.) would have arranged it very differently. It was so with Gen'l F——,— with Gen'l H——, when I annulled his hasty proclamation — with Gen'l B——, when he was recalled from New Orleans, —with the Missouri people when they called the other day. I am entirely indifferent as to his success or failure in these schemes, so long as he does his duty as the head of the Treasury Department."

He talked of the Missouri matter, and read to me the letter he had written D—— for the Committee. As it will probably be published, I forbear synopsis. It is a superb affair, perfectly just and frank, courteous but immoveable. He will not be bullied even by his friends. He tries to reason with these infuriated people. The world will hear him, if they do not. He read to me a letter which he has to-day written to Gov. G——, who, it seems, is anxious to have the President espouse his side of the quarrel, and to recognise him as the State Government, and use the federal authority to crush out the radicals, who, he says, meditate revolution and civil war in Missouri. The President answering says he will be at all times ready to extend to Missouri the protection guaranteed by the Constitution against domestic violence, whenever he (the President) shall see cause to suspect such violence as imminent. He does not so regard it at present. He thinks the instructions given to Gen'l S—— cover the case.

We got into this vein of talk through my telling him what Joe G—— says, and what I myself observed, of the tendency of public opinion in the West, almost universally, in favor of the radicals as against the conservatives in Missouri.

Talking of the military situation, he says L—— probably came up the other day thinking our army weaker than it is, and finding his mistake from the fight at B——, is holding off at present. R—— is all right, though somewhat bothered about his supplies.

October 19. The President told me this morning that R—— was to be removed from command of the Army at Chattanooga. T—— is to take his original army and G—— to command the whole force including H——'s and B——'s reinforcements. He says R—— has seemed to lose spirit and nerve since the battle of Chickamauga.

October 21. . . . B—— came in this morning with a couple of very intelligent East Tennesseeans. They talked in a very friendly way with the President. I never saw him more at ease than he is with those first-rate patriots of the border. He is of them really. They stood up before a map of the mountain country and talked war for a good while. . . .

October 22. I spoke to the President to-day about B——, his Rockville speech, and the action of the Union League of Philadelphia leaving out his name in Resolutions electing the Cabinet honorary members of the League. He says B—— is anxious to run S—— and beat W—— D——. The President on the contrary says that as D—— is the nominee of the Union Convention, and as we have recognised him as our candidate, it would be mean to do anything against him now.

Things in Maryland are badly mixed. The unconditional Union people are not entirely acting in concert. T—— seems acceptable to everyone. C—— is going to make a good run. But S—— is complicating the canvass with an embarrassing element, that of forcible negro-enlistments. The President is in favor of the voluntary enlistment of the negroes with the consent of their masters and on payment of the price. But S——'s favorite way, (or rather B——'s, whom S—— approves) is to take a squad of soldiers into a neighborhood and carry off into the army all the able-bodied darkies they can find, without asking master or slave to consent. Hence results like the case of W—— and S——. "The fact is," the President observes, "S—— is wider across the head in the region of the ears, and loves fight for its own sake, better than I do." . . .

October 24. This morning the President said that D—— has continually been telegraphing of R——'s anxiety for food; but T—— now telegraphs that there is no trouble on that score. I asked what D—— thought about R——. He said he agreed that R—— was for the present completely broken down. The President says he is "confused and stunned like a duck hit on the head," ever since Chickamauga. . . .

October 28. The President to-day wrote a letter to S—— in relation to his alleged army of returned rebels in Missouri. . . . The President added:—"I believe, after all, those radicals will carry the State, and I do not object to it. They are nearer to me than the other side, in thought and sentiment, though bitterly hostile personally. They are utterly lawless—the unhandiest devils in the world to deal with—but after all, their faces are set Zionwards." . . .

October 29. I went down to W——'s to-day and got from P——, who is here, a free ticket to New York and back for W. W——, the poet, who is going to New York to electioneer and vote for the union ticket.

Saw G—— and H——. H—— is just starting for the West on a tour of inspection. I would give my chances for —— to go with him, but N—— still stays in the sunset, and I am here with a ball and chain on my leg. . . .

I told the President that C—— would try to make capital out of this R—— business. He laughed and said, "I suppose he will, like the blue-bottle fly, lay his eggs in every rotten spot he can find." He seems much amused at C——'s mad hunt after the Presidency. He says it may win. He hopes the country will never do worse. I said he should not, by making all C——'s appointments, make himself *particeps criminis.* He laughed on, and said he was sorry the thing had begun, for though the matter did not annoy him, his friends insisted that it ought to.

October 30. . . . The President and Mrs. L—— went to see F——. About midnight, the President came in. I told him about D——'s note and asked if D—— had not always been a C—— man. He said:—"Yes, until recently, but he seems now anxious for my reëlection." I said O—— was expected here to-day, and told the President the story of P—— and O——. He went on and gave me the whole history of the visit they made to S——,—B——, O——, and H——,—of the appointment of B——,—of the way O—— rode him—of his final protest, and the break.

I said "O—— now was determined to have the Custom House cleaned out."

"He will have a good time doing it."

He went on telling the history of the Senate raid on S——,—how he had and could have no adviser on that subject, and must work it out by himself,—how he thought deeply on the matter,—and it occurred to him that the way to settle it was to force certain men to say to the Senators *here* what they would not say elsewhere. He confronted the Senate and the Cabinet. He gave the whole history of the affairs of S—— and his conduct, and the assembled Cabinet listened and confirmed all he said.

"I do not now see how it could have been done better. I am sure it was right. If I had yielded to that storm and dismissed S——, the thing would all have slumped over one way, and we should have been left with a scanty handful of supporters. When C—— sent in his resignation I saw that the game was in my own hands, and I put it through. When I had settled this important business at last with much labor and to my entire satisfaction, into my room one day walked D. D. F—— and G. O——, and began a new attack upon me to remove S——. For once in my life I rather gave my temper the rein, and I talked to those men pretty d——d plainly. O—— may be right in being cool to me. I may have given him reason this morning.

"I wish they would stop thrusting that subject of the Presidency into my face. I don't want to hear anything about it. The *Republican* of to-day has an offensive paragraph in regard to an alleged nomination of me by the mass-meeting in New York last night."

November 1. . . . . This evening Gen'l S——, accompanied by Gen'l G—— and Judge K——, came in to insist upon some order which would prevent disloyal people from voting at the ensuing Maryland election. Before going into the President's room (K—— and G—— sitting with me in the ante-room) K—— spoke very bitterly of

B——'s working against the Union party in Maryland.

After they were gone I handed the President B——'s R—— speech, telling him I had read it carefully, and saving a few intemperate and unwise expressions against leading Republicans which might better have been omitted, I saw nothing in the speech which would have given rise to such violent criticism.

"Really," says the President, "the controversy between the two sets of men represented by him and by Mr. S—— is one of mere form and little else. I do not think Mr. B—— would agree that the States in rebellion are to be permitted to come at once into the political family and renew the very performances which have already so bedeviled us. I do not think Mr. S—— would insist that when the loyal people of a State obtain the supremacy in their councils and are ready to assume the direction of their own affairs, that they should be excluded. I do not understand Mr. B—— to admit that J—— D—— may take his seat in Congress again as a representative of his people; I do not understand Mr. S—— to assert that J—— M—— B—— may not. So far as I understand Mr. S—— he seems in favor of Congress taking from the Executive the power it at present exercises over insurrectionary districts, and assuming it to itself. But when the vital question arises as to the right and privilege of the people of these States to govern themselves, I apprehend there will be little difference among loyal men. The question at once is presented, in whom this power is vested; and the practical matter for decision is how to keep the rebellious populations from overwhelming and outrooting the loyal minority."

I asked him if B—— was really opposed to our Union ticket in Maryland. He said he did not know anything about it—had never asked. . . .

Nov. 2. . . . . The President says B—— has been tendered F——'s department, while F—— goes to relieve B——, who resigns. It is not yet known whether B—— will accept. I asked about R——. The President says he sees no immediate prospect of assigning him to command;—that he had thought, when the trouble and row of this election in Missouri is over, and the matter will not be misconstrued, of sending R—— to Missouri and S—— into the field. He says that it was because of G——'s opposition that R—— is not in the Army of the Cumberland. When it was decided to place G—— in command of the whole Military Division, two sets of orders were made out, one contemplating R——'s retention of the command of his own army, and the other his relief. G—— was to determine the question for himself. He said at once that he preferred R—— should be relieved,—that he (R——) never would obey orders. This consideration of course involves a doubt as to whether R—— should be placed in command of a district from which G—— must, to a certain extent, derive supplies and reinforcements on occasion.

To-night S—— sent for copies of the correspondence between the President and B——. The Tycoon came into my room with the despatch in his hands, clad in an overcoat, pure and simple, reaching to his knees, and sleepily fumbled for the papers in his desk till he found them, and travelled back to bed. . . .

Sunday, 8 Nov. The President tells me that M—— is at last after the enemy and that G—— will attack to-morrow.

Went with Mrs. E—— to G——'s gallery

and were soon joined by N—— and the President. We had a great many pictures taken. Some of the President the best I have seen. N—— and I immortalised ourselves by having ourselves done in group with the President.

In the evening S—— came in. He feels very easy and confident now about affairs. He says New York is safe for the Presidential election by a much larger majority, that the crowd that follows power have come over; that the copperhead spirit is crushed and humbled. He says the Democrats lost their leaders when T—— and D—— and B—— forsook them and went south; that their new leaders, the S——s, V——s and W——s, are now whipped and routed. So that they have nothing left. The Democratic leaders are either ruined by the war, or have taken the right-about, and have saved themselves from the ruin of their party by coming out on the right side. . . .

He told the Democratic party how they might have saved themselves and their organisation, and with it the coming Presidential election—by being more loyal and earnest in support of the administration than the Republican party—which would not be hard, the Lord knows!

Nov. 12. . . . In the evening Miss C—— and Gov. S——'s wedding. A very brilliant-looking party. K—— looked tired out and languid, especially at the close of the evening, when I went into the bridal chamber to say good night. She had lost her old severity and formal stiffness of manner, and seemed to think she had *arrived.* McD——, S——, S——, S——, C—— and others present. The President came for a few minutes.

Nov. 18. We started from Washington to go to the consecration of the Soldiers' Cemetery at Gettysburg. On our train were the President, S——, U—— and B——; N—— and myself; M—— and Admiral R——; B—— and Capt. I—— and Lieut. M—— and C——; Mrs. W——; W. McV——; McD—— of C——; and one or two others. We had a pleasant sort of a trip. At Baltimore S——'s staff joined us.

Just before we arrived at Gettysburg, the President got into a little talk with McV—— about Missouri affairs. McV. talked radicalism until he learned that he was talking recklessly. The President disavowed any knowledge of the E—— case; said that B—— said to him, as indeed he said to me, that E—— was inefficient and must be removed for that reason.

At Gettysburg the President went to Mr. W—— who expected him, and our party broke like a drop of quicksilver spilt. McV——, young S—— and I foraged around for a while—walked out to the College, got a chafing dish of oysters, then some supper, and, finally, loafing around to the Court House where L—— was holding a meeting of marshals, we found F——, and went around to his place, Mr. F——'s, and drank a little whiskey with him. He had been drinking a good deal during the day, and was getting to feel a little ugly and dangerous. He was particularly bitter on M. B——. McV—— was telling him that he pitched into the President coming up, and told him some truths. He said the President got a good deal of that, from time to time, and needed it.

He says:—"H——, you are a fortunate man. You have kept yourself aloof from your office. I know an old fellow now seventy, who was Private Secretary to M——. He thought there was something solemn and memorable in it. H—— has laughed through his term."

He talked very strangely, referring to the

affectionate and loyal support which he and C—— had given to the President in P——, with references from himself and others to the favors that had been shown the C—— party whom they regard as their natural enemies. F—— seems identified now fully with the C—— interest, though, when C—— was nominated, he called him a heavy weight to carry, and said that C——'s foolish attack nominated him.

We went out after a while following the music to hear the serenades. The President appeared at the door, said half a dozen words meaning nothing, and went in. S——, who was staying around the corner at H——'s was called out, and spoke so indistinctly that I did not hear a word of what he was saying. F—— and McV—— were still growling about B——.

We went back to F——'s room, having picked up N——, and drank more whiskey. N—— sang his little song of the "Three Thieves," and we then sang John Brown. At last we proposed that F—— should make a speech, and two or three started out, S—— and B—— and N——, to get a band to serenade him. I staid with him; so did S—— and McV——. He still growled quietly, and I thought he was going to do something imprudent. He said, "if I speak, I will speak my mind." The music sounded in the street, and the fuglers came rushing up, imploring him to come down. He smiled quietly, told them to keep cool, and asked, "are the recorders there?" "I suppose so, of course," shouted up the fugler. "Ascertain!" said the imperturbable Forney: "Hay, we'll take a drink." They shouted and begged him to come down. The thing would be a failure; it would be his fault, etc. "Are the recorders congenial?" he calmly insisted on knowing. Somebody commended prudence. He said sternly, "I am always prudent." I walked down stairs with him.

The crowd was large and clamorous. The fuglers stood by the door in an agony. The reporters squatted at a little stand in the entry. Forney stood on the threshold, J. Young and I by him. The crowd shouted as the door opened. Forney said; "My friends these are the first hearty cheers I have heard to-night. You gave no such cheers to your President down the street. Do you know what you owe to that great man? You owe your country—you owe your name as American Citizens."

He went on blackguarding the crowd for their

apathy, and then diverged to his own record, saying he had been for Lincoln in his heart in 1860,—that open advocacy was not as effectual as the course he took—dividing the most corrupt organisation that ever existed—the pro-slavery Democratic party. He dwelt at length on this question, and then went back to the Eulogy of the President, that great, wonderful, mysterious, inexplicable man, who holds in his single hands the reins of the republic; who keeps his own counsels; who does his own purpose in his own way, no matter what temporising minister in his Cabinet sets himself up in opposition to the progress of the age.

And very much of this.

After him W. McV—— made a most touching and beautiful spurt of five minutes, and Judge S—— of P—— spoke effectively and acceptably to the people.

"That speech must not be written out yet," says Y——. "He will see further about it when he gets sober," as we went up stairs. We sang John Brown and went home.

In the morning I got a beast and rode out with the President and suite to the Cemetery in the procession. The procession formed itself in an orphanly sort of way, and moved out with very little help from anybody; and after a little delay Mr. E—— took his place on the stand,—and Mr. S—— made a prayer which thought it was an oration—and Mr. E—— spoke as he always does, perfectly; and the President, in a firm, free way, with more grace than is his wont, said his half-dozen lines of consecration,—and the music wailed, and we went home through crowded and cheering streets. And all the particulars are in the daily papers.

I met Gen'l C—— after coming in and he, McV—— and I, went down to dinner on board the U. C. R. R. Car. I was more than usually struck by the intimate jovial relations that exist between men that hate and detest each other as cordially as do those P—— politicians.

We came home the night of the 19th.

Nov. 22. This evening S—— read to the President a despatch from C. C——, in which he discussed the whole field of American politics —European diplomacy—and the naval improvements of the century. This man is certainly the most wonderful ass of the age. He recently sent a despatch to S——, criticising in his usual elusive and arrogant style, the late Oration of

S—— on Foreign Relations, concluding in regular diplomatic style by saying:—"You will read this to Mr. S——, and if he desires it, give him a copy."

S—— says:—"It is saddening to think of the effect of prosperity on such a man. Had not we succeeded, and he prospered, he would always have been known as a brave, sincere, self-sacrificing and eloquent orator. I went all the way to K—— to see and to encourage him. It is prosperity that has developed that fearful underlying vanity that poisons his whole character."

I asked Mr. S—— if he heard of the three revolutions of Matamoras, of which we have been talking to-day. He said:—"Yes! I have received a despatch about it from Gov. B——. I am surprised that a man so sagacious and cautious should have been on the brink of doing so imprudent a thing."

"He was about to fire on them then?" said the President.

"Yes!" said S——. "Our consul at Matamoras asked for protection, and he brought his guns to bear on the Castle for that purpose. I wrote to him at once that that would be war; that if our consul wanted protection he must come to B—— for it. Firing upon the town would involve us in a war with the Lord knows who."

"Or rather," said the President, "the Lord knows who not."

I happened to mention the Proclamation of Emancipation, and S—— said:—"One-half the world are continually busying themselves for the purpose of accomplishing Proclamations and Declarations of War, etc., which they leave to the other half to carry out. Purposes can usually better be accomplished without Proclamations. And failures are less signal when not preceded by sounding promises.

"The slave States seem inclined to save us any further trouble in that way," he continued. "Their best men are making up their minds that the thing is dead. B—— has written an admirable letter in answer to some slaveholders who ask him how he, a pro-slavery man, can support a war whose result will be the abolition of slavery. He tells them the war must be prosecuted, no matter what the result; that it will probably be the destruction of slavery, and he will not fight against it, nor greatly care to see the institution ended."

The President added, as another cheering incident from Kentucky, that J. B—— has asked for permission to enlist three thousand negroes for teamsters, paying them wages and promising them freedom.

The President is very anxious about B——.

Nov. 24. . . . . To-night the President said he was much relieved at hearing from F—— that there was firing at Knoxville yesterday. He said anything showing that B—— was not overwhelmed was cheering:—"Like Sallie Carter, when she heard one of her children squall, would say 'there goes one of my young ones, not dead yet, bless the Lord!'"

HAY TO NICOLAY.

Executive Mansion,
Washington, Nov. 25, 1863.

MY DEAR NICO:

G——'s and W——'s despatches are so cheering this morning that I sent you a cautious despatch this morning. H—— (fighting J——) (Fightinger than ever) has done gloriously; carried the north slope of Lookout Mountain and gobbled a thousand prisoners. T—— and S—— have also done all they attempted, and G—— is to advance to-day along his whole line.

B—— has sent a courier through to W—— and says he is all right as yet; is not hungry or thirsty, and has not quite begun his share of the fighting.

Everything looks well.

Don't, in a sudden spasm of good-nature, send any more people with letters to me requesting favors from S——. I would rather make the tour of a small-pox hospital.

HAY TO NICOLAY.

Executive Mansion,
Washington, Nov. 26, 1863.

MY DEAR NICOLAY:

The newspapers of this morning have told you all you want to know, and so I send you no telegram. The news is glorious. Nature was against us, but we won in her spite. Had not the rapid current and drift swept away H——'s pontoons, he would have utterly destroyed them.

G—— will immediately send a column to relieve B——, and if possible destroy L——.

The President is sick in bed. Bilious.

DIARY.

Nov. 27, 1863. I dined to-day at W——'s with Mr. E——. He is a very delightful old gentleman in his personal and family relations. His talk to his grandchildren was very winning and graceful.

Nov. 28. The Secretary of State came in this morning and gave me his contribution to the President's Message, relating exclusively to Foreign Affairs.

He then said he had a matter to submit which was strictly confidential:—"I saw a great while ago that the President was being urged to do many things which were to redound to the benefit of other men, he taking the responsibility and the risk. I preferred to leave to these men the attitude they coveted, of running before, and shouting for the coming events. I preferred to stay behind, to do with and for the President what seemed best, to share with him the criticism and the risk, and to leave the glory to him and to God.

"Among other measures to unite good men and to divide the opposition was the Loyal League Association of the country. I saw very early that they would be valuable in bringing over to our side the honest War Democrats, and I therefore encouraged them as far as possible with my influence and my money. Soon I discovered a wheel within the enterprise—a secret, Know Nothing, Masonic Order with signs and pass-words. They asked me for money. They sent to me from California for charters. Not to make trouble I complied with all requests. You will see for what purpose this machine is being used." Here he handed me a scrap of paper on which was scrawled in T. Weed's handwriting:—"Loyal Leagues, into which Odd Fellows and Know Nothings rush, are fixing to control delegate appointments for Mr. Chase." Seward, still scribbling, said:—"If you want to be cheated, join a secret society. They are all swindlers. If I have an idiosyncrasy it is a hatred of secrets. The Consul at London tells me that he has received trustworthy information of an alliance between France and the rebels; but his sources of information being secret, he cannot give his authority. I answer, asking him what right he has to have a secret from the President concerning public affairs, and directing him to lay his information, whatever it may be, before the American Minister at London."

He handed me a paper upon which he had copied this extract:—"The more I reflect, the less I am inclined to trust the P—— proposition. The public men of that State are queer."

I am to give both to the President.

Dec. 9. . . . . In the evening J—— and U——, and N—— and I were talking politics and blackguarding our friends in the Council Chamber. A great deal had been said about the folly of the E——-B—— letter—the R——-B—— speech, etc.—when the President came in. They at once opened on him, and after some talk he settled down to give his ideas about the B—— business. He said:—

"The B——s have, to an unusual degree, the spirit of clan. Their family is a close corporation. F—— is their hope and pride. They have a way of going with a rush for anything they undertake;—especially have M—— and the Old Gentleman. When this war first began, they could think of nothing but F——; they expected everything from him; and upon their earnest solicitation he was made a General, and sent to Missouri. I thought well of F——. Even now I think he is the prey of wicked and designing men, and I think he has absolutely no military capacity. He went to Missouri, the pet and *protégé* of the B——'s. At first they corresponded with him and with F——, who was with him, fully and confidently thinking his plans and his efforts would accomplish great things for the country. At last the tone of F——'s letters changed. It was a change from confidence to doubt and uncertainty. They were pervaded with a tone of sincere sorrow, and of fear that F—— would fail. M—— showed them to me, and we were both grieved at the prospect. Soon came the news that F—— had issued his Emancipation Order, and had set up a Bureau of Abolition, giving free papers, and occupying his time apparently with little else. At last, at my suggestion, M. B—— went to M—— to look at, and talk over matters. He went as the friend of F——. I sent him as F——'s friend. He passed on the way, Mrs. F—— coming to see me. She sought an audience with me at midnight, and taxed me so violently with many things that I had to exercise all the awkward tact I have, to avoid quarreling with her. She surprised me by asking why their enemy, M. B——, had been sent to M——. She more than once intimated that if Gen'l F—— should conclude to try conclusions with me, he could set up for himself."

(J—— says:—"It is pretty clearly proven that F—— had at that time concluded that the Union was definitely destroyed, and that he should set up an independent government as soon as he took M—— and organized his army.")

"The next we heard was that F—— had arrested F. B——, and the rupture has since never been healed."

"During F——'s time, the *M—— D——*, which had always been B——'s organ, was bought up by F——, and turned against F. B——. This took away from F——, after his final break with F——, the bulk of the strength which had always elected him. This left him ashore. To be elected in this state of things he must seek for votes outside of the Republican organization. He had pretty hard trimming and cutting to do this consistently. It is this necessity, as it appears to me, of finding some ground for F—— to stand on, that accounts for the present, somewhat anomalous, position of the B——s in politics."

J——:—"The opinion of people who read your Message to-day is that, on that platform, two of your ministers must walk the plank—B—— and B——."

Lincoln:—"Both of these men acquiesced in it without objection. The only member of the Cabinet who objected to it was Mr. C——."

Dec. 10. . . . . S—— speaks of the Message with great gratification. It satisfies his idea of proper reconstruction without insisting on the adoption of his peculiar theories. The President repeated, what he has often said before, that there is no essential contest between loyal men on this subject, if they consider it reasonably. The only question is:—Who constitute the State? When that it is decided, the solution of subsequent questions is easy.

He says that he wrote in the Message originally that he considered the discussion as to whether a State has been at any time out of the Union, as vain and profitless. We know that they were—we trust they shall be—in the Union. It does not greatly matter whether, in the meantime, they shall be considered to have been in or out. But he afterwards considered that the 4th Section, 4th Article of the Constitution, empowers him to grant protection to States in the Union, and it will not do ever to admit that these States have at any time been out. So he erased that sentence as possibly suggestive of evil. He preferred, he said, to stand firmly based on the Constitution rather than work in the air.

Talking about the M—— matter, he said these radical men have in them the stuff which must save the State, and on which we must mainly rely. They are absolutely uncorrosive by the virus of secession. It cannot touch or taint them. While the conservatives, in casting about for votes to carry through their plans, are tempted to affiliate with those whose record is not clear. If one side must be crushed out and the other cherished, there could be no doubt which side we would choose as fuller of hope for the future. We would have to side with the radicals.

"But just there is where their wrong begins. They insist that I shall hold and treat Gov. G—— and his supporters—men appointed by loyal people of M—— as representatives of M—— loyalty, and who have done their whole duty in the war faithfully and promptly,—who, even when they have disagreed with me, have been silent and kept about the good work,—that I shall treat these men as copperheads and ruinous to the Government. This is simply monstrous."

"I talked to these people in this way, when they came to me this fall. I saw that their attack on G—— was malicious. They moved against him by flank attacks from different sides of the same question. They accused him of enlisting rebel soldiers among the enrolled militia; and of exempting all the rebels, and forcing Union men to do the duty; all this in the blindness of passion. I told them they were endangering the election of Senators; that I thought their duty was to elect H—— and G. B——; and nothing has happened in our politics which has pleased me more than that incident."

He spoke of the newborn fury of some of these men,—of D—— stumping against R—— in '56 on the ground that R—— was an abolitionist;—of *ci-devant* rebels coming here in the radical Convention. Not that he objected; he was glad of it; but fair play! let not the pot make injurious reference to the black base of the kettle; he was in favor of short statutes of limitations.

In reply to a remark of A——'s about the improved condition of things in K——, and the necessity of still greater improvement, and the good disposition of the K—— congressmen, the President said he had for a long time been aware that the K——'s were not regarding in good faith the Proclamation of Emancipation and the laws of Congress, but were treating as slaves the escaped freedmen from Alabama and Mississippi; that this must be ended as soon as his hands grew a little less full. . . . .

Dec. 12. I met at the Theatre S. S. C——, who was speaking of the statesmanship and success of Gov. S——, attributing much to the *bonhommie* and affability of his manners. He says S—— sent for him the other day and asked him if he wanted to retain his place on the Committee of Foreign Relations, and if he wished to designate what gentlemen on the Democratic side should be associated with him, promising to speak to C—— for him. This frank kindliness seemed to have won C—— over very much personally. S—— is unquestionably gaining in popularity very fast. M—— said of him the other day:—"Il est très sage." The diplomatic body have all apparently stopped abusing him, and those who do not like, have been forced to respect.

Dec. 13. The President, speaking to-day about M—— matters, said he had heard some things of S—— which had very much displeased him:—That while W—— was in M——, he saw or thought he saw that S—— was working rather energetically in the politics of the State, and that he approached S—— and proposed that he should use his influence to harmonize the conflicting elements so as to elect one of each wing, G—— B—— and H——. S——'s reply was that he would not consent to the election of G—— B——. Again when G—— B—— was about coming to Washington, he sent a friend to S—— to say that he would not oppose his confirmation, if he (S——) would, so far as his influence extended, agree to a Convention of M—— to make necessary alterations in her State Constitution. S——'s reply, as reported by B—— to the President was that he would not consent to a State Convention. These things, the President says, are obviously transcendent of his instructions and must not be permitted. He has sent for S—— to come to Washington and explain these grave matters.

The President is inclined to put R—— in S——'s place, and to give to Gen'l C—— the Department of Kansas. But H—— and S—— stand in his way, and he has to use the strong hand so often with those impractical gentlemen that he avoids it when he can. . . .

To-night H—— arrived and spent the evening with the President. The conversation at first took a professional turn, the President showing a very intimate knowledge of those plays of Shakespeare where Falstaff figures. He was particularly anxious to know why one of the best scenes in the play—that where Falstaff and Prince Hal alternately assume the character of the king—is omitted in the representation. Hackett says it is admirable to read, but ineffective on stage;—that there is generally nothing sufficiently distinctive about the actor who plays Henry to make an imitation striking.

Hackett plays with stuffing of india-rubber;—says Shakespeare refers to it when he says: "How now! blown Jack!" Hackett is a very amusing and garrulous talker. He had some good reminiscences of H——, C—— (the former he admires, the latter he thinks a dull man), McC—— and P——. . . .

Tuesday, Dec. 15. The President took S——, N—— and me to F——'s with him to see Falstaff in *Henry IV*. D—— came in after a while. Hackett was most admirable. The President criticised his reading of a passage where Hackett said, "mainly *thrust* at me," the President thinking it should read "mainly thrust at *me*." I told the President I thought he was wrong; that "mainly" merely meant "strongly," "fiercely." The President thinks the dying speech of Hotspur an unnatural and unworthy thing—as who does not. . . .

Thursday, Dec. 17. One morning this week I went to the State Department. . . . Found S—— very busy over the complication arising from the "Chesapeake piracy." He said S—— had just come in and said with great glee:—"This proves my position to be correct, that England was wrong in conceding belligerency to these people." "Of course," said S——: "but how the devil does that help the matter?" S—— was delighted to have his theory vindicated even by such trouble.

Monday, Dec. 23. I took to the Senate to-day

the nomination of S—— as Major General. The President had previously spoken to some of the Senators about it. He is anxious that S—— should be confirmed so as to arrange this M—— matter promptly. I told S——, W——, H—— and D——. Senator F—— also agreed to do all he could to put the matter properly through. But on the nomination being read in Executive Session, H—— of M—— objected to its consideration and it was postponed. S—— and D—— tell me it will certainly go through when it is regularly taken up. L—— came up to the President about it, and told him this. L—— is very anxious to have the K—— part of the plan at once carried out. M—— says that G. B—— gave to S—— to present to the Senate the radical protest against S——'s confirmation, and that S—— presented it to-day. The President sent for S——, but he was not at his lodgings. The President is very much disappointed at B——. After three interviews with him he understood that B—— would not oppose the confirmation. It is rather a mean dodge to get S—— to do it in his stead. . . . .

The President to-night had a dream:—He was in a party of plain people, and, as it became known who he was, they began to comment on his appearance. One of them said:—"He is a very common-looking man." The President replied:—"The Lord prefers common-looking people. That is the reason he makes so many of them."

Dec. 24. . . . . I dined to-day with S. S. C——. He spoke of G——'s foolish C—— explosion the other night at W. P——'s Cooper Institute meeting, and said C—— was working night and day. He has gotten nearly the whole strength of the New England States. If there is any effort made in O—— he can be beaten there. He has little strength in his own State.

I asked him whom his party would nominate. "Gen'l McC——! We will run McC——. He is our best ticket. He lost some prestige by his W—— letter. But it was necessary. He never would have gotten the nomination without it."

"You don't agree with the *H——* on G——?"

"G—— belongs to the Republicans. We can't take him after his letter to W——. But for that, we might have taken him. The Republicans won't take him either. They have got his influence, and have no further use for him."

"If I were a soldier I should much prefer commanding the U. S. Army for life, to four years in the Executive Mansion. I think G—— would."

"So would McC——, I know."

I met him again to-night in the Theatre. He says he is getting tired of Washington. He wants to spend a few years in Europe. He will go, if McC—— is next President;—thinks he will anyhow. Says it is delightful to be in the minority; you are not bored by your people for office.—"Glad you like it!" quoth I. "We will try to keep you so."

Dec. 25. A lonesome sort of Christmas. I breakfasted, dined and supped alone. Went to the Theatre and saw *Macbeth* alone.

The President to-day got up a plan for extending to the people of the rebellious districts the practical benefits of the Proclamation. He is to send record-books to various points to receive subscriptions to the Oath, for which certificates will be given to the man taking the oath. He has also prepared a placard himself giving notice of the opening of the books and the nature of the oath required.

He sent the first of the books to P—— to

be used in Virginia. The second he will probably send to Arkansas.

The President was greatly amused at G——'s hasty C—— explosion and its elaborate explanation in the T——. He defended Gov. C—— from P——'s unjust attacks, saying that he thought C——'s banking system rested on a sound basis of principle; that is, causing the capital of the country to become interested in the sustaining of the National credit. That this was the principal financial measure of Mr. C——, in which he (L——) has taken an especial interest. Mr. C—— had frequently consulted him in regard to it. He had generally delegated to Mr. C—— exclusive control of those matters falling within the province of his Department. This matter he had shared in to some extent. . . .

Dec. 28. I received to-night letters from P—— and S—— asking me to come down to Florida and be their Representative in Congress.

Talked with the President about the matter of the reconstruction of Florida. He wants me to take one of his Oath-books down to Point Lookout, and get the matter going there, and after that he will appoint me a Commissioner to go to Florida and engineer business there. By their meeting at St. Augustine, the other day, there seems a prospect of getting the State under way early next Spring. I will go down and form my plans after I get there as to my own course. . . .

Jan. 1, 1864. . . . . I left W——'s yesterday and went to live at Club to-day.

Point Lookout. The President and Secretary of War to-day (Jan. 2, 1864), commissioned me to go down to Point Lookout, and deliver to Gen'l M—— the book of oaths and the accompanying blanks, and explain to him the mode in which they are to be used. Gen'l B—— was ordered by telegraph to meet me there and consult as to the manner of carrying out the President's plan for pardoning and enlisting the repentant rebels. I bore a letter for Gen'l B——'s instruction.

I went on board a little tug at the Seventh Street Wharf, and rattled and rustled through the ice to Alexandria where I got on board the Clyde, most palatial of steam tugs, fitted up with a very pretty cabin and berths heated by steam and altogether sybaritic in its appointments.

The day was bitterly cold, and the wind was malignant on the Potomac. I shut myself up in my gorgeous little cabin and scribbled and read and slept all day. The captain thought best to lay to for a while in the night, so we put in at Smith's Creek, and arrived at Point Lookout in the early morning. I went to the head-quarters of the General, accompanied by a young officer who asked my name and got it. I felt little interest in his patronymic, and it is now gone into the oblivion of those ante Agamemnona. It was so cold that nobody was stirring. A furry horse was crouching by the wall. "Hello, Billy! cold! Ain't it?" said my companion. Billy was indignantly silent. We stumbled on over the frozen ground past the long line of cottages that line the beach, built by the crazy proprietor of the land who hoped to make here a great watering-place which would draw the beauty and fashion of the country away from Long Branch, and make Newport a Ranz des Vaches. We came up to a snug-looking frame house which had been the dwelling of the adventurous lunatic. A tall young man, with enormous blonde moustache and a general up-too-early air about him, hove in sight, and my guide and friend introduced me. "Yes,

I have heard of you, Mr. Hale. I got a despatch from the General saying you would be here. When did you arrive, Mr. Kay? Rather cold weather! Any ice on the river, Mr. Day?" All this in a voice like a rumbling of distant thunder, measured and severe, and with a manner of preternatural solemnity. "The General will soon be up, Mr. Hayes." My mild insinuation as to my cognomen having brought him that near to my christening at last.

He disappeared, and coming back beckoned me out. I followed him across a little entry into a room opposite. There stood in the attitude in which, if Comfort ever were deified, the statues should be posed,—parted coat-tails,—a broad plenilunar base exposed to the grateful warmth of the pine-wood fire,—a hearty Yankee gentleman, clean-shaven,—sunny and rosy,—to whom I was presented, and who said laconically, "Sit there!" pointing to a warm seat by a well-spread breakfast table. I had an appetite engendered by a day and night of river air, and I ate breakfast till the intelligent contraband, who served us, caught the infection and plied me with pork-steaks till hunger cried quarter. The General told a good yarn on a contraband soldier who complained of a white man abusing him:—"I doesn't objeck to de pussonal cuffin, but he must speck de unicorn."

The General's flock are a queer lot. Dirty, ragged, yet jolly. Most of them are still rebellious, but many are tired and ready to quit, while some are actuated by a fierce desire to get out of the prison, and by going into our army, avenge the wrongs of their forced service in the rebel ranks.

They are great traders. A stray onion,—a lucky treasure-trove of a piece of coal,—is a capital for extensive operations in Confederate trash. They sell and gamble away their names with utter recklessness. They have the easy carelessness of a ——— about their patronymics. They sell their names when drawn for a detail to work, a great prize in the monotonous life of every day. A small-pox patient sells his place on the sick-list to a friend who thinks the path to Dixie easier from the hospital than the camp. The traffic in names on the morning of Gen'l B———'s detail of 500 for exchange was as lively as Wall Street on days when Taurus climbs the Zenith, or the "Coal Hole" when gold is tumbling ten per cent. an hour.

They live in a 30-acre lot fenced around by themselves. They put up the fence with great glee, saying, "they would fence out the d——d Yankees and keep respectable."

Rather a pleasant place, on a pleasant day, is Point Lookout. To-day it was dreary and cold. I could not but think of the winter life of the sanguine lunatic who built the little village intended for the summer home of beauty and chivalry, and destined for the malodorous abode and the unfragrant belongings of a great hospital in busy war-times.

My little boat got frightened at the blow that freshened in the evening, and I sent her up to snooze the night away in Smith's Creek.

In the dusk of the evening Gen'l B—— came clattering into the room where M—— and I were sitting, followed by a couple of aides. We had some hasty talk about business:—he told me how he was administering the oath at Norfolk; how popular it was growing; children cried for it; how he hated the Jews; how heavily he laid his hand on them;—"A nation that the Lord had been trying to make something of for three thousand years, and had so far utterly failed." "King John knew how to deal with them—fried them in swine's fat."

After drinking cider we went down to the Hudson City, the General's flagship. His wife, niece and excessively pretty daughter; tall, statuesque and fair, and named, by a happy prophecy of the blonde beauty of her maturity, Blanche, were there at tea. I sent my little web-footed sulky word to get home as she could, and sailed with the B——'s for Baltimore.

At night, after the ladies had gone off to bed—they all said *retired*, but I suppose it meant the same thing in the end,—we began to talk about some queer matters. B—— had some odd stories about physical sympathies; he talked also about the Hebrew jurisprudence and showed a singular acquaintance with biblical studies; his occasional references to anatomy and physiology evidently surprised the surgeon, to whom he respectfully deferred from time to time. He talked till it grew late and we dispersed to bed. I slept on the guards; a pleasant bed-room, but chilly; and listened till I slept, to the cold and shuddering roar of the water under the wheels.

At Baltimore we took a special car and came home. I sat with the General all the way and talked with him about many matters; Richmond and its long immunity. He says he can take an army within thirty miles of Richmond without any trouble; from that point the enemy can either be forced to fight in the open field south of the city; or submit to be starved into surrender.

He was very severe on McC—— for his action about the New Orleans expedition. He says that before the expedition was resolved on, by the President, McC—— said it would require 50,000 men; after it was resolved on, he said 5,000 would be enough. He said he did not like to attack McC——. *Nil nisi bonum*, etc. But he might have to exploit that matter sometime.

I told him of the night of October 21.

He gave me some very dramatic incidents of his recent action in Fortress Monroe, smoking out adventurers and confidence men, testing his detectives, and matters of that sort. He makes more business in that sleepy, little Department than anyone would have dreamed was in it.

Jan. 8. N—— and I visited to-night the Secretaries of the Interior and of the Treasury. U—— talked about the vacancy occasioned by the death of C. B. S——. Said he understood S—— to be for him, when he was asking it for himself. O—— is an admirable man for the place, but U—— does not want to lose him from the Department.

We found at C——'s a most amusing little toy, "the Plantation Breakdown." The Secretary and his daughter were busily engaged exhibiting it to some grave and reverend old fellows who are here at the meeting of the Society of Arts and Sciences. In the course of conversation the Secretary said to me:—"It is singularly instructive to meet so often as we do in life and in history, instances of vaulting ambition, meanness and treachery, failing after enormous exertions; and integrity and honesty march straight in triumph to its purpose."

A noble sentiment, Mr. Secretary!

Jan. 9. C—— has written to the President that the entire Union force of the P—— Legislature, House and Senate, have subscribed a request that the President will allow himself to be re-elected, and that they intend visiting Washington to present it. He says:—"I have kept my promise."

The indications all look that way. The loud Lincoln men, who are useful only as weather-gauges to show the natural drift of things, are laboring hard to prove themselves the original friends of the President. M. D—— is talking about the C—— plot to ruin him and Lincoln. He says P—— is to be at the head of the new F—— party that is soon to be placed in commission; and much of this. On the other hand, W. McV——, who dined with me to-day, says that the strugglers now seem to get ahead of each other in the nomination. The New Hampshire occurrence startled the Union League of P——. They saw their thunder stolen from their own arsenals. They fear their own endorsement will be *passée* before long, and are now casting about to get some arrangement for putting him in nomination at once.

W. told a very funny story about F—— and C—— in conversation about politics on the train. F—— bibulously insisting that if he had beaten C—— for the Senate, there would have been no war.

Jan. 13. I received to-day my commission as A. A. G. from the War Department, and accepted it, taking the oath of allegiance before Notary C——.

Made a visit or two.

Went into the President's room and announced myself ready to start. "Great good luck and God's blessing go with you, John!" How long will you stay, one month or six months?

New York, Jan. 15. On board the Fulton. The embarcation of the 54th Boys. Variety of complexions—redheads,—filing into their places on deck—singing, whistling, smoking and dancing—eating candy and chewing tobacco. Jolly little cuss, round, rosy and half-white, singing:—

Oh John Brown dey hung him
We're gwine to jine de Union Army
Oh John Brown dey hung him
We're gwine to Dixie's land.

Way down by James' River
Old massa's grave is made
And he or me is sure to fill it
When he meets de black Brigade.

We're gwine to trabbel to de Souf
To smack de rebels in de mouf.

Tuesday, 19. A cold, raw day. Passed Charleston early in the morning. Fort Sumter lit up by a passing waft of sunshine. A shot fired from Cumming's Point as we passed. The weather—demoralized by Yankee contact—growing so cold as to drive passengers below stairs to euchre.

Wednesday, Jan. 20. On arriving at Hilton Head yesterday afternoon I found that Gen'l G——'s Headquarters were now at Hilton Head. I went on shore, met Col. S——, and made an appointment to be presented to Gen'l G—— later. Took tea at the Port Royal House and was told by the gentlemanly proprietor that I had better forage on my friends for a bed. Was presented to the General and delivered my letter to Gen'l G——. He seemed perplexed rather, and evidently thought he was expected to undertake some immediate military operation to effect the occupation and reconstruction. He dwelt on the deficiency of transportation in the Department and the immobility of his force for the purposes of land attack. He has only now after great efforts succeeded in mounting a regiment of infantry for cavalry service, etc., etc. I told him it was not the President's intention to do anything to embarrass his military operations; that all I wished from him was an order directing me to go to Florida and open my books of record for the oaths; as preliminary to future proceedings.

He said we would speak farther of it. Meanwhile I will wait for my papers delayed at New York.

Jan. 23, Saturday. Saturday night I went on board the Ben Deford with the General to visit Folly and Morris Islands. Col. J——, Major B——, Capt. R—— and F—— were in the party.

In the morning we were at Pawnee Landing, Folly River. We mounted and rode to Gen'l T——'s headquarters; saw model of Fort Wagner. T—— joined G—— and we went up the beach to Light House Inlet; saw the scene of the crossing by S——; crossed and went in ambulances to Wagner; spent some time there. From Wagner walked up to Gregg, leaving our ambulance. Saw the mortar batteries before getting there. From Gregg had a good view of Fort Sumter—silent as the grave—flag flying over it—a great flag flying over the battery on Sullivan's Island. The city, too, was spread out before us like a map; everything very silent; a ship lying silent at the wharf. No sign of life in Ripley, Johnson or Pinckney.

Jan. 27. The Atlantic arrived this morning from the North vice the Arago transferred to New Orleans, and brought my books and my whiskey.

I am happy—modifiedly, as a worm must be.

Feb. 1st and 2nd. Evening of February 1st Gen'l T—— and I got on board a noisy little tug at the wharf which took us to the Ben Deford. We went upstairs and drank a few whiskey punches, and then to sleep. In the morning found ourselves off Stone;—tide too low to let us over the bar;—were rowed ashore,—Gen'l T——, Turner and I. Stopped at lower end of Folly for an ambulance; rode to Gen'l T——'s headquarters and took horses to ride to Light House Inlet; crossed in a boat and walked up to Col. D——. Col. D. full of a plan for capturing the Sumter garrison.

We went in ambulance to Wagner. The sound of firing had been heard all the morning. It grew more frequent, and Davies told us it was directed at a stranded blockade-runner. Just as we got in sight of Wagner a white smoke appeared in the clear air (the fog had lifted suddenly) and a sharp crack was heard. It seemed as if a celestial pop-corn had been born in the ether. "There's a shell from Simkins," said Turner. We went on, and there were more of them. As we got to Wagner we got out and sent the ambulance to a place of safety under the walls. They were just making ready to discharge a great gun from Wagner. The Generals clapped hands to their ears. The gun was fired, and the black globe went screaming close to the ground over the island, over the harbor, landing and bursting near the helpless blockade-runner stranded half-way from Fort Beauregard to Fort Moultrie. We walked up the beach. Heretofore we had from time to time seen little knots of men gathered to look at the fight, but now the beach was deserted. Once in a while you would see a fellow crouching below a sandhill keeping a sharp lookout. We soon came to Batteries Seymour, Barton and Chatfield, which were firing vigorously. We mounted the parapet and took a good look at the steamer. She was already a good deal damaged by one shell amidships.

Feb. 2. The enemy's fire was getting pretty warm. They had the range perfectly; most of the shell burst in or over the works; but the men were so well protected that all the time we were there but three were hit, and they were said to be imprudent. The men dodged and broke to cover at the flashing of the enemy's battery, but the officers exposed themselves with perfect insouciance.

The shells had singular voices. Some screamed frightfully; some had a regular musical note like Chu-chu-weechu-weechu-*brrr;* and each of the fragments a wicked little whistle of its own. Many struck in the black, marshy mud behind us, burying themselves, and casting a malodorous shower into the air. Others burrowed in the sand. One struck the face of C——, while I was standing on the parapet, with a heavy thud, and in a moment afterward threw a cloud of sand into the air. I often saw in the air a shell bursting,—fierce, jagged white lines darting out first, like javelins—then the flowering of the awful bud into full bloom,—all in the dead silence of the upper air;—the crack and the whistle of the fragments.

Col. D—— took us to see the great 300-

pounder Parrot. At a very little distance, an ugly-looking hole where a shell had just burst; —beside the gun traces in the sand of hasty trampling and wagon-wheels;—dark stains soaking into the sand;—a poor fellow had just had his leg taken off by a piece of a shell.

I saw them putting a crushed and mangled mass into an ambulance. He was still and pale. The driver started off at a merry trot. A captain said:—"D—— you, drive that thing slower!"

Two or three young fellows were playing with their horses in the parade. The horses joining in the fun threw riders over their heads and started off.

The ill-starred boat got badly pounded, her machinery and works battered in. She seemed sinking before we left. The navy were off nearly two miles, but still made passable shooting. Their ricochet shots, however, were generally failures.

With a good glass we could see a good many anxious spectators on the rebel side.

Chatfield to boat, 2,600 yards.
Wagner " " 3,000 "
Monitors, 2 miles.

We walked back on the beach to Wagner. A shell exploded close behind us. I made a bad dodge. Walked all over Wagner and got a sympathetic view of the whole affair.

Feb. 9, Jacksonville. . . . . We came to Jacksonville, gay with flags and busy with shipping at noon. I landed and found no General, no staff, no means of information. Ignorance the densest. Met D——, who took me to Mrs. ———. I saw in a few moments' glance the wretched story of two years. A lady, well-bred and refined, dressed worse than a bound girl, with a dirty and ragged gown that did not hide her trim ankles and fine legs. A white-haired, heavy-eyed, slow-speaking old young man. A type of thousands of homes where punishment of giant crimes has lit on humble innocents. I put on my seven-leaguers and rode with K—— and P—— in the afternoon around the pickets. P—— selected points for fortifications. We saw two negro regiments, one at dress parade, gay with banners, one in camp, fragrant with salt-horse. Some firing in the front, with ultimate intentions of mutton or fresh pork. As we came home we saw a train going to provision Gen'l G——'s advance;—a pretty dowdy walking in the silent street,—and some blue-bellied vandals making themselves agreeable to one of the few remaining families.

Feb. 10. . . . . Yesterday I had a number of copies of the Proclamation posted through the town. The few citizens gathered around, the lettered reading, the unlettered listening with something that looked like a ghost of interest. . . . At 2½ p. m. Gen'l G—— and staff came clattering into the cabin of the Ben Deford. They seemed greatly elated by the success of the expedition, and were full of Col. H——'s achievement in the capture of artillery beyond Camp Finegan. In the afternoon Lieut. M—— came in with his railway train from Baldwin. He had four mules for locomotive who had a playful habit of humping themselves and casting off their riders. He had a young woman on board to whom he showed the usual courtesies of railroad Conductors.

Feb. 11. By direction of Gen'l G—— I went to the prisoners confined in the guard-house, read to them the Proclamation, and said I had come to inform them "of this executive act, and extend to you its benefits. I have in my possession a book for the record of oaths. I have certificates entitling those signing the book to the benefit of the act. If you sign, you will be released or allowed to return to your houses, if they are not, etc. If not, you will be sent North as prisoners of war for exchange. By signing it you will entitle yourselves to all your rights as citizens of the United States. It is a matter for your choice. There is to be neither force nor persuasion used in the matter. It is a matter that you must decide for yourselves. There has been some doubt expressed as to whether you will be protected. I am authorized to promise that you will be. The occupation does it for the present. Men enough. Inducement is peace and protection and reëstablishment of your State Government."

When I had finished the little I had to say, they crowded around me asking innumerable questions. I got away and had an office fixed up in the quartermaster's block and waited for my flock. They soon came, a dirty swarm of grey coats, and filed into the room, escorted by a negro guard. Fate had done its worst for the poor devils. Even a nigger guard didn't seem to excite a feeling of resentment. They stood for a moment in awkward attitudes along the wall. I could not but think that the provost had made a mistake and sent me his whole family, as A—— said he thought eight or ten of them could be induced to take the oath of allegiance. But I soon found they had come up in good earnest to sign their names. They opened again in a chorus of questions which I answered as I could. At last a big good-natured fellow said, "This question's enough. Let's take the oath!" They all stood up in line and held up their hands while I read the oath. As I concluded, the negro sergeant came up, saluted, and said:—"Dere's one dat didn't hole up his hand."

They began to sign,—some still stuck and asked questions, some wrote good hands, but most bad. Nearly half made their mark.

. . . . The General received to-day a despatch from S——, saying that H—— fell into an ambush at the South Fork of the St. Mary's, and lost twenty-five in killed and wounded. The enemy got away with slight loss. S—— is informed and seems to believe that there is a large rebel force at Lake City, larger than his own. The General gives no opinion. He says, "S—— has positive orders not to get whipped."

Feb. 12. Received orders from the General to go to St. Augustine with despatches for Col. O—— to move his force, except two companies, to Picolata. (S—— asked last night for the 54th Mass. without delay. "One company is enough for St. Augustine." "Cool for a subordinate," said Q. A.) I went over to H—— and transferred my blasphemy business to him, and made ready at once to go to the Helen Getty. I concluded to go by way of Fernandina to get near my base of supplies. . . .

My first day's operations in Jacksonville were such as to give me great encouragement. I enrolled in all sixty names—some of them men of substance and influence. The fact that more than fifty per cent. of the prisoners of war were eager to desert and get out of the service shows how the spirit of the common people is broken. Everybody seemed tired of the war. Peace on any terms was what they wanted. They have no care for the political questions involved. Most of them had not read the oath, and when I insisted on their learning what it was, they would say listlessly:—"Yes, I guess I'll take it." Some of the more intelligent cursed their politicians and especially South Carolina; but most looked hopefully to the prospect of having a government to protect them after the anarchy of the few years past. There was little of what might be called loyalty. But what I build my hopes on is the evident weariness of the war, and anxiety for peace.

Feb. 21, Hilton Head. Got over bar this morning soon after day. B—— woke me up with the miserable news of H——'s death, loss of seven pieces, capture of four hundred wounded, and our total repulse about seven miles beyond Sanderson. He has despatches from T—— to G——. Arrived at Hilton Head about 9½ after a good run of 14½ hours. Delivered our news to Gen'l G——. The General was much shocked. He said:—"This comes of disobeying orders." He dwelt on this for some time. He said afterwards:—"I should rather he had lost these men in obedience to orders than in disobedience."

S—— has been very unsteady and queer since the beginning of this campaign. He has been subject to violent alternations of timidity and rashness, now declaring Florida loyalty was all bosh, now lauding it as the purest article extant; now insisting that B—— was in his front with the whole confederacy, and now asserting that he could whip all the rebels in Florida with a good brigade. He was ordered to fortify St. Mary's and Baldwin, but pushed out beyond Sanderson instead and got severely punished.

Feb. 22. . . . There was a ball to-night at Beaufort, gotten up by young officers there in honor of the 22d. Gen'l G—— went up for a few moments to lend his influence to counteract the gloom which was overspreading the camp. We got there early and loafed about till the dancing began. The room was exquisitely decorated; several very clever pictures, eagles, etc., were done on the walls with magnolia leaves; flags of all nations, from the Navy, etc.

I left with Gen'l G—— and went on board the Hospital Ship, filled with wounded; went through hold and up-stairs where the artillery boys were. Saw many desperately wounded; Col. R—— mortally, clutching at his bed-clothes and passing garments; picked up, bed and all, and carried away, picking out his clothes from a pile by shoulder-straps—"Major?" "No! Lieutenant-Colonel." H——, M——, D—— and E——, all very chipper and jolly; M—— shot in toes and hat (like a parenthesis) and sabre; H—— between seat and saddle, and in fore-arm. M—— proposed to H—— "to go to party; I'll do dancing, and you hugging."

Suddenly Gen'l S——, who had been much moved by R——'s appearance, started off up to the ball. He arrived during a moment's pause in the Lanciers. He stamped his foot: "Let the music stop!" and it did. "The ball cannot go on. Lights to be out in half an hour." A friend of the General asked:—"Can we eat supper?" "Anyone who has the heart to eat at such a time." All had a heart of that peculiar construction, for all ate. He came back glowing with the triumph of a generous action performed, and asked us up to his room, where we drank champagne and whiskey, and ate cake. Coming out found the grumbling feasters and went to Hilton Head after two o'clock.

Feb. 24. Rode out with T——, who returned last night, and represents S—— as plucky and defiant. He brought his troops off the field splendidly, according to all accounts.

Feb. 28, Sunday. The Arago came in this

morning. The papers of the 23d and 24th attack my coming here as a political trick. Q. A. G. is much troubled at it. I had some talk with T——. He thinks I had better stay. . . . We got on the Dictator at midnight. . . .

Feb. 29. This morning, as we neared Fernandina, I persuaded Gen'l G—— to go on to Jacksonville and send boat back here for us. We landed. . . .

March 1, Fernandina. I opened my books this morning and got a few more names. Some refused to sign on the ground that they were not repentant rebels. . . . The Dictator came in this afternoon and reported to me for orders. I will start for Key West in the morning.

March 2. . . . . We got on board the Dictator for an early start. The wind moans ominously round the state-room doors, presaging a rough day to-morrow. . . .

March 3. We went out to the bar and passed it. I heard the sea hammering on the guards, and turned over for another nap. Came back to

Fernandina. The sea was very heavy; a steady line of breakers rolling in over the bar without a break in three fathoms water. . . . I spent part of evening on board the Peconic. Trash for a little while till I got opportunity to talk to Judge F—— who seems a sincere and candid man with clear views. He thinks the time is not yet come for Florida. I am very sure that we cannot now get the President's 10th, and that to alter the suffrage law for a bare tithe would not give us the moral force we want. The people of the interior would be indignant against such a snap-judgment taken by incomers and would be jealous and sallow.

March 5. . . . . Did not get up until tea to-day. "In bunco tutissimus ibis!" There has been quite a heavy swell. To-night the phosphorescent show is the finest I have yet seen. A broad track of glory follows the ship. By the sides abaft the wheels, the rushing waves are splendid silver, flecked here and there with jets of flame; while outside the silvery trouble, the startled fish darting from our track mark the blue waters with curves and splashes of white radiance. Occasionally across our path drifts a broad blotch of luminous brilliancy, a school of fishes brightening the populous waters.

March 6. A beautiful Sunday; the purest southern day; the air cool but cherishing and kindly; the distant shore fringed with palms and cocoanuts; the sea a miracle of color; on the one hand a bright vivid green; on the other a deep dark blue; flaked by the floating shadows cast by the vagrant clouds that loaf in the liquid sky.

Florida Keys. Passed Hillsboro and New River Inlet in the morning, and made Cape Florida at noon. We struck out seaward there, skirting the inner edge of the Gulf-Stream where the pure emerald of the water was marred by the darker waves of the Gulf. Lighter around the vessel grew the pale green of the sea; more vivid and brilliant the shine in shore. When we passed the shoals off the Cape and took our southerly course outside the reefs I thought I had never seen so splendid a prodigality of coloring in any marine picture. On our left, towards the horizon, rolled the dark azure of the Gulf-Stream; before us, and to our right, as far as the distant shore, the vivid emerald of these strange Floridian waters, the darker vegetation of the coral keys throwing its pale beauty into finer relief, while the sunny skies were flushed with a faint auroral radiance of pearl and pink, such as tinges the polished lips of the sea-shells of this coast.

Leaning over the starboard rail, gazing with a lazy enjoyment at this scene of enchantment, at the fairy islands scattered like a chain of gems on the bosom of this transcendent sea, bathed in the emerald ripples and basking in the rosy effulgence of the cherishing sky; the white sails flitting through the quiet inlets; the soft breeze causing the sunny waters to sparkle and the trees to wave, I thought that here were the Isles of the Blessed; within the magic ring of these happy islands the syrens were singing, and the maids were twining their flowing hair with sprays of the coral. Anchored in everlasting calm, far from the malice of the sky, or the troubling eyes of men, they sported through the tranquil years of the everlasting summer, in the sacred idleness of the immortals.

My friend Canis Marinus begged to differ. He said:—"There's the Ragged Keys; full o' mud-torkles and rattle-snakes; them little boats is full of Conks—come up for to sponge."

Indian Key. At dusk we came to anchor off Indian Key, a rather famous place where a horticultural lunatic lived, planted and died. We rowed ashore. As we neared the island, a gruff voice hailed us:—"Who are you?" "R——!" shouted our pilot, which seemed satisfactory. We scraped heavily on the coral bottom as we went in, and brought up at a ricketty old wharf. There had once been a rather lively place here. Large buildings fitted up for hospital purposes in the old wars. Now occupied by Captain B—— and a family of spongers. We asked for fish. B—— said it was *Sabbath;* caught no fish to-day. Asked for cocoanuts. Said hadn't any gathered. "Pretty ugly job gathering on 'em in the night." Our little purser volunteered for the service, and he, S—— and I went out. He and I scaled alternate trees and sent down the heavy clusters. We plunged into a tangled abattis of some thorny thing they called manilla, which scratched and pierced like the d——.

We came in bearing our spoils and found the whole family in the great barn-like room of the store. White-headed, apathetic — open-mouthed — silent — indolent and stupid. We bought sponges and shells of them galore, and went back to our ship.

B—— came after us for a newspaper and a gass with R——. They talked about wrecks and the profits thereof—of weddings and elopements—of crops and wealth,—at intervals of ten minutes between interlocutions. Brains hardening into an unlovely mould in a lonely life on one of these coral islands.

Monday, March 7, 1864, Key West. We steamed away as it grew light and arrived at Key West about noon. The Key lies bathed in the quiet ripples of the pale green water, whitened by the coral. So bright green that I cannot describe the gem-like shine of the distant waters. The sea-gulls that soar above the sea have their white breasts and inside wings splendidly stained with green by the reflection of the gleaming water.

I went ashore, and after several inquiries found that Gen'l W—— lived half a mile from the dock. I went to a hotel to inquire about a carriage, and was referred to a Jew druggist,—who pointed to a bay rat hitched to a shay in front of his door, and implored me for pure love of God to be back by two. I drove out by the beach to the barracks; passed two black sentries, and found the General's Adjutant, Capt. B——, and soon thereafter Gen'l W——. I was expected, Gen'l B——s' orders having arrived some time ago. I arranged my matters in half an hour.

. . . . In the evening S—— and I went out to see a "popular nigger" named Sandy. Some young "Knavies" were there. They chatted a moment, ordered some sapodillos (which tasted like Castile soap and rotten apples), and then went away saying they were going to see the ladies. Whereat Sandy chuckled and guffawed to the imminent danger of his supper, which he had been eating quietly, sensibly refusing to let our entrance disturb him.

Sandy talked mostly of his influential friends. "Captains and Colonels and them things," and gingerly of the rebellious and fugacious. S. asked him if he were bothered much. "No! not sence I broke dat feller's jaw in tree pieces. I b'lieve he was a rebel—a passel of 'em,—a dozen, sah, come to debbil me; dey tore down my fence panels, and I went out to see. I ain't feared o' nobody. But a man got to be lively when he's fighting a passel, it's a busy time ob de year den.

I hit one ob 'em and he straightened out like a log; broke his jaw in tree pieces; and de rest, dey run. I nebber complains; de officers, dey got dere hands full; mustn't trouble bout every little tittle. I's a darkey sort ob person. I takes off hat to everybody; but dey got to luff me alone."

March 8, Tuesday. I walked round the town this morning,—met several of the citizens who said they were pure and disinterested, and other people were unscrupulous scamps;—seems the usual topic of conversation here with strangers within their gates. . . . .

March 9, Wednesday. . . . . I found a very decent darkey with a very decent buggy belonging to a v. d. Dr. S——; and they, all together, took me riding to my engagements. The only blot of decency on the Key West escutcheon. Otherwise they are a race of thieves and a degeneration of vipers.

We cast off about noon, and night came on us before we had made Indian Head, which was to be our anchorage for the night, as we wanted to be in the lee of Alligator Bank and reef to avoid the fresh gale now blowing in the gulf. We all stood wide-legged and anxious on the forecastle as men will about little things on ships,—Joe heaving the lead,—the Captain leaning to the breeze, his alpaca coat bagging like a seedy balloon,—old R—— confident and oracular,—till S—— who had been hanging like a pointer dog over the rail, sung out—"Light ho! 4." This was old B——, and we at once knew where we were. We anchored and lay there quietly.

I finished my poem, "Northward," begun to-day on leaving Key West.

March 11. . . . . We reached Fernandina between four and five, entering the muddy water of this coast soon after dinner. We found there had been a heavy hailstorm here this morning. . . .

March 12, Saturday. A fine day. Got away from Fernandina at half past five a. m. and arrived at Hilton Head at three p. m.

March 19. . . . . The General tells me he intends to ask of the War Department permission to take the 10th Army Corps away from here and lead it in the field himself. H—— has asked him how many troops he can spare, reserving enough for purely defensive operations. He says he can spare eight or nine thousand. Now, the effective force of the 10th Corps is eleven thousand men, and the troops composing it are such as have been longest in the Department, and the medical director advises that they be moved first. Gen'l G—— will make this application by to-day's steamer.

We got on board at about four o'clock and soon after weighed anchor. We lay in the stream until Gen'l G—— boarded us in a tug, and gave me despatches for H—— and C—— of the tenor aforesaid.

Wednesday, 23. Lay to, soon after midnight. A full attendance at breakfast. Three inches of snow on deck; effeminate southerners of six months' standing, shivering like Italian greyhounds. . . . . We drove to the hotel and played soldier like young idiots coming home from school. . . . .

. . . . Arrived at Washington, half past six.

March 24. I arrived at Washington this morning, finding N—— in bed at 7 o'clock in the morning. We talked over matters for a little while and I got some ideas of the situation from him.

After breakfast I talked with the President. There was no special necessity of presenting my papers, as I found he thoroughly understood the state of affairs in Florida, and did not seem in the least annoyed by the newspaper falsehoods about the matter. Gen'l H——, I learn, has continually given out that the expedition was the President's and not his (H——'s),—so F—— tells me. The President said he has not seen G——'s letters to H——, but said he had learned from S—— that they had nothing to bear out H——'s assertion. I suppose H—— is badly bilious about G——. G——, the President says, is Commander-in-Chief, and H—— is now nothing but a staff officer. In fact, says the President, "when McC—— seemed incompetent to the work of handling an army and we sent for H—— to take command, he stipulated that it should be with the full power and responsibility of Commander-in-Chief. He ran it on that basis till P——'s defeat; but ever since that event he has shrunk from responsibility whenever it was possible."

April 24. To-day the President, loafing into

my room, picked up a paper and read the *R——* *E——'s* recent attack on J—— D——. It amused him. "Why," said he, "the *E——* seems about as fond of J—— as the *W——* is of me."

. . . . E. L. S——, son of Lord S——, has been here for a week. I took him over to Arlington and showed him the African. He asked more questions than I ever dreamed of in similar circumstances. He applied a drastic suction to every contraband he met with, and came back with brain and note-book crammed with instructive miscellany. He has been exhausting everybody in the same way, till his coming is dreaded like that of the schoolmaster by his idle flock. He is a most intelligent gentleman—courteous and ready—a contrast to most Englishmen in his freedom from conceit and prejudice.

He leaves town to-day. I gave him my autograph book; we exchanged Cartes "like two young shepherds, very friendly and pastoral."

HAY TO C. G. HALPINE.

April 13, 1864.

MY DEAR H——:

I thank you for your kind and most unjust letter. I did call at your house on Bleecker Street, and you were not at home—nor was M. le General. I am too old a soldier to pass through your camp without reporting.

I thank you for offering to set me right with the pensive public. But the game is not worth so bright a candle. The original lie in the *H*—— was dirty enough, and the subsequent commentaries were more than usually nasty. But the Tycoon never minded it in the least, and, as for me, at my age the more abuse I get in the newspapers, the better for me. I shall run for constable some day on the strength of my gory exploits in Florida.

I am stationed here for the present. I fear I shall not get away soon again. I have a great deal to do. It is the best work that I can do if I must stay here.

To-night (April 24) Gen'l B—— came up with me from Willard's to see the President.

They talked about the opening campaign more than anything else. . . . He gave some interesting reminiscences of the siege of Knoxville (Tad laughing enormously whenever he saw his father's eye twinkle, though not seeing clearly why).

B—— and S—— are the only ones in motion in accordance with the Order for a general movement on the 23d.

April 25. This morning B—— came in with F——, a fine handsome fellow who looks like a soldier at least. . . . If I can get away during this campaign I think I will go either with B—— or G——.

On the evening of the 25th F——, who had been frequently telegraphed by B—— to come down to Fort Monroe, determined to go, and asked me to go with him. We started for the Navy Yard at 5.30, passing W——'s while B——'s splendid column was moving down 14th Street across the Long Bridge into Virginia. This is the finest looking and best appointed force I have ever yet seen. A little gorgeous and showy, reminding one of the early regiments who went shining down to Bull Run and the Peninsula as if to a picnic. The 8th N. J. Cavalry looked fine and yellow in their new cloaks and gold-braided breasts. The officers looked so superbly outlandish that it surprised one to hear them speaking in a Yankee accent, pure American as C. C—— calls it. The black regiments looked well, and marched better than others—as in fact they always do.

We went down the river among the twilight "shadders" and got some fish and dined off shad-roe and shad. F—— had brought with him some of his choice Oolong tea. . . . We got to Fortress Monroe in the morning, and W—— and I visited the "Iroquois," Capt. R. R——, while F—— went to see the General. Coming ashore we skirmished for some time about the walls of the Fortress before we could find the right entrance. We went in; saw S——, and K—— who was lounging round with an air intensely *ennuyée*, and who said:—"There are plenty of indications here which to a green hand would presage an early movement; but we *blasé* fellows don't seem to see it; we are familiar with large promise and scanty performance."

Joined B—— and F—— on the ramparts. B—— said he was walking there for the first time in several months; preferring to take necessary exercise on horseback. He spoke highly of the negro troops—especially of their walking powers. They start off and trot slouchingly without wasting any muscle in grace of action, he said, illustrating the shuffling step, on the ramparts, bending his knees, and dragging his feet over the oniony grass. He spoke of the delight with which B. O—— ate the good dinners he got while at the Fort—saying that one breakfast he got at S——'s would have cost $2,000 in Richmond.

. . . . I had a good deal of a talk with S——; one of "the best staff a man was ever blessed with,—S——, T——, S—— and W——," as B—— says. S—— is sanguine about the coming movement. "We will fasten our teeth," he says, "on his line of supplies, and he must leave his positions to come and beat us off;"—relying on G——'s not being the man to let that be done quietly. . . .

F—— seemed troubled sorely by the prospect. He fears the details have not been sufficiently studied; that the forces are to bulge ahead and get badly handled; that they rely on help from the navy in places where the navy cannot possibly help,—but rather "will be useless as an elephant with his trunk unscrewed and his tusks unshipped;" that going up the James between the precipitous banks, a few riflemen on the banks will produce a panic that nothing can remedy. He seemed surprised that the navy should not have been informed of the intended movement until to-day; or that G—— should have sanctioned, and concluded that G—— must be letting the thing slide on without suggestion from him, to squelch it before it was consummated, or, relying upon his other plans, might have given this column up to the fate of a reconnoissance in force which will have accomplished its object if it diverts from his front a force large enough to destroy it. . . .

28 April. Had considerable talk with the President this evening. He understands that the day arranged for G——'s movement is to be the 2d prox.—Monday. S—— has asked for a little more time, says that he can't fully come up to his part in the programme before the 5th. S—— is at work on his. The stories of G——'s quarrelling with the Secretary of War are gratuitous lies. G—— quarrels with no one.

The President told a queer story of M——. "When McC—— lay at Harrison's Landing, M—— came one night to the President and waked him up at the Soldiers' Home to urge upon him the immediate flight of the army from that point —the men to get away on transports, and *the horses to be killed,* as they could not be saved. Thus often," says the President, "I, who am not a specially brave man, have had to restore the sinking courage of these professional fighters in critical times.

"When it was proposed to station H—— in general command, he insisted, to use his own language, on the appointment of a General-in-Chief who should be held responsible for results. We appointed him, and all went well enough until after P——'s defeat, when he broke down,—nerve and pluck all gone,—and has ever since evaded all possible responsibility,—little more, since that, than a first-rate clerk."

G. M—— was here this evening and told a good story about A. J—— and his fearful excitement when B—— was proposing to give up Nashville to the enemy. He found him walking up and down the room, supported by two friends. "M——, I'm glad to see you," he said. The two friends left, and he and M—— were alone. "We're *sold,* M——, we're *sold;*" fiercely reiterating. "He's a traitor, M——," and such,

"——." At last, suddenly, "Pray, M——!" And they knelt down and prayed, A—— joining in the responses like Methodists. After they had done, he said:—"M——, I feel better. M——, I'm not a Christian,—no church,—but I believe in God,—in the Bible,—all of it—M——, but *I'll be d—— if Nashville shall be given up*."

The President was much amused by a story I told him of G——.

The venomous old Count says:—"I despise the anti-Lincoln Republicans. I say I go against Lincoln, for he is no fit for be President; dé say dé for one term (holding up one dirty finger) bimeby dé beat Lincoln, den dé for two term (holding up two unclean digits): dé is cowards and Ass!"

A despatch just received from C—— stating that the Harrisburgh convention had elected Lincoln delegates to Baltimore properly instructed.

The President assents to my going to the field for this campaign if I can be spared from here.

April 30, 1864. . . . . The President came loafing in as it grew late and talked about the reception which his H—— letter had met with.

He seemed rather gratified that the *T——* was in the main inspired by a kindly spirit in its criticism. He thought of, and found, and gave to me to decipher G——'s letter to him of the 29th July, 1861. This most remarkable letter still retains for me its wonderful interest as the most insane specimen of pusillanimity that I have ever read. When I had finished reading, N—— said:—"That would be nuts to the H——, B—— would willingly give $10,000 for that." To which the President, tying the red-tape round the package, answered,—"I need $10,000 very much, but he couldn't have it for many times that."

The President has been powerfully reminded by Gen'l G——'s present movements and plans, of his (President's) old suggestion so constantly made and as constantly neglected, to B—— and H—— et al., to move at once upon the enemy's whole line so as to bring into action our great superiority in numbers. Otherwise, by interior lines and control of the interior railroad system, the enemy can shift their men rapidly from one point to another as they may be required. In this concerted movement, however, great superiority of numbers must tell; as the enemy, however successful where he concentrates, must necessarily weaken other portions of his line and lose important positions. This idea of his own, the President recognised with especial pleasure when G—— said it was his intention to make all the line useful—those not fighting could help the fighting:—"Those not skinning, can hold a leg," added his distinguished interlocutor.

It seems that B——'s unhappy Red River expedition was undertaken at the order and under the plan of Gen'l S——, who, having lived at Alexandria, had a nervous anxiety to repossess the country. G—— assented from his confidence in S——, and H—— fell into the plan. Had not this wasteful enterprise been begun, B—— would now be thundering at the gates of Mobile and withdrawing a considerable army from S——'s front at Chattanooga.

S—— has asked for an extension from the 2d to the 5th to complete his preparation against D——. He says that T——'s and S——'s armies will be within one day's march of Dalton by to-night, and that McP—— will be on time.

A little after midnight, as I was writing those last lines, the President came into the office laughing, with a volume of Hood's Works in his hand, to show N——, and me the little caricature, "An unfortunate Bee-ing," seemingly utterly unconscious that he, with his short shirt hanging about his long legs, and setting out behind like the tail feathers of an enormous ostrich, was infinitely funnier than anything in the book he was laughing at. What a man it is! Occupied all day with matters of vast moment, deeply anxious about the fate of the greatest army of the world, with his own fame and future hanging on the events of the passing hour, he yet has such a wealth of simple *bonhommie* and goodfellowship, that he gets out of bed and perambulates the house in his shirt to find us that we may share with him the fun of poor Hood's queer little conceits. . . . .

May 9. Received to-day the first despatches from G——. The President thinks very highly of what G—— has done. He was talking about it to-day with me, and said:—"How near we have been to this thing before, and failed! I believe if any other General had been at the head of that army, it would have now been on this side of the Rapidan. It is the dogged pertinacity of G—— that wins." It is said that M—— observed to G—— that the enemy seemed inclined to make a

Kilkenny cat fight of the affair; and G—— answered "Our cat has the longest tail."

HAY TO CHARLES EDWARD HAY.

Washington, D. C.
May 8, 1864.

MY DEAR C——:

I have received and read with great pleasure your long letter about the good fortune that has come to you.[1] I congratulate you very heartily and say God bless you and her whom you have chosen.

I knew her very intimately when I was in Springfield, and have rarely met anyone so young who was so sensible, so good and true. I think I have never known a girl more sincere and conscientious. It is with none but the brightest anticipations and hopes for your future that I congratulate you and her.

I do not know whether you have yet made up your minds as to time and seasons. I want

[1] Charles Hay married Mary Ridgely, May, 1865.

very much to see you and talk over a thousand things that it is inconvenient to write about. I hope that you will conclude to delay for a while the consummation of your intentions. You are both very young. You can of course trust each other fully. I doubt if you will ever meet a nicer girl anywhere, and I think it will puzzle her to find a better fellow. So now in your jolly youth, you had better wait awhile, don't you think? You will be a Captain some of these fine mornings. You are now third on the list of Lieutenants. Why not wait that long at least?

Although I know nobody whom I would sooner have chosen for a sister than her you have chosen for me, I cannot think of losing you, my dear boy, without a feeling of sadness. We have not been very much together, but we have been friends as well as brothers, and so the past is very much endeared to me. The woods and hills of dear old Warsaw, the rivers of Florida and the sands of South Carolina are all fastened on my heart by your companionship. Although I liked Col. W.[1] very much, I was miserable at losing Mary Hay, and now you are about to obey the

[1] Mary Hay married Col. Woolfolk.

universal law and pass out of our exclusive possession. Of course I rejoice with you and applaud your choice. I am glad you have chosen so early and so wisely. But our home grows more desolate day by day as all of your dear ones leave it, not to return. I believe Gus and I, some of these days, will come back to Warsaw, jolly old cumberers of the ground, and pass with Father and Mother the last quiet days of their green old age. And you and yours will always be joyfully welcomed in my heart and my home.

May 13. . . . . J. L—— came into my room this morning and said the President must now chiefly guard against assassination. I pooh-poohed him, and said that while every prominent man was more or less exposed to the attacks of maniacs, no foresight could guard against them. He replied by saying that he had, by his caution and vigilance, prevented his own assassination when a reward of a hundred thousand dollars had been offered for his head. . . . .

May 14. . . . . I have not known the President so affected by a personal loss since the death of B——, as by the death of Gen'l Wadsworth. While deeply regretting the loss of S——, he added:—"S——'s devotion and earnestness were professional. But no man has given himself up to the war with such self-sacrificing patriotism as Gen'l Wadsworth. He went into the service, not wishing or expecting great success or distinction in his military career, and profoundly indifferent to popular applause, actuated only by a sense of duty which he neither evaded nor sought to evade."

The President came in last night in his shirt and told us of the retirement of the enemy from his works at Spottsylvania, and our pursuit. I complimented him on the amount of underpinning he still has left, and he said he weighed 180 pounds. Important if true.

21 May. . . . . B—— is turning out much as I thought he would—perfectly useless and incapable for campaigning. He quarrels with G—— and S——, and makes rather a nuisance of himself.

I said to the President to-day that I thought B—— was the only man in the army in whom power would be dangerous. McC—— was too timid and vacillating to usurp; G—— was too sound and coolheaded and too unselfish; B—— also; F—— would be dangerous if he had more ability and energy.

"Yes," says the American; "He is like Jim Jett's brother. Jim used to say that his brother was the d——d-st scoundrel that ever lived, but in the infinite mercy of Providence he was also the d——d-st fool."

June 5. For a day or two the house has been full of patriots on the way to Baltimore who wish to pay their respects, and engrave on the expectant mind of the President their images in view of future contingencies. Among the genuine delegations have come some of the bogus and the irregular ones. C. B—— is here with Louisiana in his trousers' pocket. He has passed through New York and has gotten considerably stampeded by the talk of the trading pettifoggers of politics there. He feels uneasy in his seat.

The South Carolina delegation came in yesterday. The President says "let them in." "They are a swindle," I said. "They won't swindle me," quoth the President. They filed in; a few sutlers, cotton-dealers and negroes presented a petition and retired.

Florida sends two delegations; neither will get in. Each attacks the others as unprincipled tricksters.

L—— hurt himself badly yesterday by falling from his carriage on the pavement. I went to see him this morning; found him bruised but plucky. Says he intends to go to Baltimore to-morrow. Says he feels inclined to go for C—— for the Vice-Presidency, on personal grounds. Says he thinks Lincoln rather prefers J—— or some War Democrat as calculated to give more strength to the ticket.

N—— started over to-day in company with C——. . . .

June 6. . . . . Got a letter from N—— at Baltimore; answered by mail and telegraph. The President positively refuses to give even a confidential suggestion in regard to Vice-Presidency, Platform or Organization.

Everybody came back from Convention tired but sober. N—— says it was a very quiet Convention. Little drinking—little quarrelling—an earnest intention to simply register the expressed will of the people, and go home. They were intolerant of speeches—remorselessly coughed down the crack orators of the party.

HAY TO NICOLAY.

Washington, D. C.
June 20, 1864.

MY DEAR NICOLAY:

I went blundering through the country after leaving you, missing my connections and buying tickets until I landed in Baltimore without a cent; had to borrow money of the Eutaw to pay for my dinner and hack. Got home tired, dusty and disgusted.

The Tycoon thinks small beer of R——'s mare's nest. Too small, I rather think. But let 'em work! V——'s sudden Avatar rather startles the Corps here away. B. M—— asks me how much we gave F—— for importing him.

Society is *nil* here. The L——s go to-morrow —last lingerers. We mingle our tears and exchange locks of hair to-night in Corcoran's Row, —some half hundred of us.

I went last night to a Sacred Concert of profane music at Ford's. Young Kretchmar and old Kretchpar were running it.—H——s and H—— both sang;—and they kin if anybody kin. The Tycoon and I occupied private box, and both of us carried on a hefty flirtation with the M—— Girls in the flies.

Madame is in the North. The President has gone to-day to visit G——. I am all alone in the White pest-house. The ghosts of twenty thousand drowned cats come in nights through the south windows. I shall shake my buttons off with the ague before you get back. . . .

DIARY.

Thursday night, June 9, the President came into my room just before bed-time, and said that R—— had been sending despatches requesting that an officer of his staff might be sent to Washington to lay before the President matters of great importance in regard to a conspiracy to overthrow the government. He asked for this permission on account of the outrage committed upon Major

B—— of his staff, who was some time ago court-martialed for coming to Washington under Gen'l R——'s orders. Recently Gov. Y—— has joined in R——'s request asking that S—— shall be sent for. "If it is a matter of such overwhelming importance," said the President, "I don't think S—— is the proper person to whom to entrust it. I am inclined to think that the object of the General is to force me into a conflict with the Secretary of War, and to make me overrule him in this matter. This, at present, I am not inclined to do. I have concluded to send you out there to talk it over with R—— and to ascertain just what he has. I would like you to start to-morrow."

He gave me in the morning, before I was out of bed, this note to deliver to R—— :—

Executive Mansion,
Washington, June 10, 1864.

MAJOR-GENERAL R——

Major John Hay, the bearer, is one of my Private Secretaries, to whom please communicate in writing or verbally, anything you would think proper to say to me.

Yrs truly,

A. LINCOLN.

Friday afternoon, June 10. I left Washington and passed through Harrisburg at midnight; Pittsburgh, noon on the 11th; through Mingo, Cadiz, to Cincinnati, where I arrived on Sunday morning. I washed my face and went out; saw a plain, old church covered with ivy, and congratulated myself that there I would find some decent people worshipping God *comme il faut;* and was horribly bored for my worldliness. After dinner, where I met a rascally looking Jew, who was dining with a gorgeous lorette, and who insisted on knowing me and recognising me from a picture in *Harper's Weekly*, I strolled out to make visits. The A——'s were not at home, except young L——. I plunged into the bosom of a peaceful family, and demanded to see the wife of a quiet gentleman on the ground that she was a young lady now travelling in Europe. He commiserated my wild and agitated demeanor, and asked me to dinner.

I left Cincinnati Sunday evening and came to St. Louis about 11 o'clock Monday morning. The road is a very pleasant one, though rather slow. I sat and wrote rhymes in the same compartment with a pair of whiskey smugglers. I reported to Gen'l R—— immediately upon my arrival. After waiting some time in an ante-room full of officers, among them Gen'l D——, a young, nervous, active looking man; Gen'l E——, whom I had known before, a man of great coolness and steadiness of judgment; R—— came out and took me to his room. I presented my letter; he read it, and nodded:—"All right—got something to show you—too important to talk about—busy just now—this orderly business—keep me till four o'clock—dine with us at the L—— —half-past five—then talk matter over at my room there. Hay, where were you born? How long have you been with the President?" etc. And I went away. He is a fine, hearty, abrupt sort of talker, heavy-whiskered, blond, keen eyes, with light brows and lashes, head shunted forward a little; legs a little unsteady in walk.

We dined at the L—— quietly at six o'clock: R——, Major B—— and I. The General was chatty and sociable; told some old army stories; and drank very little wine. The dinner had nothing to tempt one out of frugality in diet, being up to the average badness of hotel dinners.

From the dining room I went to his private room. He issued orders to his intelligent contraband to admit no one. He seated himself in a queer combination chair he had—which let you lounge or forced you to a rigid pose of business as you desired,—and offered me a cigar. "No? long-necked fellows like you don't need them. Men of my temperament derive advantage from them as a sedative, and as a preventer of corpulence." He puffed away and began to talk, in a loud, easy tone at first, which he soon lowered, casting a glance over his shoulder and moving his chair nearer.

There is a secret conspiracy on foot against the Government, carried on by a society called the Order of the American Knights, or, to use their initials—O. A. K. The head of the Order, styled the high priest, is in the North, V——, and in the South, S. P——. Its objects are, in the North to exert an injurious effect upon public feeling, to resist the arrest of its members, to oppose the war in all possible ways; in the border States to join with returned rebels and guerilla parties to plunder, murder and persecute Union men and to give to rebel invasion all possible information and timely aid. He said that in Missouri they had carefully investigated the matter by means of secret service men who had taken the oaths, and they had found that many recent massacres were directly chargeable to them; that the whole Order was in a state of intense activity; that they numbered in Missouri 13,000 sworn members; in Illinois, 140,000; in Ohio and Indiana almost as large numbers, and in Kentucky a very large and formidable association.

That the present objective point was the return and the protection of V——. He intends, *on dit*, that the district convention in his district in Ohio shall elect him a delegate to the Chicago Convention. That he is to be elected and come over from Canada and take his seat, and if the Government should see fit to re-arrest him, then his followers are to unite to resist the officers and protect him at all hazards.

A convocation of the Order was held at W——, C——, in the month of April under his personal supervision; to this came delegates from every part of the country. It is not definitely known what was done there. . . . .

I went over to S——'s office, and he read to me his voluminous report to R—— in regard to the workings of the Order, and showed me some few documents. . . . We went back and finished the evening at R——'s rooms. I said I would go back to Washington and lay the matter before the President, as it had been presented to me, and I thought he would look upon it as I did, as a matter of importance. I did not make any suggestions; I did not even ask for a copy of S——'s report, or any of the papers in the case:—1st, because my instructions placed me in a purely receptive attitude; and,—2d, because I saw in both R. and S. a disposition to insist on S——'s coming to Washington in person to discuss the matter without the intervention of the Secretary of War. Two or three motives influenced this, no doubt. R—— is bitterly hostile to S——; he is full of the idea that S—— has wronged him, and is continually seeking opportunities to thwart and humiliate him. Then S—— himself is rather proud of his work in ferreting out this business, and is not unwilling to come to Washington to impress the President with the same sense; they wish a programme for future opportunities determined; and finally they want money for the secret service fund.

Gen'l R—— wrote a letter to the President Monday night, which I took on Tuesday morning, and started back to Washington.

. . . . I had bad luck coming back. I missed

a day at Springfield, a connection at Harrisburgh, and one at Baltimore, leaving Philadelphia five minutes after the President, and arriving at Washington almost as many hours behind him. I saw him at once, and gave him the impressions I have recorded above. The situation of affairs had been a good deal changed in my transit by the Avatar of V—— in Ohio. The President seemed not over-well pleased that R—— had not sent all the necessary papers by me, reiterating his want of confidence in S——, declining to be made a party to a quarrel between S—— and R——, and stating in reply to R——'s suggestion of the importance of the greatest secrecy, that a secret which has already been confided to Y——, M——, B——, B—— and their respective circles of officers, could scarcely be worth the keeping now. He treats the northern section of the conspiracy as not especially worth regarding, holding it a mere political organization, with about as much of malice and as much of puerility as the Knights of the Golden Circle.

About V—— himself he says that the question for the Government to decide is whether it can afford to disregard the contempt of authority and breach of discipline displayed in V——'s unauthorized return. For the rest it cannot result in benefit for the Union cause to have so violent and indiscreet a man go to Chicago as a firebrand to his own party. The President had some time ago seriously thought of annulling the sentence of exile, but had been too much occupied to do it. F. W—— said to him on one occasion that he could do nothing more politic than to bring V—— back; in that case he could promise him two Democratic candidates for President this year. "These War Democrats," said F. W——, "are scoundrelly hypocrites; they want to oppose you, and favor the war, at once, which is nonsense. There are but two sides in this fight,—yours and mine: War and Peace. You will succeed while the war lasts, I expect, but we shall succeed when the war is over. I intend to keep my record clear for the future."

The President said one thing in which I differ from him. He says:—"The opposition politicians are so blinded with rage, seeing themselves unable to control the politics of the country, that they may be able to manage the Chicago Convention for some violent end, but they cannot transfer the people, the honest though misguided masses, to the same course." I said:—"I thought the reverse to be true: that the sharp managers would go to Chicago to try to do some clever and prudent thing, such as nominate G—— without platform; but that the bare-footed democracy from the heads of the hollows, who are now clearly for peace would carry everything in the Convention before them. As it was at C——: —the New York politicians who came out to intrigue for G—— could not get a hearing. They were as a feather in the wind in the midst of that blast of German fanaticism. I think my idea is sustained by the action of the Illinois Convention which endorses V—— on his return and pledges the party strength to protect him. In the stress of this war, politics have drifted out of the hands of politicians, and are now more than ever subject to genuine popular currents."

The President said he would take the matter into consideration and would write to-morrow, the 18th, to B—— and H—— about V——, and to R—— at an early day.

June 21. To-day the President started down the river with F—— to have a talk with Gen'l G—— and Admiral L——. . . .

June 23. The President arrived to-day from the front, sunburnt and fagged, but still refreshed and cheered. He found the army in fine health, good position, and good spirits; G—— quietly confident; he says, quoting the Richmond papers, it may be a long summer's day before he does his work, but that he is as sure of doing it as he is of anything in the world. S—— is now on a raid, the purpose of which is to sever the connection at junction of the Richmond and Danville Railroads at Burk's, while the army is swinging around to the south of Petersburg and taking possession of the roads in that direction.

G—— says he is not sufficiently acquainted with H—— to say with certainty whether it is possible to destroy him; but that he has confidence in him that he will not be badly beaten. When McP—— or S—— or S—— or W—— is gone on any outside expedition, he feels perfectly secure about them, knowing that, while they are liable to any of the ordinary mischances of war, there is no danger of their being whipped in any but a legitimate way.

B—— says of G—— that he seems to arrive at his conclusions without any intermediate reasoning process—giving his orders with the greatest rapidity and with great detail. Uses the theoretical staff-officers very little.

June 24. To-day a Resolution came from the Senate asking information about War and Treasury Orders concerning exportation of arms to Mexico. I did not like to act without consulting S——, so took the papers to him, asking if it would be well to send copies to Secretaries of War and Treasury or not. He said,—"Yes! send the Resolution to the Secretary of War; a copy to the Secretary of the Treasury; asking reports from them, and then when the reports are in,——

"Did you ever hear Webster's recipe for cooking a cod? He was a great fisherman and fond of cod. Some one once asking him the best way to prepare a cod for the table, he said:—'Denude your cod of his scales—cut him open carefully—put him in a pot of cold water—heat it until your fork can pass easily through the fish—take him out—spread good fresh butter over him liberally,—sprinkle salt on the butter—pepper on the salt—and—send for George A—— and me.'

"When the Reports are in, let me see them!"

He got up, stumped around the room enjoying his joke, then said:—"Our friends are very anxious to get into a war with France, using this Mexican business for that purpose. They don't consider that England and France would surely be together in that event. France has the whip-hand of England completely. England got out of the Mexican business into which she had been deceived by France, by virtue of our having nothing to do with it. They have since been kept apart by good management; and our people are laboring to unite them again by making war on France. Worse than that, instead of doing something effective, if we must fight, they are for making mouths and shaking fists at France, warning and threatening and inducing her to prepare for our attack when it comes."

C——, the artist, who is painting the picture of the "Reading the Proclamation," says that S—— protested earnestly against that act being taken as the central and crowning act of the administration. He says slavery was destroyed years ago; the formation of the Republican party destroyed slavery; the anti-slavery acts of this administration are merely incidental. Their great work is the preservation of the Union, and, in that, the saving of popular government for the world. The scene which should have been taken was the Cabinet Meeting in the Navy Department when it was resolved to relieve Fort Sumter. That was the significant act of the Administration:—the act which determined the fact that Republican institutions were worth fighting for. . . . .

DIARY.

July, 1864.

. . . . Got in to New York at 6 o'clock the 16th, Saturday, and, while I was washing my face, came up G——'s card. I went down to the parlor and delivered the (President's) letter to him. He didn't like it, evidently; thought he was the worst man that could be taken for that purpose; that as soon as he arrived there the newspapers would be full of it; that he would be abused and blackguarded, etc., etc. Then he said, if the President insisted on his going he would go, but he must have an absolute safe-conduct for four persons, saying the President's letter would not protect him against our own officers. This seemed to me reasonable, and I had even presented the matter to the President in the same way. I wrote the despatch, and sent it to Washington. About noon came the answer. I then wrote the safe-conduct and took it to the *T*—— office. I left the names blank, and was going to let G—— fill them up, but he said "no," in his peculiar, querulous tone:—"I won't write a word. I expect to be pitched into everywhere for this; but I can't help it." I was going to write a safe-conduct for "H. G—— and four others;" but he would not permit it. "I want no safe-conduct. If they will catch me and put me in Fort La Fayette, it will suit me first-rate." I wrote the names in and gave it to him. "I will start to-night," said he; "I shall expect to be in Washington Tuesday morning if they will come."

He was all along opposed to the President proposing terms. He was in favor of some palaver anyhow; wanted them to propose terms which we could not accept, if no better, for us to go to the country on; wanted the government to appear anxious for peace, and yet was strenuous in demanding as our ultimatum proper terms.

As I left his office, Mr. C—— entered.

I went back to Washington, arriving there Monday morning (July 18). A few hours after I arrived, a despatch came from G——. I took it to the President. He told me a few minutes afterwards to hold myself in readiness to start if it became necessary,—that he had a word to say to Mr. S—— in regard to the matter. In the afternoon he handed me the note, and told me to go to the Falls, see G——, and deliver that note, and, to say further, that if they, the commissioners, wished to send any communications to Richmond for the purpose indicated, they might be sent through Washington, subject to the inspection of the government; and the answer from Richmond should be sent to them under the same conditions. Provided that if there was anything either way objectionable to the government in the despatches sent, they would be returned to the parties sending them without disclosure.

I went over to see S——;—he repeated about the same thing, adding that I had better request the commission to omit any official style which it would compromise our government to transmit; that they could waive it in an unofficial communication among themselves, and not thereby estop themselves of every claim.

I left Washington Monday evening,—arrived in New York too late Tuesday; took the evening Tuesday train and arrived at Niagara Wednesday morning (July 20) at 11½. Saw G—— at once at the International Hotel. He was evidently a good deal cut up at what he called the President's great mistake in refusing to enter into negotiations without conditions. He thinks it would be an enormous help to us in politics and finance to have even a semblance of negotiations going on;—that the people would hail with acclaim such a harbinger of peace. He especially should have, as he said, shown his hand first. That he should have waited their terms—if they were acceptable, closed with them,—if they were not, gone before the country on them.

I, of course, combatted these views, saying that I thought the wisest way was to make our stand on what the moral sentiment of the country and the world would demand as indispensable, and in all things else offering to deal in a frank, liberal and magnanimous spirit as the President has done;—that the two points to insist on are such points,—that he could not treat with these men who have no powers, that he could do no more than offer to treat with any who came properly empowered. I did not see how he could do more.

Mr. G—— did not wish to go over. He had all along declined seeing these people and did not wish to give any handle to talk. He thought it better that I should myself go over alone and deliver the letter. I really thought so too—but I understood the President and S—— to think otherwise, and so I felt I must insist on G——'s going over as a witness to the interview. We got a carriage and started over.

We got to the Clifton House and met G. S—— at the door. I wrote G——'s name on my card and sent it up to H——, C—— being out of town at St. R——'s.

S—— is a seedy-looking rebel, with grizzled whiskers and a flavor of old clo'. He came up and talked a few commonplaces with G——, as we stood by the counter. Our arrival, G——'s well-known person, created a good deal of interest, the bar-room rapidly filling with the curious, and the halls blooming suddenly with wide-eyed and pretty women. We went up to H——'s room, where he was breakfasting or lunching—tea and toasting—at all events. He was a tall, solemn, spare, false-looking man, with false teeth, false eyes, and false hair.

Mr. G—— said:—"Major H—— has come from the President of the United States to deliver you a communication in writing and to add a verbal message with which he has been entrusted." I handed him the note, and told him what the President and S—— had told me to say, and I added that I would be the bearer of anything they chose to send by me to Washington, or, if they chose to wait, it could go as well by mail.

He said:—"Mr. C—— is now absent at St. Catherine's. I will telegraph to him at once, and inform you in the morning."

We got up to go. He shook hands with G——, who "hoped to meet him again;" with me; and we went down to our carriage. S—— was on the piazza. He again accosted G——; made some remark about the fine view from the House, and said, "I wanted old B—— to come up, but he was afraid to come." G—— answered:—"I expect to be blackguarded for what I have done, and I am not allowed to explain. But all I have done has been done under instructions."

We got in and rode away. As soon as the

whole thing was over, G—— recovered his spirits and said he was glad he had come,—and was very chatty and agreeable on the way back and at dinner.

After dinner I thought I would go down to Buffalo and spend the night. Went down with young D——, formerly of F——'s staff. I found him also deeply regretting that the President had not hauled these fellows into a negotiation neck and ears without terms. He gave me some details of what G—— had before talked about,—the political campaign these fellows are engineering up here. He says C—— is to write a letter giving three points on which, if the Democracy carry the fall elections, the South will stop the war and come back into the Union. These are: 1st. Restoration of the Union. 2d. Assumption of Confederate Debt. 3d. Restriction of slavery to its present limits and acknowledgment of *de facto* emancipation. On this platform it is thought Judge N—— will run. . . .

HAY TO NICOLAY.

Warsaw, Illinois,
August 25, 1864.

. . . . We are waiting with the greatest interest for the hatching of the big peace-snake at Chicago. There is throughout the country, I mean the rural districts, a good, healthy Union feeling, and an intention to succeed in the military and the political contests; but everywhere in the towns the copperheads are exultant, and our own people either growling and despondent or sneakingly apologetic. I found among my letters here, sent by you, one from J. M——, inconceivably impudent, in which he informs me that on the 4th of next March, thanks to Mr. Lincoln's blunders and follies, we will be kicked out of the White House. The d——d scoundrel needs a day's hanging. I won't answer his letter till I return and let you see it. Old Uncle J—— is talking like an ass,—says if the Chicago nominee is a good man, he don't know, etc., etc. He blackguards you and me—says we are too big for our breeches,—a fault for which it seems to me Nature or our tailors are to blame. After all your kindness to the old whelp and his cub of a son he hates you because you have not done more. I believe he thinks the Executive Mansion's somehow to blame. . . . .

Land is getting up near the stars in price. It will take all I am worth to buy a tater-patch. I am after one or two small pieces in Hancock for reasonable prices, 20 to 30 dollars an acre. L—— paid $70,000 for a farm a short while ago, and everybody who has greenbacks is forcing them off like waste paper for land. I find in talking with well-informed people a sort of fear of Kansas property, as uncertain in future settlement and more than all uncertain in weather. The ghost of famine haunts those speculations.

You were wrong in thinking either M— or C. H—— at all copperish. They are as sound as they ever were. They of course are not quite clear about the currency, but who is?

Our people here want me to address the Union League. I believe I won't. The snakes would rattle about it a little, and it would do no good. I lose my temper sometimes talking with growling Republicans. There is a diseased restlessness about men in these times that unfits them for the steady support of an administration. It seems as if there were appearing in the Republican party the elements of disorganization that destroyed the Whigs.

If the dumb cattle are not worthy of another term of Lincoln, then let the will of God be done, and the murrain of McC—— fall on them.

DIARY.

Sept. 23, 1864. Senator H—— thinks that B——'s support is so important, especially considered as to its bearing on the soldier vote, that it would pay to offer him a foreign mission for it, and so told me. F—— has also had a man talking to the cannie Scot who asked plumply, "Will I be a welcome visitor at the White House if I support Mr. Lincoln?" What a horrible question for a man to be able to ask! So thinks the President apparently. It is probable that B—— will stay about as he is, thoroughly neutral, balancing carefully until the October elections, and will then declare for the side which he thinks will win. It is better in many respects to let him alone.

Sept. 24. This morning I asked the President

if the report of the resignation of B—— were true. He said it was.

"Has D—— been appointed to succeed him?"

"I have telegraphed to him to-day—have as yet received no answer."

"What is Mr. B—— going to do?"

"He is going up to Maryland to make speeches. If he will devote himself to the success of the national cause without exhibiting bad temper towards his opponents, he can set the B—— family up again."

"W. D—— is taking the stump also. I doubt if his advocacy of you will be hearty enough to be effective."

"If he and the rest can succeed in carrying the State for emancipation, I shall be very willing to lose the electoral vote."

HAY TO NICOLAY.

Executive Mansion,
Washington, Sept. 24, 1864.

MY DEAR NICO:

Your despatch was just brought in. I took it to the President, and he told me to tell you, you had better loaf round the city a while longer. You need some rest and recreation and may as well take it in New York as anywhere else. Besides, you can't imagine how nasty the house is at present. You would get the painters' colic in twenty-four hours if you came home now.

Politicians still unhealthily haunt us. Loose women flavor the anteroom. Much turmoil and trouble. . . . The world is almost too many for me. I take a dreary pleasure in seeing P—— eat steamed oysters by the half-bushel. He has gotten a haven of rest in the family of some decayed Virginian gentry; really a very lucky chance, good, respectable, and not dear.

S—— must be our resource this winter in clo'. If you don't want to be surprised into idiocy, don't ask C—— and L—— the price of goods. A faint rumor has reached me and paralyzed me. I am founding a "Shabby Club" to make rags the style this winter. Write to me some morning while you are waiting for your cocktail, and tell me how's things. Give my love to the fair you are so lucky as to know.

Isn't it bully about S——?

DIARY.

Sept. 25, Sunday. Yesterday N—— who has been several days in New York telegraphed to the President that T. W—— had gone to Canada, and asking if he (N.) had better return. I answered he had better amuse himself there for a day or two. This morning a letter came in the same sense. The President, when I showed it to him, said,—"I think I know where Mr. W. has gone. I think he has gone to Vermont not Canada. I will tell you what he is trying to do. I have not as yet told anybody.

"Some time ago, the Governor of Vermont came to me 'on business of importance' he said. I fixed an hour and he came. His name is S——. He is, though you wouldn't think it, a cousin of B. S——. B. is large, blonde, florid. The Governor is a little, dark sort of man. This is the story he told me, giving Gen'l B. S—— as his authority.

"When Gen'l McC—— was here at Washington, B. S—— was very intimate with him. They had been together at West Point, and friends. McC—— had asked for promotion for B. from the President, and got it. They were close and confidential friends. When they went down to the peninsula, their same intimate relations continued, the General talking freely with S—— about all his plans and prospects; until one day F. W—— and one other politician from New York appeared in camp and passed some days with McC——. From the day that this took place S—— saw, or thought he saw, that McC—— was treating him with unusual coolness and reserve. After a little while he mentioned this to McC—— who, after some talk, told B. he had something to show him. He told him that these people who had recently visited him, had been urging him to stand as an opposition candidate for President; that he had thought the thing over, and had concluded to accept their propositions, and had written them a letter (which he had not yet sent) giving his idea of the proper way of conducting the war, so as to conciliate and impress the people of the South with the idea that our armies were intended merely to execute the laws and protect their property, etc., and pledging himself to conduct the war in that inefficient, conciliatory style. This letter he read to B——, who, after the reading was finished, said earnestly:—'General, do you not see that looks like treason?

and that it will ruin you and all of us.' After some further talk, the General destroyed the letter in B——'s presence, and thanked him heartily for his frank and friendly counsel. After this he was again taken into the intimate confidence of McC——. Immediately after the battle of Antietam, W—— and his familiar came again and saw the General, and again B—— saw an immediate estrangement on the part of McC——. He seemed to be anxious to get his intimate friends out of the way, and to avoid opportunities of private conversation with them. B—— he particularly kept employed on reconnoissances and such work. One night S—— was returning from some duty he had been performing, and seeing a light in McC——'s tent, he went in to report. Several persons were there. He reported and was about to withdraw when the General requested him to remain. After everyone was gone, he told him those men had been there again and had renewed their proposition about the Presidency:—that this time he had agreed to their proposition, and had written them a letter acceding to their terms, and pledging himself to carry on the war in the sense already indicated. This letter he read then and there to B. S——.

"Immediately thereafter B. S—— applied to be transferred from that army.

"At very nearly the same time, other prominent men asked the same; F——, B—— and others.

"Now that letter must be in the possession of F. W——, and it will not be impossible to get it. Mr. W—— has, I think, gone to Vermont to see the S——s about it."

I was very much surprised at the story and expressed my surprise. I said I had always thought that McC——'s fault was a constitutional weakness and timidity which prevented him from active and timely exertion, instead of any such deep-laid scheme of treachery and ambition.

The President replied:—"After the battle of Antietam I went up to the field to try to get him to move, and came back thinking he would move at once. But when I got home he began to argue why he ought not to move. I peremptorily ordered him to advance. It was nineteen days before he put a man over the river. It was nine days longer before he got his army across, and then he stopped again, delaying on little pretexts of wanting this and that. I began to fear he was playing false,—that he did not want to hurt the enemy. I saw how he could intercept the enemy on the way to Richmond. I determined to make that the test. If he let them get away, I would remove him. He did so, and I relieved him.

"I dismissed Major K—— for his silly, treasonable talk because I feared it was staff-talk, and I wanted an example.

"The letter of B—— furnishes another evidence in support of that theory. And the story you have heard N—— tell about S——'s first visit to McC——, all tallies with this story."

Sept. 26. B—— has gone into Maryland stumping. He was very much surprised when he got the President's note. He had thought the opposition to him was dying out. He behaves very handsomely, and is doing his utmost. He speaks in New York Tuesday night.

B——, in spite of some temporary indiscretions, is a good and true man and a most valuable public officer. He stood with the President against the whole Cabinet in favor of reinforcing Fort Sumter. He stood by F—— in his Emancipation Decree, though yielding when the President revoked it. He approved the Proclamation of January, 1863, and the Amnesty Proclamation, and has stood like a brother beside the President always. What have injured him are his violent personal antagonisms and indiscretions. He made a bitter and vindictive fight on the radicals of Missouri, though ceasing it at the request of the President. He talked with indecorous severity of Mr. C——, and with unbecoming harshness of S——, saying on street-corners "this man is a liar, that man is a thief." He made needlessly enemies among public men who have pursued him fiercely in turn. W. R—— said to-day that H—— was going to placard all over Maryland this fall:—"Your time has come!" I said, "he won't do anything of the kind, and moreover M. B—— will do more to carry emancipation in Maryland than any one of those who abuse him."

N—— got home this morning, looking rather ill. I wish he would start off and get hearty again, coming back in time to let me off to Wilmington. He says W—— said he was on the track of the letter and hoped to get it. . . . .

Sept. 29. . . . . W—— has just returned here from the North. He says New York is absolutely safe; that W—— is advising his friends to bet; that D. R—— is despondent—saying the Democratic party are half traitors.

Things looked very blue a month ago. A meeting was held in New York (to which Geo. W—— refers) of Union men opposed to Lincoln, and it was resolved that he should be requested to withdraw from the canvass. But Atlanta and the response of the country to the Chicago infamy set matters right. . . . .

G—— is moving on L——. This morning early the President telegraphed to G—— expressing his anxiety that L—— should not reinforce E—— against S——. G—— answered that he had taken measures to prevent it by attacking L—— himself. He is moving in two columns; O—— south, and B—— north of the James. S—— was much excited on hearing the news and said "he will be in Richmond to-night." "No," said the President; "H——, what do you think?" H—— answered that he would not be surprised if he got either Richmond or Petersburg by the manœuvre.

Oct. 2. To-day I received a letter from W. N. G—— saying certain of his friends had agreed to press his name for Judge of the District Court, Western Missouri, in place of Judge W——. He adds, however, that, in case Judge B——, Attorney-General, should desire the appointment, he would not stand in his way, believing that B——'s appointment would be very advantageous and satisfactory to the Union people of the State. He requested me to make this known both to Mr. B—— and the President. I read his letter to the President, and, at the same time referred to the recent indiscreet announcement made by C——, that in the event of a reëlection the President would call around him fresh and earnest men. He said: "They need not be especially savage about a change. There are now only three left of the original Cabinet with the Government." He added that he rather thought he would appoint Mr. B—— to the vacant judgeship if he desired it. He said he would be troubled to fill his place in the Cabinet from Missouri, especially from among the radicals. I thought it would not be necessary to confine himself to Missouri; that he might do better farther South by taking Mr. H—— from Kentucky.

He did not seem to have thought of that before. But said at once: "That would do very well; that would be an excellent appointment. I question if I could do better than that. . . . I had always thought, though I had never mentioned it to anyone, that if a vacancy should occur in the Supreme Bench in any Southern District, I would appoint him, . . . but giving him a place in the Cabinet would not hinder that."

I told him I should show G——'s letter to Judge B——, to which he assented.

Oct. 7. I showed B—— the letter to-day. He said some friends of his had previously spoken to him in the same sense; that he was friendly to G——; thought well of him as a gentlemam and a lawyer, and knew of no one whom he would sooner see appointed. That he would not take the office himself in any case. That he had earnest antagonisms in that State; he was fighting those radicals there that stood to him in the relation of enemies of law and order. "There is no such thing as an honest and patriotic American radical. Some of the transcendental, red-Republican Germans were honest enough in their moon-struck theorising; but the Americans imprudently and dishonestly arrogate to themselves the title of unconditional loyalty, when the whole spirit of the faction is contempt of, and opposition to law. . . . While the present state of things continues in Missouri, there is no need of a Court,—so says Judge T——, and I agree with him."

HAY TO NICOLAY.

Executive Mansion,
Washington, Oct. 10, 1864.

MY DEAR NICOLAY:

How are your mails for this morning. We are very busy. . . .

Pennsylvania fellows are very confident. You will know the result before this gets here.

K—— was here this morning. He seemed to be in a great hurry, as he only staid two hours and a half, and didn't talk about himself more than nine-tenths of the time.

No fun—no Christmas! Thank God you are not here. We are dreary enough. The weather is nasty.

DIARY.

Oct. 11. . . . I was mentioning old Mr. B——'s very calm and discreet letter of October 5 to the President to-day contrasting it with M——'s indiscretions; and the President said:—"Yes, they remind me of ———. He was sitting in a bar-room among strangers who were telling of some affair in which his father, as they said, had been tricked in a trade, and he said, 'That's a lie!' Some sensation. 'What do you mean?' 'Why the old man ain't so easy tricked. You can fool the boys but ye can't the old man.'"

. . . . At eight o'clock the President went over to the War Department to watch for despatches. I went with him. We found the building in a state of preparation for siege. S—— had locked the doors and taken the keys up-stairs, so that it was impossible even to send a card to him. A shivering messenger was passing to and fro in the moonlight over the withered leaves who, catching sight of the President, took us around by the Navy Department and conducted us into the War Office by a side door.

The first despatch we received contained the welcome intelligence of the election of E—— and H—— in the C—— district. This was from S—— at C—— who also promised considerable gains in Indiana, made good a few minutes after by a statement of 400 gain in Noble County.

Then came in a despatch from S—— stating we had 2500 in the city of Philadelphia and that leading Democrats had given up the State. Then S—— was seen to be crowding S. C—— very hard in the C—— district, in some places increasing B——'s colossal vote of last year.

The President, in a lull of despatches, took from his pocket the Nasby papers, and read several chapters of the experiences of the saint and martyr, Petroleum V. They were immensely amusing. S—— and D—— enjoyed them scarcely less than the President, who read on, *con amore*, until nine o'clock. At this time I went to S——'s, to keep my engagement. I found there B—— and his wife; Cols. C—— and W——, A. B—— and M—— . . . . D—— was also there. We broke up very early. D—— and I went back to the Department.

We found the good Indiana news had become better, and the Pennsylvania had begun to be streaked with lean. Before long the despatches announced with some certainty of tone that M—— was elected by a safe working majority. The scattering reports from Pennsylvania showed about equal gains and losses. But the estimates and the flyers all claimed gains on the Congressmen. Reports began to come in from the hospitals and camps in the vicinity, the Ohio troops about ten to one for Union, and the Pennsylvania less than three to one. Carver Hospital, by which S—— and L—— pass every day, on their way to the country, gave the heaviest opposition vote, —about one out of three. L—— says,—"That's hard on us, S——,—they know us better than the others." Co. K, 150th P. V., the President's personal escort, voted 63 to 11 Union.

I am deeply thankful for the result in Indiana. I believe it saves Illinois in November. I believe it rescues Indiana from sedition and civil war. A copperhead Governor would have afforded a grand central rallying point for that lurking treason whose existence C—— has already so clearly demonstrated. . . . I should have been willing to sacrifice something in Pennsylvania to avert that calamity. I said as much to the President. He said he was anxious about Pennsylvania because of her enormous weight and influence, which, cast definitely into the scale, would close the campaign, and leave the people free to look again with their whole hearts to the cause of the country.

HAY TO NICOLAY.

Executive Mansion.
Washington, Oct. 13, 1864.

MY DEAR NICOLAY:

I suppose you are happy enough over the elections to do without letters. Here are two. I hope they are duns to remind you that you are mortal.

Indiana is simply glorious. The surprise of this good thing is its chief delight. Pennsylvania has done pretty well. We have a little majority on home vote as yet, and will get a fair vote from the soldiers, and do better in November. The wild estimates of F—— and C——, founded on no count or thorough canvass, are of course not fulfilled, but we did not expect them to be.

Judge T—— died last night. I have not heard anything this morning about the succession. It is a matter of the greatest personal importance that Mr. Lincoln has ever decided.

W. D——s' clique was badly scooped out in the mayoralty election at Baltimore yesterday. C—— (regular Union) got nearly all the votes cast. . . .

HAY TO NICOLAY.

Nov. 7, 1864.

I have nothing to say till the day after to-morrow. God save the Republic!

DIARY.

Nov. 8. The house has been still and almost deserted to-day. Everybody in Washington, not at home voting, seems ashamed of it and stays away from the President.

I was talking with him to-day. He said:—"It is a little singular that I, who am not a vindictive man, should have always been before the people for election in canvasses marked for their bitterness:—always but once. When I came to Congress it was a quiet time. But always besides that, the contests in which I have been prominent have been marked with great rancor. . . . ."

During the afternoon few despatches were received. At night, at seven o'clock, we started over to the War Department to spend the evening. Just as we started we received the first gun from Indianapolis showing a majority of 8,000 there, a gain of 1,500 over M——'s vote. The vote itself seemed an enormous one for a town of that size, and can only be accounted for by considering the great influx, since the war, of voting men from the country into the State centres where a great deal of army business is done. There was less significance in this vote on account of the October victory which had disheartened the enemy and destroyed their incentive to work.

The night was rainy, steamy and dark. We splashed through the grounds to the side door where a soaked and smoking sentinel was standing in his own vapor with his huddled-up frame covered with a rubber cloak. Inside, a half-dozen idle orderlies; up-stairs the clerks of the telegraph. As the President entered, they handed him a despatch from F—— claiming ten thousand Union majority in Pennsylvania. "F—— is a little excitable." Another comes from F——, Baltimore, giving 15,000 in the city, 5,000 in the State. "All Hail, Free Maryland. That is superb!" A message from R—— to F——, followed instantly by one from S—— to L——, claiming Boston by 5,000, and R—— and H——'s elections by majorities of 4,000 apiece. A magnificent advance on the chilly dozens of 1862.

E—— came in, shaking the rain from his cloak, with trousers very disreputably muddy. We sternly demanded an explanation. He had done it watching a fellow-being ahead, and chuckling at his uncertain footing. Which reminded the Tycoon of course. The President said:—"For such an awkward fellow, I am pretty sure-footed. It used to take a pretty dexterous man to throw me. I remember, the evening of the day in 1858, that decided the contest for the Senate between Mr. Douglas and myself, was something like this, dark, rainy and gloomy. I had been reading the returns and had ascertained that we had lost the legislature, and started to go home. The path had been worn hog-backed, and was slippery. My foot slipped from under me, knocking the other one out of the way, but I recovered myself and lit square; and I said to myself: '*It's a slip and not a fall.*'"

The President sent over the first fruits to Mrs. L——. He said, "She is more anxious than I."

We went into the Secretary's room. Mr. W—— and F—— soon came in. They were especially happy over the election of R——, regarding it as a great triumph for the Navy Department. Says F——,—"There are two fellows that have been specially malignant to us. H—— and W. D——, and retribution has come over them both." "You have more of that feeling of personal resentment than I," said Lincoln. "Perhaps I may have too little of it, but I never thought it paid. A man has not time to spend half his life in quarrels. If any man ceases to attack me, I never remember the past against him. It has seemed to me recently that W. D—— was growing more sensible to his own true interests, and has ceased wasting his time by attacking me. I hope, for his own good, he has. He has been very malicious against me, but has only injured himself by it. His conduct has been very strange to me. I came here his friend, wishing to continue so. I had heard nothing but good of him; he was the cousin of my intimate friend Judge D——. But he had scarcely been elected when I began to learn of his attacking me on all possible occasions. It is very much the same with H——. I was much disappointed that he failed to be my friend. But my greatest disappointment of all has been with

G——. Before I came here I certainly expected to rely upon G—— more than any other one man in the Senate. I like him very much. He is a great strong fellow. He is a valuable friend, a dangerous enemy. He carries too many guns not to be respected on any point of view. But he got wrong against me, I do not clearly know how, and has always been cool and almost hostile to me. I am glad he has always been the friend of the Navy, and generally of the Administration."

. . . Towards midnight we had supper. The President went awkwardly and hospitably to work shovelling out the fried oysters. He was most agreeable and genial all the evening, in fact. . . . Capt. T—— came up with a band about half past two, and made some music. The President answered from the window with rather unusual dignity and effect, and we came home.

Nov. 11. . . . . At the meeting of the Cabinet to-day the President took out a paper from his desk, and said:—"Gentlemen, do you remember last summer I asked you all to sign your names to the back of a paper of which I did not show you the inside? This is it? Now, Mr. Hay, see if you can get this open without tearing it." He had pasted it up in so singular style that it required some cutting to get it open. He then read as follows:—

Executive Mansion,
Washington, Aug. 23, 1864.

This morning, as for some days past, it seems exceedingly probable that this Administration will not be re-elected. Then it will be my duty to so co-operate with the President elect, as to save the Union between the election and the inauguration; as he will have secured his election on such ground that he cannot possibly save it afterwards.

A. LINCOLN.

This was indorsed:—

William H. Seward,
W. P. Fessenden,
Edwin M. Stanton,
Gideon Welles,
Edw. Bates,
M. Blair,
J. P. Usher.

The President said:—"You will remember that this was written at a time (six days before the Chicago nominating Convention) when as yet we had no adversary, and seemed to have no friends. I then solemnly resolved on the course of action indicated above. I resolved, in case of the election of Gen'l McC——, being certain that he would be the candidate, that I would see him and talk matters over with him. I would say, "General, the election has demonstrated that you are stronger, have more influence with the American people than I. Now let us together, you with your influence, and I with all the executive power of the government, try to save the country. You raise as many troops as you possibly can for this final trial, and I will devote all my energies to assisting and finishing the war."

S—— said:—"And the General would answer you '*Yes, Yes;*' and the next day when you saw him again, and pressed these views upon him, he would say, '*Yes, Yes;*' and so on forever, and would have done nothing at all."

"At least," added L——, "I should have done my duty and have stood clear before my own conscience."

The speeches of the President at the last two serenades are very highly spoken of. The first I wrote after the fact, to prevent the "loyal Pennsylvanians" getting a swing at it themselves. The second one, last night, the President himself wrote late in the evening, and read it from the window:—"Not very graceful," he said: "but I am growing old enough not to care much for the manner of doing things."

To-day I got a letter from R—— breathing fire and vengeance against the Custom House which came so near destroying him in his district. I read it to the President. He answered that it was the spirit of such letters as that, that created the faction and malignity of which R—— complained.

It seems utterly impossible for the President to conceive of the possibility of any good resulting from a rigorous and exemplary course of punishing political dereliction. His favorite expression is:—"I am in favor of short statutes of limitations in politics."

12 Nov., 1864. I started for G——'s headquarters. We left the Navy Yard at two o'clock in the afternoon. The party consisted of F——,

D——, W——, M. B——, P——, I——, F——, I——, T. W——, F——, a Chinese English merchant, and R—— of the *G*——. The day was sad, blowy, bleak, and a little wet.

We dined, and some played cards and all went to bed. When we got up in the morning, we were at Hampton Roads. We made no stay there, but after communicating with the Admiral D. D. P——, we started up the James River, he following in his flagship, the Malvern. He overtook us about noon or a little after, and came on board with Captain S—— of the Navy. P—— is a good-looking, lively man, a very off-hand talker, a man not impressing me as of a high order of talent,—a hale-fellow; a slight dash of the rowdy.

In the afternoon we passed by the island of Jamestown. On the low, flat, marshy island, where our first colony landed, there now remains nothing but ruins. An old church has left a solitary tower as its representative. A group of chimneys mark the spot of another large building. On the other side of the river, there is high, fine, swelling land. One cannot but wonder at the taste or judgment that selected that pestilential site in preference to those breezy hills. They probably wished to be near their boats, and also thought a river was a handy thing to have between them and the gentle savages that infested the shores of the James.

Fort Powhatan we saw also—where a battalion of negroes flaxed out F. H——'s command of the F. F. V's.

We arrived at City Point at three o'clock. There are very few troops there but quite a large fleet lying in the river.

We went ashore; walked through the frame building standing in place of that blown up by the late fearful explosion. We climbed the steep hill, whose difficulty is mainly removed by the neat stairs that Yankee care has built since our occupation of the Point. At the top of the hill, we found a young sentry who halted us, and would not let us go further, till P——, throwing himself on his dignity, which he does not use often, said: "Let that General know that Admiral P—— and Mr. F—— are here to see him." He evidently impressed the sentry, for he said, after an instant's hesitation:—"Go ahead! I reckon it's all right."

A common little wall-tent being indicated, we went up to beard the General. At our first knock he came to the door. He looked neater and more careful in his dress than usual; his hair was combed, his coat on, and his shirt clean, his long boots blackened till they shone. Everybody was presented.

After the conference was over we went back to the boat; the General accompanied us. We started down the river and soon had dinner. . . . . After dinner we all gathered around G—— who led the conversation for an hour or so. He thinks the rebels are about at the end of their tether, and said:—"I hope we will give them a blow this winter that will hasten their end."

He was down on the Massachusetts idea of buying out of the draft by filling their quota with recruits at $300, from among the contrabands in Sherman's army. "S——'s head is level on that question," he said in reply to some strictures of Mr. F——; "he knows he can get all these negroes that are worth having anyhow, and he prefers to get them that way rather than to fill up the quota of a distant State and thus diminish the fruits of the draft." S—— does not think so hopefully of negro troops as do many other Generals. G—— himself says they are admirable soldiers in many respects; quick and docile in a charge; excellent in fatigue duty. He says he does not think that an army of them could have stood the week's pounding at the Wilderness and Spottsylvania as our men did; "in fact no other troops in the world could have done it," he said.

G—— is strongly of the belief that the rebel army is making its last grand rally; that they have reinforced to the extent of about 30,000 men in Virginia, L—— getting 20,000 and E—— getting 10,000. He does not think they can sensibly increase their armies further. He says that he does not think they can recover from the blows he hopes to give them this winter.

He is deeply impressed with the vast importance and significance of the late Presidential election. The point which impressed him most powerfully was that which I regarded as the critical one—the pivotal centre of our history—the quiet and orderly character of the whole affair. No bloodshed or riot,—few frauds, and those detected and punished in an exemplary manner. It proves our worthiness of free institutions, and our capability of preserving them without running into anarchy or despotism.

G—— remained with us until nearly one

o'clock at night—Monday morning—and then went to his own boat, the "Martin," to sleep till day. B——, D——, and B——, of his staff, were with him.

. . . . We left Fort Monroe at 3½, and arrived at Washington Tuesday morning, the 15th, at 7 a. m.

18 Dec. . . . When the President came in, he called B—— and B—— into his office, meeting them in the hall. They immediately began to talk about A——'s Bill in regard to States in insurrection. The President had been reading it carefully, and said that he liked it with the exception of one or two things which he thought rather calculated to conceal a feature which might be objectionable to some. The first was that under the provisions of that bill, negroes would be made jurors and voters under the temporary governments. "Yes," said B——; "that is to be stricken out, and the qualification 'white male citizens of the United States' is to be restored. What you refer to would be a fatal objection to the bill. It would simply throw the Government into the hands of the blacks, as the white people under that arrangement would refuse to vote."

"The second," said the President, "is the declaration that all persons heretofore held in slavery are declared free. This is explained by some to be, not a prohibition of slavery by Congress, but a mere assurance of freedom to persons actually there in accordance with the Proclamation of Emancipation. In that point of view it is not objectionable, though I think it would have been preferable to so express it."

The President and Gen'l B—— spoke very favorably with three qualifications of A——'s Bill. B—— is especially anxious that the Bill may pass and receive the approval of the President. He regards it as merely concurring in the President's own action in the important case of Louisiana, and recommending an observance of the same policy in other cases. He does not regard it, nor does the President, as laying down any cast-iron policy in the matter. Louisiana being admitted and this Bill passed, the President is not estopped by it from recognizing and urging Congress to recognize, another state of the South, coming with constitution and conditions entirely dissimilar. B—— thinks that the object of Congress in passing the Bill at all, is merely to assert their conviction that they have a right to pass such a law, in concurrence with the executive action. They want a hand in the reconstruction. It is unquestionably the prerogative of Congress to decide as to qualifications of its own members: —that branch of the subject is exclusively their own. It does not seem wise, therefore, to make a fight upon a question purely immaterial; that is, whether this bill is a necessary one or not, and thereby lose the positive gain of this endorsement of the President's policy in the admission of Louisiana, and the assistance of that State in carrying the Constitutional Amendment prohibiting slavery.

B—— talked more than both Lincoln and B——; and somewhat vehemently attacked the radicals in the House and Senate, who are at work upon this measure, accusing them of interested motives and hostility to Lincoln. The President said:—"It is much better not to be led from the region of reason into that of hot blood, by imputing to public men motives which they do not avow."

HAY TO CHARLES EDWARD HAY.

Executive Mansion,
Washington, 31 March, 1865.

MY DEAR C——:

I have been a little neglectful of my duties to you lately. I have written almost no letters except on business for some time.

I am getting very hurried as the time approaches for me to give my place in the Executive Office to some new man. The arrears of so long a time cannot be settled in a day.

You have probably seen from the papers that I am to go to Paris as Secretary of Legation. It is a pleasant and honorable way of leaving my present post which I should have left in any event very soon. I am thoroughly sick of certain aspects of life here, which you will understand without my putting them on paper, and I was almost ready, after taking a few months' active service in the field, to go back to Warsaw and try to give the Vineyard experiment a fair trial, when the Secretary of State sent for me and offered me this position abroad. It was entirely unsolicited and unexpected. I had no more idea of it than you have. But I took a day or two to think it over, the matter being a little pressing,—as the Secretary wanted to let Mr. B—— know what he was to expect,—and at last concluded that I would accept. The President requested me to stay with him a month or so longer to get him started with the reorganised office, which I shall do, and shall sail probably in June.

Meanwhile N——, whose health is really in a very bad state, has gone off down the coast on a voyage to Havana, and will be gone the "heft" of the month of April, and I am fastened here, very busy. I don't like to admit and will not yet give up that I can't come on to your "happiest-day-of-your-life;" but I must tell you that it looks uncommonly like it just now. But whether I come or not, I will be with you that day in my love and my prayers that God will bless you and yours forever.

I very much fear that all my friends will disapprove this step of mine, but if they know all that induced me to it they would coincide.

HAY TO ALBERT RHODES.

Paris, Sept. 7, 1865.

MY DEAR RHODES:

I have just received your lively letter of the last of August from which I infer that the agony of tearing yourself loose from your adored Paris has been met in a heroic spirit and survived. "Parigi O cara" is very hot and nasty now. "All in a hot and copper sky. The bloody sun at noon blisters and broils the asphalt pave as hot as Hell in June," as our mutual friend the Ancient Mariner says. I feel deep sympathy for fat women at this season. They pay a heavy tax for your admiration.

Your anxiety in regard to Mr. P—— I am happy to relieve by stating, that he has returned in an astounding state of Teutonic health. He was detained by sickness in Bonn but is now quite well.

I congratulate you on making the acquaintance of Mrs. L——. One of the cleverest women I know. And thoroughly feminine and amiable.

I saw in the street the other day a handsome Spaniard named B——, Secretary of Legation at

Stockholm, who asked tidings of you. I said you were in England. He looked polite commiseration and we drifted apart.

DIARY.

Paris, Sept. 25, 1866.

The Reverend Dr. S——, Professor of Dogmatic Theology in the Propaganda Fide College at Rome, called to-day and talked a good while about American and Roman politics. I am not in the condition to give anybody the most direct and valuable instructions about our politics, and I hope the Doctor got some more definite idea from my talk than there was in it. I got one idea from him which was definite enough, to wit, the condition of absolute uncertainty in which the Roman politicians are as to the future. He says the Pope really is not fixed in any plan. It seems to be now certain that the French will withdraw in December. Then, what will happen, remains to be seen. If the enemies of the Temporal Power are willing to allow him to exercise the sovereignty over the little patch of earth around the Eternal City, he can still retain his position and prestige in the Catholic World. If on the contrary he is made the object of violent attack from without, he will retire from Rome. There are unquestionably many revolutionists in Rome. But it is not from them that danger is apprehended. The Romans are themselves too weak, too destitute of enterprise to accomplish anything. The friends and foes of the Pope in Rome are of the same feeble stamp. The only thing to be feared is the flood swelling in from Italy and submerging Rome. But, I asked, is it considered impossible, among reasonable men around the Pope, to treat with the King of Italy and to obtain from him the protection he would doubtless gladly accord? The Doctor shook his head and said slowly, "I do not see how it can be done. There are some compromises which would destroy the very essence of the principle in question. These cannot be made. Such compromises are different from merely accepting the logic of events."

I asked about the Pope's projected retirement to Malta. He said that several years ago, the Pope in conversation with the English representative at Rome, said in allusion to some danger then

contemplated, "I suppose if I am driven out of Rome you will let me come to Malta, would you not?" Upon that the envoy wrote to his government, and Earl R—— immediately answered that whenever his Holiness desired it an English Man-of-War would be at his service at Civita Vecchia to take him to Malta. This despatch still exists and Dr. S—— says it is the only document that has passed between the two governments on the subject.

I asked if O—— R—— was a Catholic. He said no, Lady Wm. R——, his mother, is.

I referred to the hope that the Catholics in America had, to see the Pope among them. He said the matter had sometimes been thought of, but that it seemed impracticable, as the Pope should occupy a more central position in reference to Christendom.

Col. R—— informed me to-day of S——'s engagement to Mrs. S—— H——. He wrote a letter to Mrs. A—— announcing his engagement but did not even mention the lady's name. This is eminently characteristic. The great point with S—— is that *he* is to be married. If the lady happens to get married about the same time, all

the better for her. But this is quite a secondary consideration.

W—— tells me that once, while S—— was sick, he said to him, "S——, you ought to marry and have a woman to take care of you." S—— answered, "Don't talk of that, W——! I am left behind."

W—— tells me another very good thing on S——. When the question of the admission of Louisiana and Arkansas, in President L——'s time, was before the Committee, B—— opposed it, giving his reasons. S—— agreed with him and urged him to make a speech to that effect in the Senate. "No," said B——, "I am what you call a copperhead and a speech from me to that effect will do the question more harm than good. You make the speech." "I can't," said S——, "have got too many irons in the fire now." "If you will deliver a speech I will write it," says B——. "Agreed," said S——. B—— wrote the speech and S——, after putting a quotation from Milton in, delivered it. While he was giving it to the Senate in that high-priced style of his, old C——, the nestor and pride of the Senate, suddenly pricked up his ears and began to listen, a thing he seldom

did when the great Bostonian had the floor. His seat was near B——'s, toward whom he leaned, and nudging him, said, "B——, listen! Hanged if the fellow is not arguing!"

I believe this to be a copperhead fiction, but it is very good, "all same so," as Japanese Tommy used to say.

Just before going to Biarritz, B—— says, the Emperor went to the Palais de l'Exposition. He seemed to be very bilious. On coming in sight of the Champ de Mars, he said: "Call that a palace! Looks like a gasometer!" When he came to the high, closed fence, surrounding the park, he says: "What does this mean? Tear it down! The people have a right to see the building." They explained and he compromised by tearing holes in the fence at intervals. On each side of the North entrance were neat brick structures for the officers of the Exhibition. Here his bile biled over. "Otez-moi ça. What the Devil do you spoil the view so for? Tear them down!" and this week you see workmen demolishing with pick and shovel what they built laboriously last week with chisel and trowel.

The Emperor never was the meekest of men, but

his temper is sour this autumn as the disappointed vintage of Burgundy.

Sept. 27. Yesterday Mr. B—— was one of the party that accompanied L. L. M. M. on the visit to the iron-clad fleet at Biarritz. I wish F—— had been there.

L—— gives an odd reverse to the brilliant account of the Russo-American festivities of this summer. He says the persons in charge of it swindled the government infamously. That the appropriations were most munificent, but that the arrangements made were paltry and shabby.

Sept. 30. This morning I found at the Legation a despatch from Mr. S—— (sent through the French Ministère de l'Interieur) saying: "Resignation accepted—Gen'l D—— appointed successor—leaves here 28 October"—dated Washington, 29th September, 12.45 at night. I sent copy to Biarritz.

The morning papers contained the bare announcement. The *Patrie* in the afternoon contained an attack on Mr. B—— for his ultra American stiffness in the Mexican question.

The *Constitutionel* this morning shows by its

announcement that it has been made acquainted with S——'s despatch.

The General (Dix), immediately after his arrival, was presented by Mr. B—— to the Marquis de M—— and a few days afterwards received from the Grand Master of Ceremonies a letter informing him that he would be received by the Emperor on Sunday, the 23d, at two o'clock. He afterwards received a note from the Duke de Fascher la Pajerie informing him that the Empress would receive him immediately after his audience with the Emperor.

I hired a carriage and two servants in the Rue Boissy d'Anglas for H—— and myself. It was a highly respectable looking affair, not fresh enough to look hired, with a couple of solemn flunkies that seemed to have been in the family for at least a generation. We went to the General's and in a few moments came in the Baron de la J——. He said he was very much crowded to-day with *besogne,* that he had five Ministers to bring to the Palace and that therefore we would please excuse his hurry. Upon which we all rose and went to the door, where we found a court carriage, the Imperial arms blazing on the panels and the harness, drawn by four horses and accompanied by two mounted outriders. Everything covered with tawdy, tarnished gold lace. It seemed like the Triumphal Car in a flourishing circus. Into this vehicle mounted the General and the Chamberlain, H—— and I following in our sham-private *remise* and we had the honors of a stare from the *badauds* on the asphalt of the Champs Elysées as the party lumbered down to the Tuileries. We were all in our Army uniform.

Arrived there we were shown to a warm, cheery anteroom, with a superb wood fire and a fine view of the Tuileries gardens and the river and the Arch of Triumph. The Colombian Minister had already arrived. He and his Secretary stood conversing with one of the fine violet-colored Chamberlains. Another received us and talked of nothing in particular—the weather, which was sharp for Paris—skating, monuments, acquaintances. One torment of diplomatic life is that you never know the names of these agreeable fellows. They lose all identity in their violet coats and Imperial moustaches. You do not hear their names when you are presented to them, and if you look upon the official list of the officers of the Emperor's household you only find that you may take your choice of a dozen names for the man you are looking after.

F——, the British Minister *ad interim*, came in. I presented him to Gen'l D——. They talked Alabama, Fenians and stuff. Then a long gaunt Bavarian, P—— de P——, and his Secretary, who seemed moved by rusty springs—in military uniform; a thin, wiry, blue-blooded Brazilian—a Peruvian and some more. B——, at least a half head taller than anybody but F——, who is not tall by the way—only long.

There came some more violet people and moved us into a larger saloon. They were presented to the Duc de C——,—a jaunty old gentleman, lean and shaven and wigged—long also. He bowed lavishly and seemed distressed that nobody would sit down. B—— in a few moments was called for. He entered the next room where the blaze of the Imperial presence dazzled us through the opening of the door. His audience of leave was soon over. Gen'l D——, followed by me and H——, was then ushered into The Presence. The General looked anxiously around for the Emperor, advancing undecidedly, until a little man who was standing in front of the Throne stepped forward to meet him. Everybody bowed profoundly as the Duc de C—— gave the name and the title of the General. The little man bowed, and the General, beginning to recognize in him a dim likeness to the Emperor's portrait, made his speech to him. I looked around the room for a moment, admiring as I always do on ceremonial occasions in France the rich and tasteful masses of color which the various groups of Great Officers of the Crown so artistically present. Not a man's place is left to accident. A cardinal dashes in a great splash of scarlet. A cent-garde supplies an exquisite blue and gold. The yellow and the greens are furnished by the representatives of Law and Legislation, and the Masters of Ceremonies fill up with an unobtrusive violet. Yet these rich lights and soft shadows are accessory to the central point of the picture—the little man who is listening or seeming to listen to the General's address. If our Republican eyes can stand such a dazzling show, let us look at him.

Short and stocky, he moves with a queer, sidelong gait, like a gouty crab. A man so wooden looking that you would expect his voice to come rasping out like a watchman's rattle. A complexion like crude tallow—marked for Death, whenever Death wants him—to be taken sometime in half an hour, or left, neglected by the skeleton King, for years, perhaps, if properly coddled. The moustache, an imperial which the world knows, but ragged and bristly, concealing the mouth entirely, moving a little nervously as the lips twitch. Eyes stupidly watchful—furtive—stealthy, rather ignoble, like servants looking out of dirty windows and saying nobody at home and lying, as they say it. And withal a wonderful phlegm. He stands there as still and impassive as if carved in oak for a ship's figure-head. He looks not unlike one of those rude inartistic statues. His legs are too short—his body too long. He never looks well but on a throne or on a horse, as kings ought.

But the General, who has raised his voice and grown a little oratorical as he closed his speech by recalling the bonds of union which ally America and France, hands the Emperor his sealed letter of credence. He receives it and gives it to the Duc de B——, who stands at his right. His face breaks up with ungainly movements of the moustache and the eyelids. You can imagine it a sort of wooden clock preparing to strike. When he speaks you are sure of your theory. His voice is wooden; it is not so strong or as full as a year ago. He speaks rather rapidly and not distinctly. He slews half his words, as rapid writers do half their letters. He makes his set speech, which, with the General's, will appear to-morrow in the *Moniteur*, and then comes sidling up and says (smilingly, he evidently thinks, but the machinery of smiles at the corners of his mouth is apparently out of repair), "You expect many of your countrymen in Paris this year?"

"A great many, doubtless."

"There will be a regiment of your milice?"

"There has been some talk of it, etc., etc., but your Majesty will not expect them to compare with your veterans."

"But you have shown that it does not take long to make good troops."

When I and H—— (that is awkward, but I preserve the order) were presented He, clearly wishing to be very civil, as it is most rare that a monarch addresses a Secretary of Legation, said, "But you are very young to be Col-o-nel. Did you make the war in America?"

I wanted to insist that older and wickeder men than I were responsible for that crime, but I thought best to answer the intention rather than the grammar, and said I had an humble part in the war.

"Infanterie or cavalerie?"

"The general staff!"

"And you!" he said, turning to H——, and received the same answer.

We bowed and backed out of the Presence.

We were then taken to the apartments of the Empress. She was charmingly dressed in a lilac walking dress with an almost invisible bonnet. She had doubtless been to church like a good, pious lady as she is and received afterwards in her promenade costume. Time has dealt very gently with her. She is still full of those sweet winning fascinations that won her a crown. There are few partisans so bitter as not to be moved by her exquisite manner. Even the little stories at which men smile, her subjection to priests, her hanging up over old B——'s death-bed the holy rag from the baby linen of John Baptist, which extorted from the tormented old sinner his last grim smile, her vestal lamp in the Church of Our Lady of Victories and all that mummery, is not unfeminine, and people do not care to be bitter about it. To the General she was charming. She talked about the President and his trip to Chicago (which the General explained was purely a personal visit of friendship to the tomb of a friend ! ! !). When we were presented, she made the identical remark made by the Emperor, "You are young to be Colonel?" People after a dozen years of intercourse get the same ideas and ways of looking at things. She asked if the grade of Colonel was the same in our army as in the French. She spoke English with a charming Castilian accent, which is infinitely prettier than the French.

She is so winning and so lovely that one feels a little guilty in not being able in conscience to wish her eternal power for herself, her heirs and assigns.

So we left the gracious blonde Spaniard and passed down through avenues of flunkeys to the door where our own sham flunkies received us and drove us to the Rue de Presbourg.

The ceremony is concluded by giving to the Chief Piqueur a present of 250 francs.

The last time I saw the Emperor, was on the 1st of January, 1867, at the Diplomatic reception. Instead of admitting the Diplomats by a door nearest the Salle de Trone, they always manage to drag them through a long series of saloons crowded with footmen of portentous calf development and Chamberlains in purple: to strike the imagination of outside barbarians. We were pressed on as usual through these blazing hedges of tinsel, to the Reception room. It was pretty well filled when we entered and we passed a pleasant half hour talking to our acquaintances in the Corps. A good deal of interest was taken in the General, who was one of the newest arrivals, and whose venerable and gentlemanlike appearance produced a most favorable impression. At the order of the bustling Chamberlains we took our places, the United States by a queer chance finding itself between the two American Empires, Mexico and Brazil, A—— having been presented just before and the Brazilian just after Gen'l D——. The Brazilian Minister presented D—— to A——, the General thinking that much could be sacrificed to courtesy, and they began to recall an old Washington acquaintance, when the door opened and the usher shouted "L'Empereur." Everyone bowed with various degrees of abject servility. The Emperor came woodenly in. He was dressed in his usual uniform of General of Division. The Prince Imperial, a nice, slender child, with pleasant, sad eyes like his mother, came in with his august sire for the first time. The Emperor only begins to associate him with great public ceremonies. He was dressed in black-velvet coat and short, full breeches, with red stockings—the broad cordon of the Legion of Honor over his shoulder and across his little chest. He walked beside his father, bowing when we bowed, and stopping a little, fidgeting while the Sphinx talked with the wise men of the World.

But, on entering, the Emperor paused, bowed and took position — the Pope's Nuncio — Mgr. C——, made the usual formal speech of congratulations, to which the Emperor replied with his best wishes for the perpetuity of thrones and the prosperity of peoples and his hopes that the Exposition would bring the millenium this year. He evidently had his brain full of the vast results that are to accrue to him from that unsightly structure in the Champ de Mars. He then went around the circle, speaking a word to most of the Ministers. I stood next to A—— and waited with great interest to see how they met.

The Emperor came rolling up to the Mexican and stopped. Both bowed. A—— seemed rather ill at ease. The Emperor held him a moment with his dead eyes half shut. He then said in a manner which was carefully cold and insolent, "Les choses sont bien compliquees là bas." The poor devil, who doubtless feels himself lost by his advocacy of the Imperial cause in Mexico, had no reply ready to this insolent remark from his angry and ungrateful temptor. The Emperor bowed, the Prince Imperial bowed and A—— bowed. I did not dare to look at him.

I looked at the Emperor instead, who came to Gen'l D—— and was very gracious—speaking French this time—asked the General where he lived and said it was a beau quartier—the General said yes, thanks to His Majesty—and His Majesty pulled the corners of his mouth into a sort of smile and bowed to the General and bowed to me and passed to Brazil—and put a malicious little question to Brazil about its war, and then walked almost hastily past the smaller powers—pausing an instant with F—(who was below us, having been presented five minutes later the day we were)—then passed out and we loafed down to the door and waited in the uncomfortable entry for our carriages, till we were blue and ill-natured. Then made calls on the necessary nobs by writing our names in a book at their door, and at last went home and took off our livery and were glad it was over.

HAY TO ALBERT RHODES.

Paris, Oct. 19, 1866.

MY DEAR RHODES:

I offer you my warmest congratulations upon your new clustering honors. Don't get proud thereat, but always remember you are a miserable sinner, and that if you had your deserts you would be howling in ignited sulphur, instead of standing as you do in the face of an admiring world, with one foot at the Hague and one at Rotterdam, the modern Colossus of Rhodes.

Gen'l H. E—— I do not personally know—and am likewise ignorant of his Etat-Civil. If it would be of any advantage to you, I know his father, his elder brother, his brother-in-law, his brother-in-law's son's first cousin and their wives and daughters, and good eggs are the men, and winsome creatures are the girls of that family. But with Gen'l H. E—— I have not foregathered, as I have with his brother T—— and Gen'l T——, Judge T. E——, Jr., who is a monstrous good fellow.

Wishing you continuous good luck, I am,

Yours truly.

HAY TO ALBERT RHODES.

Paris, Dec., '66.

MY OWN AND ONLY RHODES:

I am going home, as the papers have stated, in a strange paroxysm of truthfulness. I leave the service of the ungrateful Republic in a week or two more.

> Vain pomps and glories of this world I hate ye.
>
> (Shakes.)

I shall try to find a place behind some respectable counter. I do not care what I sell—candles or stocks—so that profits shall accrue. I shall pull off my coat and roll up my sleeves, but I don't believe Jordan will be so hard a road to travel as it is cracked up to be.

General D—— is a most genial gentleman with a very charming family. The New Secretaries are good fellows and will keep up the high traditions bequeathed by me and P——. They are W—— H—— and J—— D——.

There is no news.

I went down to No. 30 Victory Street the other day, but I could not recall my vanished illusions.

I am falling into the sere, the yellow leaf.

I am yours.

HAY TO NICOLAY.

Washington, D. C.
February 14, 1867.

MY DEAR NICOLAY:

. . . . We had rather a rough passage. I was in the condition of every man *qui se respecte*, on such occasions, the first day or two, but afterwards experienced a salutary shock by falling in love with the prettiest woman you ever clapped eyes on, which kept me on my sea-legs the rest of the voyage.

. . . . I found Mr. S—— as admirable as ever—calm, philosophical, optimist as ever. Not a word against his enemies and slanderers; a little astonishment at the completeness of the defeat, but a perfect comprehension of it. He treats me with the most distinguished kindness, offered me any mission that was falling in;—proposed my name to the President for the reversion of Sweden, McG—— having fallen a victim to the celestial wrath of the Gods Senatorial. But the President wanted the place for a deadbeat copperhead soldier named B—— of New York. . . . S—— says the Senate will reject him. C—— squirms—don't want to be turned out—says the Senate ought not to allow it, and the Senate seem inclined to protect the poor devil by rejecting everybody who is nominated to succeed him. I am inclined to decline a nomination in that state of affairs, though S—— thinks I would be confirmed. I will wait a day or two to see what becomes of Gen. D——. The Senate is very ugly—will certainly reject C—— for A——, and talk of rejecting E—— for the H——. D——'s chances are growing every day darker. F—— and H—— both want his place. S—— has blood in his eye. He is splendid in his present temper—arrogant, insolent, implacable,—thoroughly in earnest—honest as the day. . . .

You are all right everywhere. That push

against you came from cops who want your place. S—— wrote you that letter simply to give you an opportunity to say the charges were lies. He was rather amused at the completeness of your defence—"ten times over justified," he said. Letters like that were written to nearly everyone in the service;—nobody grew furious and resigned but M——. He becomes a high-priced martyr and has the sure thing on a first-class mission two years hence. It is hard for S—— to save L——'s friends from being pushed off their stools by hungry copperheads;—he defends them whenever he can.

I am a little at sea about what I shall do. The law has been a magnificent business for the past two years—a little duller now. . . . I may go to law after I have rested a while. Everybody without exception tells me I am looking very ill. It has demoralized me a little. . . .

It is all one way here. Nobody dares for an instant oppose the current. The thing must work itself clear. I have faith in the end. . . .

HAY TO NICOLAY.

Warsaw, Ill.,
March 18, 1867.

MY DEAR NICOLAY:

I am safely lodged at last among my Lares and Penates. I find my parents as well as ever; my mother better than usual, and full of her old good spirits; my father at 66 with not a gray hair, with the ruddy cheek and ravenous appetite of a growing boy. . . .

There is little comfort in the country now. The weather is hideous; *i. e.* what people insanely call "beautiful, fresh, cold weather." A cloudless sky, white, shining distances, and a thermometer ten degrees below 0 according to Meinherr Fahrenheit. I have escaped six winters, and my good nature has been nipped and frozen in this absurd springtime.

So much for nature. Society much worse. Poverty everywhere. In the East it is still tempered by the fever of speculation, but in the West everything and everybody is as flat as a buckwheat cake *de la veille*. There is no money and no business. One endless Sunday seems to gloom over all the little towns you pass. A man can live for almost nothing here; but he just misses that, and he makes nothing. For instance a very decent fellow came to Warsaw some time ago to start a newspaper. He had a little money, within $200 of the amount. He could not raise in the town the other $200. Again, a church here gave a fair and a supper. They spent $50. They received $40. These trivial figures give you some idea of the thumb and finger with which hard times is pinching.

Moral:—You stay where you are for the present. In the East, if you are lucky, these things would work to your benefit. There are some men who are growing rich. . . . In the West you would not make your Kanawha salt. (That H has given me a world of trouble.) Nobody is keen for our book. We will have to write it and publish it on our own hook some day, when we can afford. You had better not come home till you are kicked out, and our crazy friends in the Senate have legislated all the dead-beats now in office into an eternity of bread and butter. Newspapers are all running down. The *E——* *P——*, the *J—— of C——*, and a few others are doing well. The W—— papers *nil*.

While in W——, D—— proposed a Claim and

Law business partnership. I held it under advisement. He is public printer again, appointed by the Senate, but does not intend to hold it very long. . . .

A—— is making a collection of Lincoln's letters, speeches, etc., but on his own hook. B—— encourages it, but will not give him the key to the boxes. He will keep them for the present, and still hopes for our assistance in classifying them. He has commenced practice in partnership with S——'s son—with brilliant prospects. Mrs. L—— was well—was extremely kind—insisted on my moving my traps to her house; I could not, as I only remained one day. She is living in a pretty house of her own.

DIARY.

Warsaw, Illinois.
June 3, 1867.

It would be hard for me to imagine a pleasanter spring than I have passed. I have worked enough not to feel utterly idle and *desoeuvré*. I have been idle enough to enjoy in its fullest extent the joy of the *ne rien faire*. I have taken a deep interest in the destruction of caterpillars on my apple trees—in the planting of my own little orchard of 5 acres—in the growth and welfare of my orchard that S—— has leased. S—— is a Methodist Colporteur, who peddles the Gospel with Methodist sauce in the winter and vexes the envious soil in the summer—a quaint and most worthy man. He has leased my orchard—the S—— place for ten years, for half the crop. On College Hill the D—— boys—two fine, industrious Yankees—have taken the vineyard and the ten-acre block. They seem to be thoroughly good fellows with sand in their gizzards. They are the terror of loafing and swindling laborers who don't want to give a day's work for a day's wages. One of them is somewhat damaged by rebel lead at Gettysburg. I have spent a good deal of time on the different places: digging some, planting, pruning. I find a singular love for that kind of work in myself. It is the sense of justification it gives me for not doing nothing. If I stay at home I cannot idle or read for amusement, without being haunted by the ceaseless reproach of misspent time. But in the fields, tiresome and monotonous as the work may be—such as shovelling dirt or dropping corn—it frees me utterly from the sense of responsibility for the passing hour. I am doing work, substantial, real work which will have its result doubtless some day and so I plod on and watch the sun, glad after all when my day is over and I can ramble home through the magnificent hills and valleys that surround this town.

I never was so close to nature before since I was a child. I have watched the flowers like a detective this spring. There is a little patch of wild woodlawn on my S—— place that is very sweet and solitary—full of fresh, woodsy smells and far enough from any farmyards to be utterly still—barring the birds and the grasshoppers—whose racket only makes the solitude more perfect by proof. I stumbled one day on a patch of open turf thick in blue grass and superbly illuminated with great purple pansies that had probably bloomed for years unseen by any eyes, but the bright, beady ones of orioles and jays and catbirds. It was worth the price I paid for the land, to feel that this exquisite show, so lavishly running to waste year after year, was mine. I would not pluck them—the violets and phlox, the windflowers and bluebells—because I loved them. When I crossed the fences, however, and walked down the valley pastures of my neighbors, the poaching spirit waked in me and I gathered red bud, hawthorne, apple bloom and plum blossom right and left—making what I thought an equitable return in killing about a thousand ugly green-black-yellow caterpillars that had raised their tent on the limb of a splendid crab, all pink and fragrant in its May bloom. I cut off the branch they were on and dropped it into the fresh, clear rivulet. Then at the risk of my neck I clambered up the bank by G——'s—where the surviving precipice looks like a ruined amphitheatre of the woodlawn gods that are gone—and got a handful of columbine and then came slowly down to the river and along its pebbly banks home. I can never get enough of looking at the river. It has its new, fresh beauty every morning and noon. And a new and unimagined transfiguration every sunset.

So the pleasant spring has shaken away its sands. I have scarcely any plans. I came to wait for answers from M——, who wanted me to come into his establishment—from S——, who wanted to buy my Florida property—and from B——, who wanted me to enter his firm as a Washington partner. I have answers from all—singularly unanimous—all backing out as if they had suddenly discovered that I was a leper. I am not disappointed. I could scarcely have brought myself to enter M——'s house in any case. I have a great distaste to the life of a claim agent in the Federal City where my associations have been so different, and I long ago made up my mind not to lose any sleep over my ill-starred Florida speculation.

I can scarcely say now to myself what my plans are. Let me see. Go to S——, see some publishers in New York and Boston—write L——'s book for him—write two lectures and that will pretty well fill up the summer.

If it were only myself I thought of I would stay here. I will have an income—all things succeeding—of at least $500 a year, and I can bring that up a few hundreds by writing—and have a more tranquil mind than anywhere else.

To-day voted for the second time in my life—the Republican Judicial Ticket. I had to make oath to my residence.

Went last week to a ball at K——, a Mrs. I——. It was a pretty party—toilettes very neat and fresh. The ladies all in full dress—very few gentlemen—in fact I alone, I think, was in evening dress. The talk very much as at a party anywhere else. The dancing, all quadrilles. Only one or two men in town can waltz—to the desolation of the girls, most of whom waltz well enough.

June 11, 1867. The newspapers a week or so ago announced my appointment to Austria—all, so far as I know, taking their cue from the *New York T——*; ought to be good enough authority on that matter. B—— and P—— write me very hearty letters of congratulations. I write to B——, My Dear Mr. B——, If nothing more comes of it, I am grateful to the guidance who first sent the news of my appointment on its travels, some weeks ago, since it has procured me so kind and cordial a letter from you. And another from P—— to the same tenor. I am without any further intimation of the truth or falsehood of the report—and indeed do vehemently doubt it. If it comes I may not go to Austria, but I will try to borrow money enough on my crop to go to Washington to see what it means. If it means a scandal or row about the place, *i. e.*, if M—— insists on being kicked out, another boot than mine must do it. Not that I object to the kicking out *per se*, but I don't think the fun of doing it and then parting my own coat tails for the heavy-shod Senate, will pay for a month of sea sickness.

The Senate is of late gone clean daft in its Presidentophobia. It slaughtered a dozen brave fellows because they were nominated and then confirmed another dozen wild caps for no better reason. They threw over McG—— because they thought he might be a copperhead and confirmed B——, who was a blatant one of the Five-Points' race—a gambler of highly ungrammatical habits. They confirmed D——, who was the P—— convention's incarnate, obstinate and unrepentant, and smothered R——, who did more than any mother's son of them to defeat the nominee of that movement and elect F——. They refuse to be comforted because of M——, and there are not a half a dozen Senators who would not have said of him just what that shabby blackguard McC—— said, after a week in Vienna. So, though my record is of the straightest radicalism—abolitionist when many of them were doughy of face, and ever since —they would fling mud upon me if my appointment were attended with any squeak of martyrdom. As to all that I am ignorant. I do not know where Mr. M—— is—where the Legation is—who is running it—what has become of L——. All this, if I should be appointed I would go to Washington to inquire about and decide according to my best lights and the state of my liver.

I make you a thousand impressive compliments in recognition of your kindness in asking me to your estates. It would be the greatest pleasure incident to this probationary state of existence—but it does not look probable. If I can, I will, gladly and gratefully. Make Miladi remember me and recall me to the young people whose memories have doubtless cicatrized the impression I made in past pleasant days. Your friend and servant,

J. H.

Until this thing is developed you had better write to me, Care State Dept. Mr. C—— always knows my address and is good enough to send me my letters.

Rode down to the Golden Bluffs and spent an hour or so with George W——, in his vineyard, pinching his vines. The prospect for wine this year so far is excellent.

P. S. P. M.

This afternoon I received a copy of the Secretary's letter notifying me of my appointment and asking me when, if I accept, I will be ready to start. The long delay is accounted for by the fact that the letter had been sent to Warsaw, Wisconsin, by mistake. C——'s letter is dated June 6, the original May 30. I very much fear it will be found impracticable, as I am appointed Secretary of Legation to act as Chargé d'Affaires. I do not yet know whether L—— has resigned or been dismissed. I will go to Washington and talk with both sides about the matter before I decide. It is not worth a quarrel. I do not care for a quarrel if I am to gain by it, but a squabble for a counter is poor wisdom, in spite of Robert Browning. (Statue and Bust).

HAY TO MISS ELIZABETH HAY.

Warsaw, Ill.
June 12, 1867.

DEAR AUNT:

I have a presentiment that a weary and wayworn pilgrim will knock at your door between dusk and midnight of Monday evening next, craving shelter from the warm blast of summer and the fierce rays of the moon. Deny him not—for he will bring you tidings of your brethren and friends in this country. You can recognize him by his answer to the name of John, and by a broad accent derived from a prospective residence in the city of Vienna! He is unable to go to a tavern, having expended his last kreutzer in the purchase of this half sheet of paper. You will do well to lock up your spoons, as I fear that a sojourn of several years in Washington has not had a beneficial effect on his morals. Don't set any wine before him, as he has sunk his entire fortune in an unprofitable vineyard, and bursts into tears whenever grape-juice is mentioned. Treat him kindly, for, though feeble-minded and erring, he is still a fellow-worm. But be careful about the spoons.

[John Hay was commissioned Secretary of Legation, May 20, 1867, to act as *chargé d'affaires ad interim* after the retirement of Mr. Motley, June 14, 1867, at Vienna.]

Monday, June 17, 1867. I started from home for Washington. On the train to Hamilton met Col. C—— with his dog, a singularly intelligent pointer which he had captured during the war as a pup. Met at Hamilton, where we waited two hours for the train, Pros. Atty. P——. Told me of the —— W—— family. "When a young man gits bloated—with a crick in his neck you know—he's about a gone coon."

Rode to Carthage in the same seat with R—— L——, a second cousin of the late President. He is forty-one years old, looks much older. The same eyes and hair the President had—the same tall stature and shambling gait, less exaggerated, a rather rough, farmer-looking man. Drinks hard, chews ravenously. He says the family has about run out. "We are not a very marrying set." He is dying of consumption, he said very coolly. There was something startling in the resemblance of the straight thicket of hair, and the grey, cavernous eyes framed in black brows and lashes, both features of the great dead man. He was a pioneer of our country. Knew my father since long years. Brought a load of wheat to G—— and M—— in 1842 with ox teams; got $90 in gold for it. Told me that in 1860 he had talked to "Abe" about assassination. Abe said: "I never injured anybody. No one is going to hurt me." He says he was invited by Abe to go on to Washington at the time of the inauguration but declined, thinking it dangerous—a naïvete of statement I thought would have been impossible out of the west.

Spent Tuesday, the 18th, at Springfield. Talked with C—— at length. He was rather disgusted with the extra session, but could not think of disregarding the summons. He promised to talk with W—— and Y—— about my confirmation. Thought there was no doubt about it.

When I left Springfield C—— came with me to New York. I went there, instead of directly to Washington, because I saw in the papers that the President and the Secretary of State would be there on Friday on their way to Boston. They passed up Broadway in the evening. I was on the balcony of the Metropolitan. Two or three men beside me made criticisms on the President—not kindly, but when the common council came by, they looked at each other, and said, "Don't say anything about them or they'll get out and bust your snoot."

I went late in the evening to the Fifth Avenue Hotel and saw a good many people, but not the President nor the Secretary. Most of the men I saw were balmily tight and insisted on my drinking with them. I found Mr. S—— afterwards at T—— W——'s. He explained the vacancy in the Austrian mission—asked me when I could go. "At once." He told me to go down to Washington and get my papers and start by the first steamer. "I would do so." I spoke of the Senate's possibly throwing me out, but he said that was not probable and there was no use anticipating it. He had told M—— that evening that the moderate men who did not want an extra session and who compromised on this provisional arrangement, now found themselves like a man whose reprieve had run out and who had gained nothing by the delay. He thought nothing would come by the extra session. Congress were called together on false issues, and they will see when they get here, that the President, instead of being reckless and factious, is carrying out their own law in good faith.

This is all true; but I think, as W—— said to me in the morning, it is regrettable that the President and S—— should have given room to these false issues by stirring up this row before the 4th of July.

The next day, Saturday, G—— D—— brought me a kind invitation from L—— J—— to go to the races at Jerome Park in his drag. The day was exquisite—the crowd brilliant—the mercury very fair. I became acquainted with S—— B——, a very agreeable fellow, spite of his politics. M—— was there, and, as I had outgrown my animosity, we were friendly enough. R—— was on hand. He has a great talent for talking to women. Sir Fred. B—— was also on hand, and was civil enough to say that he hoped they would not get a minister to Vienna till they took me. John M—— was strutting about, less important than of yore, waxed and dyed and holystoned like the battered old buck he is. I met the V——s, S——s, C——s and many more. Was delighted to have one more hour with Mrs. B——, who was as lively as ever. As old P—— said, Mon Dieu ! qu'elle est vive, qu'elle est vive !

Went to see the K——s and the S——s and more ladies. Saw a good many men, who were all cordial. Everybody thinks my appointment is a good thing and does not for a moment conceive that I can refuse it.

Went on board the Steamer "City of Boston," Saturday, June 29, in a highly mixed-up condition. I had dined the night before with D——, B——, F——, V—— at the Union Club, where we ate abominations, *i. e.*, homards farcis, *Gibelottes à la Maitre d'hotel*, etc., and nothing solid and honest. So I was an indigested mass. Add to that a severe sore throat, and you have me a prisoner in my berth the first two days out. Then the ship's doctor, H—— (a most clever fellow, by the way, who owns a copy of the "Princess," in which Tennyson's own rough draft of the "Home they brought" and the "He hears thy voice mid rolling drums!" are written in. They are infinitely weaker than the revised versions, (which again he has botched and spoiled in his last volume). H—— gave me a purge and lotion which brought me right up again.

When I came on deck C—— S—— began to joke. He said he did not know what kept me so long in New York till some one explained. I was curious to know where he got this news and he told me M——. How M—— ever dreamed such a thing puzzles me. S—— says M—— told him he had said to me, "You had better keep this thing and let Austria alone," and the blackguard never had mentioned the matter to me and I can't conceive where he heard it. He spoke to me at Jerome Park and said he had made a strong push for the Mexican mission. Said he thought J—— would refuse to receive O——. I said, "Then he certainly would have refused you, as you are well known to have been one of the most earnest partisans of Maximilian." He only said he thought J—— would not have dared reject him. This was every word that passed between us.

We had a pleasant celebration of the 4th of July. S——, D—— and W—— made neat speeches, S—— presided very effectively and I answered very briefly and drily to the toast "The President of the United States."

We landed at Liverpool Tuesday evening and got lodgings at the Queen's Hotel. My card and a couple of crown pieces were very effectual in getting my luggage and the H——s' out of the Customs. Wednesday morning I went out to walk. A small and dirty newsboy accosted me on the street and said, "Buy a paper, sir, got the passengers by City o' Boston, got your name in it." I bought the paper overcome by the dirty youth's sagacity. I shall go to my grave uncertain how he discovered I was a Yankee and had come over in the "City of Boston." I suppose it must have been my boots.

We got off on the London train a little before noon and arrived in the great city Wednesday evening at 5.15. I packed the H—— ladies in a cab for Charing Cross and started myself for the

L——. Found it full. They offered to send a porter to get me rooms at N——'s. N——'s grinningly announced a glut of guests. I went to Charing Cross. All full. I told my cabby to drive anywhere. He brought up at a French house, D——. They asked me if I would have a room on the first, second, third or fourth floor. I said the first. "Well, I believe we have none." The second, then. "Mon Dieu, I believe we have none on the second," etc., etc. There was one on the fourth right under the shingles baking and frying. I fled aghast. My ever-faithful cabby brought up in 8 T—— Street, near Tottenham Court Road, Hotel B——, a queer little Spanish house that had a vacant room. I took it desperately, though everything looked Séaviter. I prepared to pass the night in deadly struggles with garrotters. But it was far better than it seemed. I had a good dinner, good bed, and good breakfast and almost regretted to leave it when the next morning I had gotten a room at the splendid and comfortless L——. If ever I come to London incog., I will find that little house again.

I called at the Legation. Met M—— and A——. M—— took me to call on Mr. A——.

I passed the rest of the day shopping—hatters, boot-makers, tailors, and bankers.

Dined in the evening with Mr. and Mrs. A——. A very pleasant dinner and pleasant talk. A—— has been a great deal in Vienna. Knows it very well and likes it—was full of pleasant things about Vienna people. He seems rather more cheery and better contented with the world than M——. I should say it was because he has a wife and baby.

When I came in I found W—— and the B——s had arrived, and Mr. and Mrs. C——'s card in my box.

Friday, July, 1867. I breakfasted with the C——s. W—— B—— and I mounted an omnibus and went up High Holborn, passed the site of the New Viaduct, the foundations of the great New Market and descended near Cheapside, the road being barred by dense crowds gathering to see the Belgian Volunteers march by. We wormed through the mass to St. Paul's and walked through the vast pile. Thence through Paternoster Row and a succession of tortuous little streets till we came to Holborn again, and I took a hansom and went to the Legation. Saw Mr. A—— there—asked when the ladies received calls, found it was just the hour—went around to Portland Place and lunched with them. Mr. and Mrs. K—— were there. The piquante Madam K—— insisting that she had suddenly been attacked with water on the knee, which occasioned much glee.

We tore our friends to pieces a little while. M—— got one or two slaps that were very unexpected to me. S—— and his new wife were brushed up a little. I dine with them on Tuesday at 7.45 and on Sunday at 7.30, if I have nothing else, as the terms of the invitation kindly ran.

At 3.30 M—— came for me and Judge W—— of Pennsylvania to go with him to the House of Commons. At the door of Westminster Hall we met Tom B. P——, C——'s successor, who, as M—— found his party, suddenly increased by K—— and F——, rather cumbrous, took one of them off his hands and got K—— into the Speaker's gallery. P—— was very robust and hearty in his Americanism—rather too much so to suit the public, conservative stomach of Judge W——, who is reaction and discontent personified. P—— took us into the crypt, where Guy Fawkes collected his incendiary materials "to blow us all up," he said. It is now a most gorgeously ornate Chapel—too handsome to be good for anything.

In the vestibule I met Lord E——, looking, with his blazing head and whiskers, as if he "had just come through hell with his hat off." We talked a moment of Lord Lyons, and M—— called me to follow him. He seems to have great and unusual privileges in their Parliament Houses: he took three of us to good seats upon the floor, facing the Speaker, and giving a good view of the whole house. The members sit on either side of the hall on five benches running the whole length of the room but cut in the middle by a narrow gangway. The Speaker's chair is at the end opposite the entrance. Three clerks sit below, in front of him. The Reporters' gallery is just above and behind him, and higher still the ladies' boxes are railed off and you see them dimly behind the railing like prisoners in the gloomy twilight. Narrow galleries surround the hall, but they are vacant. They are reserved for members in case of a full house, something which rarely happens.

On the government bench, to the right of the Speaker, the most noticeable man was Disraeli, who, since the very inception of the Reform Bill which is now near its passage, has been constantly at his post, defending, explaining and fighting for the Government Measure. He has grown enormously in the public estimation in this session. It was a stroke of the shrewdest policy on the part of the present Tory Government, having gained office by defeating the Liberal Bill last year, to keep it by carrying a more liberal one this year. In the great fight now beginning between privilege and democracy in England, the Democrats will have need of all their skill and discretion, for the aristocracy seem to perceive to a great extent the meaning of the occasion, and they will throw everything away in the fight that does not seem essential. If the Republicans are not distracted by false issues they will conquer at last, by the force of numbers. But they must make a good fight or suffer long delays.

While we were there, Disraeli, Gladstone, Forster, Newdegate and several others made short conversational talks. I was very much impressed with their directness and simplicity of statement. I think the exclusion of the public, by taking away all temptation to display, has a very fine effect on parliamentary oratory. Nothing could be clearer and finer than Disraeli's and Gladstone's manner of stating their points.

The members sat with their hats on, taking them off when they rose to speak and replacing them immediately afterwards. Many had their feet on the back of the bench in front. Yet on the whole their demeanor was very attentive and respectful. They have a very decided way of expressing their approbation or disapproval of the member speaking. I admired Newdegate's coolness in holding his own and talking unmoved by a general growl of ill-natured comment, until the Speaker called him to order.

There were a dozen or so very young fellows in the Hall, who were, of course, the representatives of their families. Among the most youthful looking was Lord Amberly. .

The debate not being specially entertaining we went over to the House of Lords. We came in just behind the woolsack and took our seats on the steps of the Throne. The Lord Chancellor was in his seat. In front of him the Clerks, on either side, on benches, the Peers. The Government occupying his right; Lord Derby at their head. Nearest us, on the right, were the spiritual Lords, the Archbishop of Canterbury, an elderly and rather infirm-looking man; the Bishop of Oxford, a fine, portly prelate, whose blue riband made me think of a prize ox; the Bishop of South Wales and the Bishop of London. On our left sat the Duke of Buccleuch, a stiff, dry Scotchman, with a wen on his forehead. Next to him snored comfortably Viscount Sidney. Then came Lord Stanhope. Then the Duke of Argyll, small of stature and red of hair. M—— pointed out to us the tall, slender, finicky Marquis of Bath, who was severely nipped by the Cotton Loan; Earl Powis, a smaller Forrest without the mustache; the Duke of Richmond, a good-looking silver-haired man; Lord Stratford de Redcliffe, a rather undersized old gentleman, white-haired, bent, and not in the least the grand manner that Kinglake fancies; and the Duke of Buckingham and Chandos, the most remarkable-looking nobleman I ever saw—who looks in style, station, dress, way of getting over the ground, face and features like a brisk country grocer in New England. Yet he is one of the best bloods that the English stud can show and is a bright fellow besides, as the plucky retrieval of his estates, ruined by the waste of his father, shows. Bourgeois as he looks, he is as proud as any one of his class, they say. The

Earl of Bradford is a good-looking, youngish man. Lord Romilly and Lord Cairns, two recent additions to the lower Lords, made short, sensible speeches while we were there.

They adjourned rather early. One of the gentlemen with black calves picked up the Mace, another the Seal, a third the Lord Chancellor's scattered papers and marched out before him in solemn procession, a fourth following him and holding up the tail of his gown. We saw them safely under way and passed out the other way, through the anteroom, where we saw the superb marble of Gibson representing the Queen, supported by Justice and Grace. The room contains also a great many royal portraits. As we went out, we saw the Lord Chancellor coming solemnly up the corridor. We dropped into the doorway and the gorgeous pageant—little man staggering under the Mace, stout man carrying the Seal, and tall man bravely holding the tail of his Lordship's coat—swept before our own stricken gaze. We went out—again passing through the grand and imposing hall of William Rufus.

In the evening a man named Y——, a good-hearted grain dealer from M——, who has been to Paris ten days and comes back bored to death because he couldn't tell a cabman where to drive, and who for that eminently satisfactory reason is cutting short in a month a projected tour of a year—the moral of which is, that before you go to Paris you should ascertain what language people speak there—Y——, I say, took us to Cremorne and the Alhambra—which are dreary beyond the power of human tongue to describe. Yet they were full of the same class one finds at the Mabille and elsewhere, who have nothing better in God's world to do. When we left the Alhambra we passed down the Haymarket for quarter of an hour. The streets were full of poor old women and some not so old, painted, bedizened and miserable. The Belgians just now overflow the town and they were the objective point of these poor, lost creatures to-night. The Belges seemed rather to enjoy the attention they received, from which I conclude that the Belgian women must be hideous, or that there is a charm in novel ugliness. It was certainly in London that Pope learned that "Vice is a monster of such frightful mien," etc.

Saturday. W—— and I started out together for a ramble. We went to S——, where we saw

F——, then to the Legation. Then walked down Regent Street to Waterloo Place, skirting St. James Park by the Horseguards, the Treasury and the New Foreign Office to Westminster Abbey. We lunched in a little shop over against the Abbey on sandwiches and ale, for which we paid, both of us, 6 pence. This economy put us in high spirits and we attacked the Abbey with good heart. Entering by the North porch I was a little disappointed. The building is choked and crowded by its several tablets fitting the space between the columns of the aisles, and by the introduction of the choir forward of the transept. But the great enchantment of the place remains. Rare Ben Jonson and Garrick and Thackeray and the rest, and the busts of the greatest. Andre's alto-relief with Washington's head knocked off and pasted on again, Lamb accused Southey of doing; Milton's name at the head of a long list of titles of a well-meaning snob who placed his monument there, and the herd of magnificent cenotaphs and epitaphs of the illustrious obscure, were the little farces that relieve the more solemn suggestions of the place. When I came to the extreme west end and got a better view of the superb proportions of the nave I was consoled for my former disappointment. It is hard to imagine anything finer.

We went out into the muggy daylight and tossed up a penny to see if we should go to Hyde Park or the River. There was some attraction in the running water, I presume. The denarian oracle said River. We walked to Westminster Bridge and then took passage to London Bridge, as the clouds looked minatory. They kept their evil promise, for the rain began to fall as we came near to Southwark Bridge, "which is of iron," the haunt of Gaffer Hexam. We hurried ashore and loafed till the rain ceased, in the Cannon Street Station. Then took a cab for Charing and embarked again for Greenwich. This river omnibus is the pleasantest thing I know in the way of city locomotion. I wonder they have never adopted it in Paris. We had a fine view as we passed, of Whitehall Gardens, Somerset House, The Temple, The Tower, and the long lines of docks and warehouses that stretch from London Bridge to the Isle of Dogs. In half an hour we were at Greenwich. We ordered dinner at the Ship Tavern and strolled around the hospital buildings, first built for the weak lungs and the dyspeptic stomach of William III, who could not stand the foul air of London, but abandoned on the death of his wife, Queen Mary, and given up to the crippled sailors. Thus is humanity sometimes reconciled to the sorrows of kings.

Our dinner was to me unique. It consisted entirely of fish. Beginning with matelotte of eels, it went on with fried cutlets of salmon with piccalilli sauce, which we rejected because it tasted fishy, and ending with the *specialité* of the place, Whitebait, plain, and devilled. The peculiarity of this appetizing little beast is, that you can eat all day without getting tired. We finished about a peck of the plain, and our appetites scarcely needed the spur of the cayenne pepper to induce them to do justice to the devil.

We sat in the mellow sunset on the garden terrace and looked up and down the river. The day was hazy and the distant ships looked dim and ghostly in the vague far mist that hid the town. The sun, near its setting, poured a long, blazing lane of light over the still water which was tangled in the rigging and sails of the ships that lay at anchor before us. The exquisite harmony seemed to embrace the bright red of the sunlight, the blue waters, the white sails and the green gunwales of the little boats. At intervals the river steamers dashed by like wild, graceful creatures of the wave. Solitary oarsmen rowed their slim wherries over the light into the hazy distance. Club shellboats dashed along, their crews rising and weaving in perfect cadence. The misty haze that covered the scene was too thick for the cloudy splendors of our sunsets, but a strange and beautiful effect was created by this rosy veil of failing sunlight fading away on either side into the gray, mysterious horizon. In the grandeur of this uncertain light we came back to town.

July 14, Sunday. Went to morning service at the Church of All Saints, the new Ritualistic church in Margaret Street, a beautiful and unusual-looking building, crowded into a space too small for it, and looking very uncomfortable there. The crowd was very great: every inch of sitting and standing room was taken. The service was very finely given. The priests had rather poor voices, but the choir was good and the whole congregation joined in the hymn with fine effect.

In the afternoon I went with W—— to the Temple. We were too early and passed a pleasant half hour in rambling around the walks and gardens of that venerable pile. A series of light showers were falling, compelling us to dodge under arches and doorways like vagrant cats. We got good enough seats, just outside the rail, among the industrial classes, while the nobs who had orders sat inside and lost the effect of the fine, harmonious nave. The singing was superb. The sermon, a sensible and gentlemanlike talk about Judas.

We came away sorry to leave the quaint old place, with its exquisite tesselated floors, its arches where the Gothic is dawning, its grim bronze Templars asleep in full mail until God loosens over sea and land the thunder of the trumpets of the night.

I dined at Mr. A——s'. We talked among other things of the late extraordinary recantation speech of Earl R——. A—— says R—— has been always in his way our friend. G—— has not; has been led away by his impulses now and then.

A—— thinks D—— has forced the present bill on the Tory party, that he has led them the devil's own rigadoon of a dance. If so, I take back all the credit I have given them for shrewdness and sagacity and transfer it all to Dizzy himself.

Then A—— gave a most humorous account of the visit of the Prince of Wales to the Monitor. They evidently dislike F—— at No. 54. I hardly know why.

July 15. This morning I went to call on Mr. M——, who has been here a day or two. (I shall never have any more doubt as to the long, involved question, whether it hurts a man to cut off his head. It hurts like the devil.)

He received me very coolly and stiffly—not speaking a word in reply to my salutation. He answered in the dryest and briefest way my questions about his family. I asked when he had left Vienna, and he began to talk. He grew almost hysterical in his denunciation of the "disgusting, nasty outrage of his being turned out." His resignation has been forced from him by a trick and then snapped at, to give the place to somebody else. "But the crowning insult of all was his recent letter of recall."

He evidently thought that the Senate was going to keep him in by rejecting all nominees, and was bitterly disappointed at the turn things had taken. He wanted to stay at Vienna a few years more to make the necessary researches in the archives there for his history of the Thirty Years' War.

He said S—— had committed a great blunder in throwing away a friend. He seems most bitter on the recent correspondence, in which his resignation is accepted without any further words.

He says the Baron von B—— wrote a despatch to W——, strongly laudatory of him (M.) and directing him to offer his services as a mediator, if possible, to fix the thing up.

We talked an hour or so. As it is not possible to justify entirely the conduct of the Government in this matter, I did not attempt that, but explained to M—— how I thought he was mistaken in imputing it to any hostility on S——'s part. S——'s utter indifference to attacks and his philosophic calmness under abuse, I think, render him a little indifferent to the sufferings of his sensitive fellow creatures under the same inflictions. He never dreamed that M—— would take that letter in such dudgeon, though it must be admitted that it was a frightful one for a gentleman to write or to receive.

After an hour's talk Mr. M. grew very much more sociable and we parted in quite a cordial manner.

I walked through the National Gallery and

saw for the first time Turner. I would go to him very often if I lived in London.

Left a card on S—— and came home in a smart little shower, to which I did not object, as it justified my umbrella.

On the 18th of July, 1867, Fred W—— and I started for the southwestern railway station, main line, intending to visit

Salisbury and Stonehenge.

We got to the station exactly in time. W—— bought the tickets and I had the baggage labelled, they have no checks in England, and we got our seats just as the whistle blew. W—— was lighting a cigar as the Guard looked in and said, "you can't smoke in there." I breathed a sigh of relief until he added in hope of a tip, "you can smoke in the next compartment." W—— joyfully followed the suggestion and I followed like a lamb. There was a stout Briton in that carriage of whom W—— asked leave civilly. "Of course," said the jolly Briton, "what's the use of travelling if you can't smoke"—so they both lighted their weeds and poisoned the pure air for half an hour or so in sweet, dumb sympathy. The fool masonry of blowing clouds together thawed out the Yankee and the Englishman, and I gained from their lively chat that we passed by Hampton Court and Wellington College for the support and education of soldiers' children, an enormous building on the right: then on the left the new Micropolis, a graveyard laid out on a barren heath, intended to serve as the future accommodation of the dying Londoners, its cheapness being expected to underbid the convenient but expensive city graveyards, "and Westminster Abbey is getting too common, you know." We rattled by Aldershot and Wimbledon common, the headquarters respectively of the regulars and the militia of England. We came to Overton, where a great sheep fair was being held upon the top of a neighboring hill. Around the platform stood great numbers of drovers and sheep raisers. I could not help remarking what a different crowd that would have been in America. Here they were clean, decent, stolid fellows, dressed as befitted their vocation, talking little, walking very slowly or standing in quiet groups. In America, you would have seen nervous, quick movement, or utter rest! Loud talking, or whistling, or whittling, or some more decided way of passing the time. The old Church of Basing Stoke gave us a beautiful ruin as we passed. We arrived at Salisbury about noon. I knew we were there, for towering aloft into the clear, summer sky stood that airy and elegant spire, which gives to the city all its style and character.

We drove to the White Hart Hotel and were shown by a round, fresh, hearty girl to our room, which, to our delight, still gave us a view of the spire. We took luncheon, the tenderest round of cold roast beef, the whitest bread, the clearest ale, and then took a fly for Stonehenge. We drove through the quaint old town, gleefully pointing out the queer fronts and shrug-shouldered gables on the streets like children over new toys. There is nothing that children like so much as that which differs widely from their everyday food. There seemed in Salisbury to be no corrupting trace of the nineteenth century. Out of the town we passed into the fresh and fragrant country lanes.

HAY TO NICOLAY.

Vienna, September 2, 1867.

. . . . . This place is as bad as Paris. It is dearer than I thought it would be in some respects, cheaper in others. I have an apartment of three good rooms, kitchen and servant's room, for which I pay 1500 florins a year. The florin is worth from forty to forty-eight cents, according to the fluctuation in gold.

The great luxury is music—this is cheap, also. One of the Strauss family leads in the Volksgarten several times a week, admission forty kreutzers,—not twenty cents. Or, you can cool your nose on the bars of the enclosure and hear it for nothing—if you are not *beamter*. The opera is good—the only ballet I ever saw that was not a bore. Faust was superbly given a few nights ago. Mr. M—— has a box and has given me the reversion of it till October, in the which I am luxurious. The acting is very fine also in the Hofburg Theatre, the classic,—and Offenbach is lord over all in the other show-houses. Blue Beard, Belle Helene, and the Grand Duchess have delighted the town for the last fortnight. . . .

You ought to come and see this town. The asses say, as the asses say everywhere, that it is very unpleasant in summer—that the winter is the time. But if a man be not an ass, he knows there never was a town north of the tropics that was not pleasanter in summer than in winter.

The suburbs of this town—the environs rather—are very beautiful. I spend most of my Sundays in the mountains and valleys of this chain of the Tyrols that seems to have been caught and tamed into a wild pleasure ground.

I do nothing but read German. There is nothing to do here. L—— says there never was anything. He is a fine fellow,—lives like a bourgeois prince; received me cordially and took great pains to make me comfortable. He is in now, I think.

Mr. M—— took leave as Minister June 14, and G. A. L——, Secretary of Legation, was in charge, until relieved by John Hay, who became *Chargé d'affaires ad interim*, 20 August.

DIARY.

Vienna, September 8, 1867.

To-day was a great festival. They have grown, even in the month I have been here, so common that I take no note of them. The people, who seem in the main a rather industrious community, yet seize with the greatest avidity on all excuses for leaving their work. On these festival days the whole town shuts up shop and goes to the country. They eat a good dinner, drink a great deal of beer, and smoke many cigars, and the economies of the week vanish in the enjoyments of a day. When they go off on these excursions they are very sensible about it, enjoying themselves in a most hearty and naïve way. They do not seem to need the excitement that the Parisians crave or demand. They are contented to lie on the grass and look at the white clouds, to loaf through the balsamic woods, to live and let the world roll on. They break very easily into groups of two and are not ashamed to let the world into the confidence of their tender sentiments.

To-day's fête fell on a Sunday, and the holiday was therefore considered rather a swindle by the easy-going people, who want no cumulation of idle days, but insist on taking them in detail. Crowding two holidays into one was, as Charles Lamb once said, "an economy unworthy of the Dispensation." But it laid the obligation on every soul in Vienna to give the day up to indolence. I never saw a town so utterly idle as Vienna to-day. A New England village on Sunday is as still, but there is the earnest Sunday work going on; the Church, and the Sunday School, and the reading and the singing, fill up these sacred hours and leave no time for mere loafing. But the few Viennese that staid in town were purely idle. I saw them sitting like slouchy statues in the parks, dawdling on the quais, positively leaning against the shady walls of houses, because they were too lazy to find a seat. I saw one stalwart young porter asleep on a bench, his arms on the bundle he was carrying, his pipe clenched firmly in his teeth.

I saw in a little paper this morning that the Belvedere was open to-day. I went there, but was punished for my weak credence in a Vienna paper, by finding that the all-powerful Fest had shut the doors of the gallery. So I went away from the southern doors inclined to be critical; and my mood was justified by the first thing my eyes lit upon, the two swaybacked horses that ramp before the palace in an attitude suggesting a sudden attack of mollities ossium. A man who has once seen and thoroughly studied the Marly horses at the gates of the Champs Elysees, has his judgment formed and his verdict forestalled for any other horses that ever have been cast or hewn. All the other rampant horses I have ever seen impress me as imperfect imitations, or desperate variations of the incomparable marbles of Couston.

The Belvedere is a pretty palace and placed on a fine eminence commanding a fine view of the city, the audacious tower of St. Stephan's forming an elegant center to the picture. In front is a stiff and formal garden, covering, with frequent terraces and fine marble stairways, the descent from the palace to the tower Belvedere. This is intersected by neatly gravelled paths, of which the entrances are guarded by smiling sphynxes about whom there is nothing to suggest either mystery or cruelty. About half way down the garden, tasteful stairways on either side are adorned with twelve statues of children representing the months of the year, entirely original in conception and most graceful and pleasing in attitude and execution. The ascending view of the upper Belvedere, from the south front of the lower, is full of grace and dignity.

I think I shall be friends with the Belvedere. I spent a day there some weeks ago to get the "hang of the school house" (a Western boy who had never learned his letters, on his first day at school was asked by the schoolmistress if he could read. He replied, with the spirit of Western pluck, he reckoned he could as soon as he got the hang of the schoolhouse). I went through, rather hurriedly of course, and have not yet entirely selected my favorites. I found food for my new love of Rubens, whom I detested in Paris, but to whom I have made reverent recantation since Antwerp. In fact, the picture I was most curious to see was his Helen Forman, that odd and fantastic, artistic pillorying of a pretty woman's immodest fancy and a husband's proud and sensual love, for the disrespectful admiration of all coming time. But when, after long searching, I came to the place where it should be, I found a black frame on the wall and the number of the picture mocking me with its absence. I asked where was the picture. The attendant Meingotted and did not know. I walked through the galleries, in another room I found some works of Rubens: one of which is catalogued "Die vier Welttheile," in which a suckling tigress in the corner is enough to drive Landseer to despair. The versatility of this man Rubens is his most wonderful quality. But I was cross about the Helen Forman. As I went down to the Erdgeschoss I saw some easels in the west end and following my nose, which flared game, I came before long to the object of my search. It stood in a good light by a window and next it was a very good copy just finished. I felt as glad as if I had found a lucky stone. So she stood, those centuries ago, before her fond, jolly husband, to whom Art was its own excuse in everything. You can see in the pretty, naïve face, with its great blue eyes, full yet of childish wonder, framed in those splendid, crisp locks of gold, the struggle of love and vanity against natural modesty. She snatches up the artist's furred cloak and wraps it round her with a quick, coquettish grace—and all the warring sentiments are appeased. They are as old as Eden, the vanity, the sensualism, the suggestive concealment. And as she stands thus, in that attitude when grace and awkwardness, are, as in all real women, so charmingly blended, the fond eye of the Artist husband catches the fleeting loveliness and fixes it forever. The sweet, artless, spoiled-child face that we know so well, that walks with Rubens in the garden in the Pinocothek at Munich, that goes sailing up to Heaven in the Altar piece at Antwerp, and stands on the volet of her husband's stupendous work, The Descent from the Cross, is here most exquisitely drawn, and the enamoured artist revels in the red and white and blue and gold, of cheeks, lips, hair and eyes. And yet you see he loves no less the soft, round, pink knees and the fat, white feet.

You are glad Rubens had such a wife, and very glad he did not marry your sister.

But I was talking about something else. I was walking this afternoon out in the Josephstadt and saw a crowd in the Lerchenfeld Strasse. There was music, and the idle Viennese seemed wide awake in the neighborhood. I went up to see what it was all about, being also idle and a Viennese *pro hac vice*, and I came just in time to see a religious procession go by. Monks in dozens with shaved heads, the first honest shaved heads I have ever seen, all sorts of ecclesiastical supes, with candles, that flickered in the wind and went out. Some lit them conscientiously and shaded them with their hands. Others marched on stolidly, careless of appearances, with shameless black wicks. Six expensive-looking fellows carried a heavily embroidered baldaquin, six more lighted them with gorgeous red lamps. Under the baldaquin walked a very pompous party who from time to time stopped the procession and made a remark or so in an unknown tongue: upon which the whole procession and the majority of the bystanders ducked, beat their breasts and moaned as if in severe indigestion. A smell of incense filled the air, which to me always has an odor of good company, I don't know why. I took off my hat with the rest, and was grateful for the incense and the music.

I believe Austria is the only country on earth where the priests wear top boots. It gives them a remarkably rakish and knowing air. They feel their oats more plainly here than anywhere in the world.

The Church is enormously rich and has thus far succeeded in retaining its vast possessions free from the requisitions of the sorely pressed and almost bankrupt government. In Vienna nearly every-one of the great religious orders are still in full possession of the vast estates acquired by their predecessors in the middle ages. The Schottenhof, a reminiscence of the Scotch Benedictines of the twelfth century, the Molkenhof and others are little cities of themselves. The liberals, there are a few liberals here, are very bitter upon this non-producing and all-consuming body.

A few days ago a convention of school teachers was held here—the first of the kind ever seen in

Vienna. Like all beginnings, the character was rather rude and raw. But one most promising sign was that it spoke out freely and boldly upon the question that underlies all education—freedom from religious or political trammels. It is to be hoped that under the dead and decaying life of Austria, new forms of intellectual vigor and activity are preparing among the people, to rebuild and save the nation, after the storm of the coming revolution has destroyed the useless forms of the past, and swept the field clean for the future.

Sept. 9. The present heavily embarrassed condition of the Austrian finances naturally calls the attention of the people to these vast riches of the Church, and of late the impression has gained ground that the State must receive some financial help from the plethoric ecclesiastical establishment. There is as yet very little talk of compulsory measures. These are in fact denied in the official journals. But it is thought possible that the Emperor himself may make a solemn appeal to the Church for a free will offering to the Treasury. It would be disastrous if the Church should have the wit to take advantage of this juncture to lay upon themselves a free tax, and trade the sums thus easily raised against a re-affirmation of the Concordat.

The existence of this incubus is now seriously menaced. It is improbable that it can much longer continue to oppress and crush the life of this nation.

The Church is making frantic efforts to save it. In the mountains of the Tyrol, petitions for its preservation are circulated for signatures, and even now a Catholic convention is sitting in Innsbruck, for the purpose, as stated by their organ, Tiroler Stimme, "Den lieben Herrgott wieder in seinem lichte ihm zu sitzen." They are sitting in a hall adorned with statues of Francis Joseph and the Immaculate Conception, and the walls are hung with crucifixes and the Imperial Shields of Austria. The toothless old giant that Bunyan set away out of the active field of fight two centuries ago, has still wit enough to make the proudest monarchy of earth hew his wood and draw his water.

As I go in the early morning to take my plunge and splash in the Danube water in Leopold Stadt, I walk through the Tiefen Graben, the deep ditch which marks the site of the ancient moat of the outer fortress of the city. At the corner of the Strauch Gasse and the Freyung, stands at the angle of Monte Novo's palace, a sanguinary-looking infidel flourishing a malignant cimeter. This marks the spot when in John Smith's time, our friend John who married into one of the first families of Virginia—I prefer Brougham's version to the historical one—stood a baker's shop. John may sometimes have refreshed exhausted nature there after the slaughter of his baker's dozen of Turks, who were encamped just outside the wall, upon the famed Viennese Semmels and Spritz Krapfen. One night the bakers, preparing the city's breakfast at midnight, heard the shovels and pickaxes of the enterprising Musselmen, under their feet. They had mined thus far under the wall and into the city. The bakers gave the alarm and the Turks were cut off and crushed, caught as I have often caught moles, by sticking a spade into his hill just behind him.

The Tiefen Graben is so far below the average level of the city that about half way down its length, Wipplinger Strasse strides far above it in the air. In the T. G. you wonder what that Suspension Bridge is for, and in Wipplinger Strasse you gaze with amazement at the men and wagons burrowing at the bottom of the ditch. The Tiefen Graben runs into the Gestade, and out of this dark, foul and utterly ignoble place starts the Talzgries, which runs for a few hundred paces and ends in the broad, bright, garish sunshine and wide daylight of the Donau Arm.

Along this unclean street rolls an endless tide of Polish Jews continually supplied by little rivulets running down from the Judenplatz and the *culs de sac* of that neighborhood, not running, but trickling down the steep, stone bed of the cañons called Fischer Stiege and Marien Stiege and Wachtel Gasse, Quail Alley. These squalid veins and arteries of impoverished and degenerate blood are very fascinating to me. I have never seen a decent person in those alleys or on those slippery stairs. But everywhere stooping, dirty figures in long, patched and oily black gaberdines of every conceivable material, the richest the shabbiest usually, because oldest and most used, covering the slouching, creeping form, from the round shoulders to the splay, shuffling feet. A battered soft felt hat crowns the oblique, indolent, crafty face, and what is most offensive of all, a pair of greasy curls dangle in front of the pendulous ears. This coquetry of hideousness is most nauseous.

The old Puritan who wrote in Barebones' time on the "Unloveliness of love locks" could here have either found full confirmation of his criticism or turned with disgust from his theme. What they are all doing is the wonder. They stand idle and apathetic in the sunshine, or gather in silent, or chatty groups of three or four, take snuff and blow their aquiline noses in chorus on dubious brown handkerchiefs. They have utterly revolutionized my ideas of the Hebrew. In America we always say rich as a Jew, because even if a Jew is poor he is so brisk, so sharp and enterprising that he is sure to make money eventually. But these slouching rascals are as idle as they are ugly. It occurred to me that it might be these long coats that keep them down in life, and that the next generation if put early into roundabouts might be spry fellows. But the Jesuits moved the world in their long coats. I suppose the curse of the nation has lit on these fellows especially.

All this quarter is subject to them apparently, for the little, obscure shops in the blind alleys have Hebrew signs. This was another shock to me. Think of tallow and onions advertised in a corner grocery in the sublime and mysterious characters in which the tables of the law were carved. I saw that this morning.

To-night I walked again through those blind alleys and swarming streets. The veil of darkness made the crowd more easy and confidential. The noise of traffic was over, but the small hucksters were busy shovelling their green peaches and astringent pears into baskets, or cooping up their melancholy chickens and ducks that seemed heavyhearted and humiliated that the day had passed and they were not stewed. The talk in the streets was noisier and freer, the dinner and the darkness had loosened these awkward tongues. Porters and charwomen stood in discreet corners and squeezed each others' hard fingers. The same mysterious Hebrews glided by, a little brisker as the night gathered and loafing time was shortened. In the Gestade I came across a group of little Goths who had pulled off their trousers and were lashing each other merrily with them. Old women sat dozing on their doorsteps too tired to rest well; almost always alone. Their men were dead or off to the beer shops. While the women are young, they go with them. But with age comes with them only the brute's drudgery and the brute's repose. Under the shadow of the tall black bulk of Mary-Stairs Church, young women sat in silence with shabby and ignoble-looking men. And overhead, between the high walls of the narrow streets, you could see as clear and dark blue patches of sky, as if you stood on the icy spire of the Matterhorn.

Sept. 10, 1867. They talk in Prussia, in the interest of peace, always, of substituting Prince de R—— for C. v. d. G—— at Paris, to counteract the strong personal amiability of M——. When will these old children here learn that it is a positive disadvantage to have their Minister "beloved" at a foreign Court! Napoleon is not much of a man, yet he twisted his friend M—— around his gouty fingers, while old G——, whom he hated, bullied him out of his wits whenever he got sight at him.

Garibaldi at the Geneva Peace Congress makes a war speech! This is bold and fine. The old man has not long to live and he will go up with a flash. He loved liberty and peace so well that he is willing to fight for them. He hates war—as a doctor hates drugs, but he uses it, for the good of the world. He ought to free Rome, if Rome is worth freeing? and then die. His short cuts, by the compass of abstract right, over the field of Government and law are too destructive to the Fetishes for him to lead a quiet life even in Italy free. John Brown is a saint now. Had he lived he would have been a malignant Rad, and people would have tired of him. In America the current of national life is so healthy, that one man cannot disturb it. So that our revolutionists do not hurt anything. Error and truth, as we regard them, must never have full course. We must take both diluted.

Sept. 11, 1867. Heard to-night *Minna von Barnhelm* at the Burg. It was well played by S——, whom the ladies loved because of his good legs, by LaR—— who is said to be a son of Goethe and who really resembles him strikingly; by M—— and Schone. Either a majority of the audience understood French or they were well-bred enough to seem to, for in the long scene between Minna and Riccault de la Mortimère they listened with the same quiet attention which they always give to the play. The women were Bognar and Schneeberger—the former good, but gaspy and the latter first rate. Baumeister was excellent as the Wachtmeister.

Riccaut calls cheating at cards, "corriger la fortune."

There is too much talk in the German plays to suit us.

The liberals here would not in the least gain if Garibaldi smashed the temporal power in Rome. It would relieve them at once of the Concordat, they think.

Saphir once was advised by a friend to take measures against the cholera that had just appeared in Europe and was expected in Vienna. "Bah! not yet," he said, "Vienna is a century behind the rest of the world in everything."

Sept. 12, 1867. The papers find it as hard to get at the kernel of the King of Prussia's throne speech, as Balzac's monkey to get at the nut. Baden has done all the talking necessary for the present. All that is necessary for Prussia is to be steady.

Sept. 13, 1867. I am mentioned in the Freuenden Blatt as "Der Amerikanische Minister Camel Hey." That looks deliciously oriental: I can imagine myself in a Burnous and yellow shoes.

Began to-day to study the substratum of Viennese life.

The Peace Congress breaks up with some ill-feeling.

Sept. 14, 1867. J—— P. B——, our Secretary of Legation at Constantinople, called to-day and talked an hour or so. His long residence in Turkey has almost made a Turk of him. He espouses heartily the Turkish cause, berates Russia soundly for the secret interventions in Greece and the principalities, and denounces M—— S—— for the aid and comfort they give to the enemy in Candia. He says these two officers are in very bad odor with the Turkish Government; that matters have several times approached an open rupture. He said that the Pasha Ali complained to him of M—— having "Chanté les victoires de ces sujets la sur nos troupes." S—— is of course a hearty Hellenist.

B—— has written a book on the Dervishes which is being printed in London. He gave me a little resumé of it which seems curious.

His boy came to me at the opera in the evening. He is a very accomplished linguist. Is educated by the State Department.

Sept. 15. The Prince of Waldeck Pyrmont gives up his realm to Prussia, retaining his church interest and his resources. He is playing sovereign on half pay.

King Lear at the Burg. A general dead level of respectable acting that was very dreary in effect. I remembered Forrest's storms and tempests of passion—often overdone, sometimes in bad taste, but always full of wonderful spirit and inexhaustible physical energy; and the careful and somewhat lachrymose style of Wagner suffered very much by the comparison. The Schlegel text, though very correct and scholarly, is not Shakespeare. There is not a word of Shakespeare that can well be altered now. The blast of his mighty thought sweeping through his words for three centuries has attuned them to an immortal and perfect harmony.

I was very curious to see Shakespeare in German. It is certainly very fine. But I shall not go often.

Literature is considered here rather a low business. If a noble is clever and can write verses, he is very proud of it, but as a gentleman is proud of being able to dance a clog dance or play the banjo well. So they never put their names to their poems, but have a literary name, which is kept rigidly distinct from the one that bears sixteen quarterings. Count Anton is Anastasius Grün—Baron M—— -B—— is Fried Hahn.

Sept. 18. Last night I saw a remarkably fine performance of *Robert le Diable* at the Opera. The more I see of this work of Meyerbeer's the more I am convinced that for men standing on my musical plane this is the greatest Opera yet written. I am willing to shut my eyes and admit that *Fidelio* and *Don Juan* are finer considered in the light of abstract poetic truth. But Robert comes home harder than anything I have ever heard. It is not cheap effect—no one dare say that. It is as pure and scholarly as anybody's work. Yet from the uproarious camp scene in the beginning to the final psalm of holy triumph at the close, there is not a note that palls upon the attention of the hearer. It is a high and classic state of music "brought home to the meanest capacity." I think a great deal is due to the superb scaffolding that Scribe had erected for Meyerbeer to build his great conceptions by.

There is a vast variety of scenes and pictures embracing almost a panorama of human life and passion. The Camp, the Court, the Grave, are the scenes where we are led. Men drink, sing, gamble, love, hate, and pray. The devil plays upon the hearts of men as upon the keys of a piano. Heaven and Hell fight a grim duel for the soul of Robert and in this ghastly contest, material love strives leagued with the light, against the Devil and the Father. And all this is combined with perfect taste and a masterly subordination of accessories to the main purpose.

One great attraction of the play to the parterre was Fraulein Lucas, who danced the part of the seductive Helen in the uncanny graveyard scene. The public estimate this young woman much higher than the K. K. management of the Opera. She is relegated usually to third or fourth rate parts, but gets more applause than the prime ladies. She cannot dance, to speak of, but she is young, flexible and sinuous as a snake, with a pretty, jolly, mutine face, and whirls and writhes in passionate contortions that remind us we are on the borderline of civilization and that just at our door are the mysteries, the languors, and the splendors of the Orient.

Sept. 20. An old man was to-day sentenced to eighteen months in prison for Majestätsbeleidigung. When asked if he were satisfied he said: "Ja, das ist gerade genug, ich küss die Hand für die Strafe." He had committed the offence to get his living in jail.

HAY TO ALBERT RHODES.

Legation of the United States, Vienna.
September 25, 1867.

MY DEAR RHODES:

You know I love you, but you never write a letter without some offensive insinuation in it. When I started home before, you said I was after an "orifice"—though the Lord knows you lied. I can never prove it because the facts are against me. But I did not ask for it—and had been appointed nearly a month, before, in my out of the way den, I ever heard of it.

Now I am going home again and as lightning never strikes twice in the same spot, it is safe to conclude that they will not offer me another place. I shall not ask for one unless I get very hungry and the chickens roost too high in my neighborhood for stealing.

I sail in a week or so. I am working like the d—— to get off and shall accomplish it.

I am anxiously awaiting the appearance of your novel. There is a dead calm now in letters and you could not have a better time to speak with the certainty of being heard.

P—— made me a flying visit the other day. We may possibly go home together. He spoke of you and old times in Parigi O Cara.

If in future years you ever drift up the Mississippi (you are so cross-grained that you will never float with the stream) and come to my humble ranch, I will comfort you with apples and stay you with flagons—and you will confess how much better and decenter is the life of a laboring man with honest content, than the vicious pleasures and hollow splendors of public service.

But you will go back to diplomacy and vice and leave me in my honest poverty.

Yours,

J. H.

HAY TO NICOLAY.

Vienna, October 19, 1867.

MY DEAR NICOLAY:

I had no end of a good time after I left you. I poked around Poland, lonesomely enough, but fully compensated by the unusual and peculiar towns I passed through. Warsaw is a very respectable place—170,000 inhabitants,—with two theatres and a fair opera. I heard an opera by a Polish composer which was not bad. There was a little passage of instrumentation in it that was exquisite and brought down the house with the wildest enthusiasm. But Cracow was the quaintest and most entirely satisfactory little town I ever saw. It has only 40,000 inhabitants but it has a palace and a cathedral, and theatre (where I heard a very fair burlesque), and a regular mediæval Jews' quarter. I regretted being alone, as that prevented me from passing a day in the salt mines at Wieliesga, which are the most curious in the world. I thought it would become a little monotonous after an hour or so, hearing nothing but Polish.

I found nothing had suffered by my absence,

but in the day or two since I returned I have had a good deal to do. . . .

Send me B——'s F—— du M——. If you have an Italian grammar belonging to me, send it to me. I have forgotten.

I couldn't stand it. I bought the Cignani.

HAY TO NICOLAY.

Vienna, Nov. 24, 1867.

MY DEAR NICOLAY:

I was a little cross that your letter came just in time and the packages just too late, but in the end it made no difference at all, or rather was for the better, as I did not go to Italy and had no special need of the language. So I will cram the grammar and dictionary for the scoot I think of making this winter to Rome and back. I was gone just fifteen days, only nine of them being outside of the Imperial Royal Apostolic Empire.

W—— went with me, and a young Bostonian,—a Q——. We had a good time—a sweet season. From Vienna to Pesth, a pleasant, picturesque ride,—a very interesting day in the Hungarian capital, which is a very big town for its size, and which we did very thoroughly; Pesth to Baziasch on the Danube, a bad ride all night over a rough road. A magnificent day on the Danube to Orsova, and another to Rustchuck—over the railway all day to Varna—and by breakfast time the next morning we were staring with the delight of greenhorns at the unparalleled spectacle that greets you as you sail down the Bosphorus into Constantinople. That closes for me in this world, I verily believe, my sensations of great cities. The last is infinitely finer than anything I ever imagined. I am pretty sure there is nothing that approaches it on earth. We had perfect weather—June at its prettiest in Illinois for instance,—and this staid with us all the time. We passed a day in Asia and climbed Mt. Boulgourlou and saw the gates of the morning. We had great larks, which I have not time to write. I found time so running against me, however, that I had to give up Greece and Italy. It takes a sail of six days—though five is the time published—through the Greek archipelago and the Adriatic to get back to Trieste. I will merely tantalize you in your hyperborean home by telling you that last week at Corfu we saw hedges of roses in full bloom and oranges perfuming the air as if out of special compliment to me and S——. This is the latitude of New York. I think we had better go there and live, as I learn that at home the country is submerged by a terrible Locofoco hurricane, and we are too old to cruise over the waste waters till it comes up again. I see old T—— and B—— are still plucky, like the Doctor who killed his patient with calomel, and swore the man would have gotten well if he had doubled the doses.

I hate the water worse than any cat. It will be hard to get me on the Mediterranean again. But I feel very anxious to make that Nile trip with you. When do you think of starting? I shall try to take a flight into Italy this winter—I shall never have time to do it thoroughly, and then, if I can, next spring after I leave here, take a rapid run through Spain.

DIARY.

Christmas Eve I spent at Mrs. L——'s. There was an enormous tree and presents by hundreds. The young ladies were pretty as ever and very easy and gay. I never saw better breeding than there is in the Haute Bourgeoisie of Vienna.

They talked German to me for the first time and I was astonished at their wit and the profoundness of their criticism and observation, which I had utterly failed to see in their English. (I think the reason diplomatists are as a general rule so stupid is, that they are so much in the habit of speaking a foreign language.) The whole household praised my German so that I grew ashamed to speak it.

Dec. 26. An Italian girl came in and I understood a good deal of her talk. She wanted shekels. I took out of my pocket and gave her half of what I had. She said naïvely, "give me the other half" (datemi l'altra metá).

It was a fine afternoon and the Ring was crowded from Kärnthner Strasse to the Barracks.

More Gemütlichkeit. The Ministerial crisis here has lasted a week "on account of the holidays." All the leading statesmen went home to their Christmas tree.

The Great Princes here speak very bad German—like F——. They learn in their youth nothing but French, dogs, horses, women. They are embarrassed when they meet with cultivated men and so avoid "mixed society." Together, they are all alike.

Old Carl L——, speaking to a servant girl: "Where do you live, my pretty dear?" "In Durchlaucht's kitchen."

Minister B—— went off to the country during the ministerial crisis here for the holidays.

Dec. 30. The Ministry is published to-night as formed.

To-day Countess K—— received for the Empress at the Burg. A small, nicely furnished room. Men and ladies in brilliant uniforms, and the richest and most eclatant satins, coming and going. The brilliancy of colors was suggestive of ophthalmia. In the evening, drove out to the Augustan, where Prince Hohenlohe was receiving for the Emperor. Along the avenue to the Pavilion, pine wood torches gave a glaring light. Inside the door of the vestibule was ranged a semicircle of some dozens of splendidly-dressed menials, with heads powdered as if by a passing snow storm, to head off the unwary from improper stairs and force them into the broad way that led into Hohenlohe. He is a youngish, stiffish, very pleasant-spoken man, baldish on the bump of firmness. E—— was there, with the handsome clothes, gallant bearing and feeble face you would expect from an old youth who has squandered all of his estates that he can.

Spent the rest of the evening at Santa Q——'s, good music, some very pretty women. Talked a little with W——, and with B. F. M. L. on K——, who speaks very remarkable English for a foreigner.

Dec. 31, 1867. D—— tells me that A. L. influence prevents the marriage of W—— and O'S——: that the Empress mother gave to Mme. W—— $2000 a year to keep her from marrying a crazy L——: because they thought the example of such marriages bad.

Jan. 5, 1868. Last night dined at H——'s. The Papal Nonce was there and we had more talk than is usual. He is a most amiable old gentleman.

H—— took me in and showed me his coffin and the skeletons of his friends. One of a woman, "une bonne amie à moi," whom he chucked under the chin and made the bony head wag and grin in the candlelight and the teeth rattle. A music box played dirges. Hatchments hung all around dated 186–.

JOHN HAY TO DAVID GRAY.

Vienna, Jan. 6, 1868.

DEAR DAVID:

I have your letter of the 1st. No letters have come for you. I will inquire at the Post Office every day till the 9th.

I suppose we will both be disappointed when we meet. We have looked forward to it too long. We have grown too much alike. The same mighty impulse has rushed for years through our souls till we are filled with the same magnetism. Our lives have been sawed off clean at the same place and the stumps are too smooth to be interesting. But notwithstanding these broodings, David Gray, I long to see you as never for anybody before. I don't think that it will do any good to the tired spot—but perhaps. I have broken an engagement to meet a party of friends in Rome so as not to miss you.

You are David and I am not Jonathan, but I am thereabouts.

J. H.

DIARY.

Jan. 18. To-day Maximilian was buried. The streets all day and yesterday were impassable. The whole town seized eagerly upon this occasion for loafing. They stood quietly about in dense masses as if waiting for something, in streets distant from the church where there was something to be seen. With the patient, stupid good nature of the dummer Kerl von Wien.

I received no invitation and so had not the bore of refusing. I suppose they had gotten some hint of my instructions to T——. Possibly opened my letter.

D——, Q—— and W—— came in and talked. I read McC——'s report. It is not cheering. Called on Dr. G. He says "nothing serious."

Jan. 18, 1868.

COPY OF LETTER TO SECRETARY OF STATE.

My Dear Sir :—The remains of the Archduke Ferdinand Maximilian, of Austria, were to-day deposited in the crypt of the Capucine Church. All the streets and adjoining squares were filled with a vast crowd of citizens and strangers.

Nearly every European monarchy sent a special embassy for this occasion. The death of Maximilian was felt last summer as a sensible blow at the prestige of kings. It was, perhaps, more significant even than the execution of Louis XVI. For here the Prince of one and the agent of another most powerful Empire was defeated and punished in an attempt upon the life of a weak Republic. The confederated kings have therefore done their best to rehabilitate the dead usurper by investing his name with an authority and sanction which was denied by events.

The popular demonstration was very genuine and touching. The *Kaiser Max*, as the people all call him, was most affectionately regarded in his life, and mourned in his death by the common folk of this Empire. He was popularly considered a Democrat. He was unpopular at the Court of his brother, feared and dreaded by the bigoted aristocracy, who were always jealous of men suspected of ideas. He was liable to many of the reproaches which Shakespeare's Cæsar makes to the spare Cassius. He saw no plays. He read books. He was a great observer. Seldom he smiled. It is highly probable that the vague liberalism of a younger brother, who saw all hope of the crown vanishing in the growing family of his Senior, and which was, perhaps, more the product of ennui and reverie than any firm grasp of true political principle, was not robust enough to have greatly disturbed the serenity of the sacred circle of Austrian noblesse, nor to have afforded any sensible support to the compact phalanx of liberal publicists, who have already wrought out such an opportunity for Austria. The fears of the nobles and the trust of the people were, perhaps, equally ill-founded. But, none the less, the multitude go mourning for him to-day, and the blue blood flows more peacefully in noble veins now that they have seen him laid away in the vault of the Capucines.

I received no invitation to the ceremonies nor thought proper to make any communication on the subject to the Minister of Foreign Affairs. I suppose they have in some way received intimation of my instruction to Mr. T——. By a naïvely indiscreet speech of a country member in the Reichsrath who had once been Postmaster, it was recently made known that the Austrian Government up to a very recent period still adhered to the deplorable habit of examining suspected correspondence in the mails. Perhaps they have regarded my letter to Mr. T—— as coming within that category.

A few evenings ago in conversation with the Spanish Minister here the reports as to the Cuban purchase were mentioned. He spoke in a way to leave the impression on my mind that the matter was the subject of very serious consideration in the leading circles at Madrid. You of course are well informed as to these matters. I only mentioned this little incident, as showing that the loud talk of European journalism of the "absurdity" of the proposition in question is the result either of ignorance or fear.

Feb. 18. Last night the first and probably the only ball of the season was given at the Palace in honor of the wedding of the young Grand Duchess of Modena to Prince Louis of Bavaria. In the Diplomatic Circle I was presented to the Emperor by Baron Beust. His Majesty was especially courteous. He spoke among other things of the wonderful resources we had displayed in our recent war and of the sudden and complete peace that had followed. He spoke of the difficult position of the President, and complimented him highly on his "energy and courageous consistency."

The ball was given last night, in my opinion, to afford the Imperial family and the great officers of the Empire a valid excuse for absenting themselves from the ceremonies of the Silver Wedding of the King of Hanover, which took place at the same time with great éclat in the Cursalon, a large building in the city park. There were present about two thousand persons, mostly Hanoverians. The occasion has been awaited for some time, not without uneasiness, as it was thought not improbable that the dispossessed King might indulge in a demonstration that would seriously compromise his position with the court, both in Vienna and Berlin. But no one could have imagined that his reckless anger and vanity would lead him so far. He made a speech of the most violent character, in direct contravention of all the recent treaties made with him at such enormous cost by the Government of Prussia, and in defiance of all the laws of propriety which should have restrained him as the guest of Austria.

It is generally considered something more than a coincidence that Mr. von B—— yesterday declared, that if the Hanoverian intrigues were not speedily discontinued, the severest measures of sequestration would immediately be put in force. It remains to be seen whether, even yet, the King of Prussia can be persuaded from his rigid adherence to the dogma of divine right, to allow justice to be done to an avowed public enemy.

For a week past the public mind has been filled with anxiety by the meagre and confused advices received from the Lower Danube. I am inclined to think from all I can gather, that the stories of armed and organized bodies at present operating in Bulgaria and Servia are at least premature. But it is now no longer possible to ignore the fact that an active organization for revolutionary purposes now exists throughout all the nations forming the more southerly stratum of the great Slavic race. It is very powerful in Servia, Bulgaria and Moldavia-Wallachia—in each case probably secretly encouraged by the reigning Prince in the hope of final independence from the Suzerain Porte. It is thought possible that the first outbreak may take place in Montenegro, as being one of the points most difficult to reach by the Sultan's troops.

It is stated that numerous additions to this

revolutionary force are being recruited by secret agents in Austrian Poland and sent across the boundary to be armed and drilled in Russia.

So far, the remonstrances of the Eastern Powers have had very little effect, as the vassal-Princes give all the explanations and make all the promises required and still placidly watch the brewing of revolt under their very eyes.

Vienna, March 23.

Coming back from Italy I found the town in a jubilee over the vote in the House of Lords which virtually dooms the Concordat. A wild, good-humoured and thoroughly enthusiastic crowd roamed the streets all night of Saturday, called out the Ministers, sang the national hymn under the palace windows, cheered for the Emperor, the Government, the House of Peers, the Reichsrath—and insulted nobody and broke no windows—even those that were sulkily dark amid the illumination. But the reactionary party were furious and either silly or malicious enough to telegraph to the Emperor that a revolutionary émeute was in progress. They scared the Archduchess' mother out of bed, and aristocracy in general sat and shivered in its nightshirt until the crowd, tired with its loyal jubilee, went home to bed.

April 12. To-day I have felt like a vagabond and shall always know how to sympathize with the houseless poor.

My servant's mother being very sick I gave him congé for all day and going out myself in the morning, I heedlessly left my key at home. I was in for it, *i. e.* out for it. I did not know where the servant lived so that I might go for his key. There was nothing before me but to wait till evening. In the morning I got on well enough. I walked in the Exercier-Platz and got an appetite for breakfast, which I took at noon. Then the time began to drag. As my perverse fate would have it I had put on a hideous pair of worn-out boots for convenience in walking and had covered them an inch thick with mud. So making visits was out of the question. I went to see P——; of course, he was out. D——, of equal course, out. I walked down the Graben. It rained. I went into the Cathedral. Sat there till I got out of conceit with the bench I occupied and walked again. Dodged into Cafés, ordered a tasse and read newspapers. Thought of Maria

Stiegen and went there. There was preaching in the Czechish language. I staid till the sermon was out. The crowd was more picturesque than usual. Some of the men were dressed in skins with leather girdle and scrip. Many of the women in peasant costume. Two girls came in together, evidently sisters. Yet one was a goose and the other a swan. The one short, stout, high-shouldered, a paysanne in every respect. The other tall and svelte, wore her bright peasant dress like a comedy queen, the silk handkerchief framing a sweet, arch, piquante face. The one kept her eyes fixed on the preacher with a dull stare—the other looked briskly about the house and everything in it, turning her head when the door slammed like a young fawn. There was grace in the way in which she stood about in her thick, little, men's boots. Nothing is stranger than these differences in peasant families—except sometimes the differences of destiny they occasion.

April 18, 1868. P—— spent the evening with me. We had a long talk about old-fashioned politics. I told him of my chance shot at the Methodist preacher who wanted a Brigadier-General: and of the young Kansian, who thought the Government should have a better system of police.

He told me many picturesque incidents in the history of L——. At a time when L——'s fortunes were most desperate, R—— committed the fatal error of trying to conciliate the Jayhawkers by appointing J—— and other ringleaders to offices in the Militia. J—— L—— saw his opportunity and instantly made a stumping tour through the southern tier of counties, denouncing with the greatest audacity and bitterness his former friends and comrades, and holding up the bargain between them and the Governor to the indignation of the people. In J——'s own town, a most dramatic scene took place. L—— was savagely denouncing some lawless act of J——, when the astonished Jayhawker rose in the audience and shouted, "J—— L——, I done that by your order."

"You lie!" roared J——.

"By your written order, I say."

"You lie!" L—— repeated, with a most brazen confidence, which was not altogether unreasonable as he had managed to secure and destroy all his correspondence of that period.

He continued, "You, —— J——, are a murderer!"

"By G——, I never murdered J——," said J——, and the apt retort tickled the Kansas fancy.

L——'s audacious campaign was a great success. A legislature was returned friendly to him.

His connection with the Methodists was a very singular passage in his history.

R——, after having been his intimate friend, sad-hearted, one day, turned upon him. His paper had been publishing L——'s autobiography by instalments. Now, however, the autobiography disappeared from its columns and instead an exposal of the crimes of the Danite Band of which L—— was chief, appeared in the *Journal.* It had a tremendous effect. The contre-coup against R—— himself was so great that he was compelled to leave the state. But the exposé remained and L—— suffered vastly in public estimation. He resolved on a bold stroke. He "got religion," in Western phrase, and joined the Methodist Church. He was at once rehabilitated in the opinion of many. He fell from grace before very long. One day, a man who heard him cursing furiously, said, "Take care, L——, you'll be kicked out of the Church."

"They may kick me out, but d—— if they can keep me out," said the meek Methodist.

After he murdered J——, he suffered another great eclipse of popularity. Kansas never minded killing a man in fair fight, but this was a decidedly irregular proceeding. J—— went to draw water from a well which L—— claimed as his own property. L—— shot him coolly, brutally, cynically. Kansas looked upon the deed as "awfully low form," and rather snubbed L——. He never could stand the frown of his world. Something must be done "to get up his rep." He joined the Methodist Church again.

P—— told me an amusing incident of L——'s second conversion. He had been making a rambling exhortation one night in church before a great audience, and perorated by referring to the bloody scenes he had passed through in the Mexican war, and how he had been spared to testify, etc.,—as they all say. A drunken young editor, who was also a member of the Convention, then rose in the body of the house and proceeded boozily to the pulpit, followed by friends anxious to prevent a scandal. He anathematized them for interfering with him and began his remarks. "Feller citizens, General L—— has told you how he fought, bled, and died in Mexico. Feller citizens, *I* have fought, bled and died in Mexico, nary time." Here his friends seized him, took him in their arms and carried him down the long aisle to the door. He lay back, much at his ease, gravely repeating, in all the tones of the musical scale—"Nary time—nary time"—till his voice died away out of doors.

P—— thinks L—— had a power over men little short of magnetic. Many of his opponents feared to become acquainted with him lest they should become his friends. I have often heard this before, and always with great surprise. To me (and I knew him well) the man had no charm. He seemed coarse, mean and ignoble. His craft was too rude and bungling to deceive any one apparently. He had the sad, dim eyes and bad-toothed face of a harlot. Yet he had a certain easy *bonhomie* that made him at home everywhere.

They say in Kansas that his suicide was occasioned by the fear of detection in a corrupt contract bargain with F—— and McD——, which he had solemnly denied in the Senate, but the proof of which had subsequently come to the war office.

April 19. Finished to-day Badeau's life of Grant and sent him a note of thanks. I have read it with more interest than I read novels. It is very successfully written as a popular work. I am glad Badeau has made a strike.

Some good things in it. I think there are few things in history so ludicrous and touching at once, as B—— (when they were really beaten and the invincible West was swarming over Missionary Ridge) riding up and down his lines waving his sword and announcing a victory to his troops.

April 23. Yesterday P—— came in, and while we were talking, artillery began. He couldn't keep still, so we went out and saw a neat, little review in the Parade Platz. I thought it was the Imperial Baby, but was wrong, for to-day one hundred guns thundered the glad tidings to Austria that they had another omnivorous Hapsburg to provide for.

April 26. A letter from Mr. M—— asking

if I will stay as Secretary in case he is Minister. Answered that I could not.

April 27. Letter from Mrs. B—— which I answered and then wrote another to J. B. "Dear Mr. B. I have received and answered a letter from Mrs. B. this evening and I don't yet feel inclined to leave your company. So I will say a word or two to you—lingering with my hand on the doorknob.

"I had no idea when I came abroad last summer that I should be here so long. I thought they would fix up the vacuum (abhorred of nature and office seekers) in a few months—so I came for a flyer, principally because I was a little ashamed of having been in Europe nearly two years and having seen nothing. I have had a pleasant year of it. There is very little work to do at the Legation. I have sinned grievously against certain ten-day regulations that I have heard of. I have seen all I care to of Prussia, Poland, Turkey and Italy. I have drawn my salary with startling punctuality. I have not wearied the home office with much despatches. My sleep is infantine and my appetite wolfish. I am satisfied with my administration of this 'arduous and delicate post.' I believe that is the regular shriek of the Radical Press in alluding to the Vienna Mission. You and Mr. A—— worked while you were in harness. I am not sure but that a serious man could always find work in those two missions. But equally sure am I that no two other American diplomats can catch each other's eyes without mutual guffaws unless they have a power of facial muscle that would put the Roman Augurs to shame. Just let me get into Congress once, and take one shy at the Diplomatic appropriation bill.

"I am very glad I came. Vienna is worth while for a year. It is curious and instructive to see their people starting off in the awkward walk of political babyhood. They know what they want and I believe they will get it. The aristocracy is furious, and the Kaiser a little bewildered at every new triumph of the Democratic and liberal principle. But I don't think they can stop the machine now—though they may get their fingers mashed in the cogs. I don't think the world ever seemed getting ahead so positively and quietly before. Two years ago—it was another Europe. England has come abreast of Bright. Austria is governed by Forty-Eighters. Bismarck is becoming appalled by the spirit of freedom that he suckled with the blood of Sadowa. France still lies in her comatose slumber—but she talks in her sleep and murmurs the Marseillaise. And God has made her ruler blind drunk, that his Helot antics may disgust the world with despotism.

"If ever in my green and salad days, I sometimes vaguely doubted, I am safe now. I am a Republican till I die. When we get to Heaven we can try a Monarchy, perhaps.

"If you take the trouble to answer this, please tell me what you have been doing. I have heard a work on Franklin mentioned, but have not seen it advertised. Why don't you write a history of American Diplomacy?"

May 26. This evening in the Volksgarten there were a good many Americans. I said, in answer to some questions, I thought conviction extremely doubtful. I found myself almost entirely alone in this opinion.

May 27. F—— A—— sent me a despatch announcing the acquittal of the President.

While discussing this subject with L—— in

Venice two months ago, I said I thought impeachment would fail, because from the way the trial had begun, I was convinced it would be a purely legal one, and that on a strictly legal basis, there was no case against the President. He must be turned out, if at all, on political grounds, as an obstacle to peace and union—this could be well done in twenty-four hours—and this, in my opinion, was the only way to do it. These were my first strong impressions. They rather gave way when I saw the apparent unity of the Republican party lay in the pressure of the case. But when the news of the first adjournment came—not knowing it was for H——'s sickness—I took it that the majority was stampeded, and have had no confidence in impeachment since.

June 3. It is very curious to see how the Senators who saved the President have changed their tone. They are gradually becoming the apologists and defenders of the H. E. Forsaking the safe ground of "incompatibility of temper," on which it was certainly agreed the President was to be ousted, they have narrowed their minds to the purely legal aspect of the matter, and having cast loose from party dictation, seem already drifting out of the party jurisdiction. It would not surprise me much to see some of these new, jealous Johnson men before the year is out —not corrupted or seduced—but merely fighting themselves off their own lines into the enemy's, while the stupid devils who never had an idea in their lives, get honor and credit from their party for voting solid with the general ruck.

A most interesting letter from B—— L—— in Washington.

On the whole analyzing my own sentiments. I am not very sorry—not at all sorry at the result. I think Johnson will put some water in his whiskey now. I don't think he can do much more harm. We are still in opposition where a party always works best. Impeachment is demonstrated not to be an easy thing. The lesson may be a good one some day if we have a Republican President and a copperhead Senate. The Tenure of Office law—a fruit of haste and folly—is knocked to pieces. A two-thirds majority in both houses is anomalous.

P—— of the Department has been here for the last ten days. He made some capital puns.

Two Germans at Dombach were guilty of some little hoggishness. P—— called them sardines. P—— said, "No, they are Herren."

Drove out to Schonbrunn. The elegant world goes there now instead of to the Prater, which is quite desolate. Called on the M——'s, but could not find them.

June 7, 1868, Monday. This morning a notification came from the Duke de G——, through K——, Doyen of the Corps, that Prince Napoleon, who arrived here Friday, travelling as he is incognito, would not receive the Diplomatic Body as a body, but would be happy to see any who would call.

I went over to the Golden Lamb, Leopoldstadt, about one o'clock. I was received, I believe, by Col. R——. Count Z—— was in the antechamber with the Colonel. H—— came in before long. He introduced me and Z——. We talked a good while till W—— (Prussian), who was with the Prince came out and Z—— went in. H—— began girding at W—— about the supposed treaties and intrigues he had cooked up with the Prince. W——, to escape persecution, turned to me and talked impeachment. Z—— made a long stay. F—— P—— came in. At last Z—— emerged and I went in. The Prince received us in a pleasant, off-hand way, and we began at once to talk about America and his visit there. He remembered most of the names now prominent in politics. He spoke of S——, said he ought to have prevented the President's trip to Chicago. Said he remembered C——, a young, blackfaced man, President of the Legislative Body —he meant G——. He spoke of L—— as a man of great merit and deplored his leaving the War Office, but remembered S——, and was much pleased with what he saw of him.

After a few words about Germany and the interesting moment in which he visits it—the interview ended by my retiring.

HAY TO NICOLAY.

St. Moritz, June 30, 1868.

MY DEAR NICOLAY:

Don't write or send anything more here. I will leave the first of next week. It is a fine place to grow fat and eat large quantities of indifferent viands at a cheap *table d'hôte*. I walk nearly all day, and, Lord bless you, how I can eat. I must hie me back to the Freyung, and endeavor to find in Dreher's Bier some compensation for the gushing steel spring of Paracelsus. It is a little hard, too, just as Gen'l McC—— is expected here.

Lots of Hoheiten and Durchlauchts are coming next week, too, and I shall not bask in their glory. But if I can keep through the summer the boiled beef on my bones which I have stowed away these three weeks, I shall be more than content.

. . . How are you betting on the Fourth of July? It really seems as if some of the big wigs of the M—— Club are for C——. I still, in spite of the clamor and loud talk, believe he won't get a vote in Convention. This is hazardous prophecying so near the event, but as Joe Gargery said, when he thought Pip had swallowed a loaf of bread:—"I have seen many a bolt in my day; and, as a boy, have bolted frequent, but bless me if ever I see such a uncommon Bolt as that." The Democratic party has more bowels than brains, I admit; but they can't digest the C—— J——.

I "feel to realize" that I must come to Paris to sharpen up my dull wits,—Kriechen ein Bissel an's

Schliff,—as the exquisite Wiener Deutsch has it. I am growing Boeotian on the Schöne Blaue Donau. But I can't at this moment say when I will come. I can tell better after I have gotten back to the Freyung,—and ascertained the temper and frequency of American visitors in my absence.

P—— has come and gone before this, I suppose. There is a remarkable instance of a fellow of fine talents and ambition, sinking year after year into the baleful quicksands of routine. A few years more and all the world can't pull him out. P—— is too good for his place, and yet the place requires a first-class man. As I did not make the world, I won't tackle that paradox. The same kind Providence that creates enough crazy men to man our ships, scoops the life out of men enough to carry on the routine of government.

HAY TO NICOLAY.

St. Moritz,
August 16, 1868.

MY DEAR NICOLAY:

I answered day before yesterday your note of the second; but my mind is so weakened by sorrows and shower-baths that I can't remember what I told you. . . . . I have one word to add. In my resignation I recommended A—— at London to fill my place, and wrote to A—— advising him to pitch in for it. To-night I receive a letter from him (he not having yet received mine), asking my intentions, and saying he is to have my place when I get tired of it. They are parting my vestments among them, and for my raiment are they pitching pennies.

I am very glad of this turn. A—— is a good fellow, superfluously well qualified for the post, and is, moreover, within a day or two of Vienna. So that when he gets his papers he can come directly on and relieve me.

I hope to be out and a-rambling by the first of October. I will spend a day or two with you in Parigi O Cara; then make a straight Hemdenschweif for sunset.

It seems a thousand years till I start.

I have a modest letter from the Congressional Committee asking for war-sinews. Concussional Committee! I will send them something according to my poverty of resources.

Gen'l McC—— is here. He sails for home on the nineteenth of September. He " don't take no sort of interest."

HAY TO NICOLAY.

Liverpool, October 14, 1868.

(alludes to the Inmanner)	My boat is on the shore
(alludes to J. H. Horticulturalist)	My bark is on my tree
(announces a fact in fysic)	Seasickness is a bore
(gives financial counsel)	You bet your pile it be.

I had a rapid and prosperous voyage from Paris here. I found George Sand's Cadio at the station. It is dedicated to Harrisse.

The channel was like a duck pond. For these mercies, Laus Deo Ventorum.

I passed through London with contemptuous speed. Spent fifteen minutes in the Metropolis. Was afraid, if R—— saw me, he would make too fierce a radical of me.

I ran head-first into a piece of luck that you, of all men, will envy me. That true-hearted American and profound statesman, C. Dickens, Esq., read last night here, and I contributed six shillings to alleviate the sufferings of his honest poverty. M—— can knock the spots out of him reading, but whether it was what he read, or what he is, I don't know,—he held that house, full of placid Britons, chained tight for two mortal hours as I never saw a house held.

I got the worth of my six bob. (The pens here require mending every five minutes).

Liverpool town is a good town to pass through in a hurry. The sun takes till noon to struggle through the fog. The muffins are good.

D—— is out of town. I am gradually lowering the tone of my spirits to suit sea life. I shall have attained the proper indifference to life in about an hour.

My tug is by the shore
My ship is on the sea
As I cannot write no more
Here's a treble health to thee,
To Madame and the Babee.

Hurrah for the elections!

DIARY.

Buffalo, January 27, 1869.

Delivered last night a lecture before the Y. M. C. Association on "The Progress of Democracy in Europe." Had a fair house—very attentive and good-natured audience. Was reasonably successful—especially pleased at the absence of trepidation and duration of my voice.

After the lecture I went to a large party at Mrs. W—— W——'s. Pretty women, handsome toilettes, etc.

January 28. Dined last night with Mr. J—— G——. He told a good story on B——. B. F. B. had a scheme at Charleston for harmonizing the party by a compromise between the two wings: laid it before R—— and asked him, "Isn't that an honest and fair proposition?" R—— said, "B——, you know what I think of a man with a cast in his eye. I never saw but three that were thoroughly fair and trustworthy, and they are you, R—— and B—— (of the H——)."

HAY TO E. C. STEDMAN.

Warsaw, Illinois.
February 11, 1869.

MY DEAR MR. STEDMAN:

I want to burden you somewhat. You are busy and I am idle. To him that hath much work, shall more be given, and he that hath none shall shirk even that he hath. If you think it is not too bad, will you put it in an envelope and send it to the editor of the *G——*; if you think it is too bad, say so, and send it to your abject servant.

I was in New York a day or two recently. I looked into Broad Street but you were out of your lair. I passed an evening at the C—— Club in the constant hope of seeing you come in, but had to go without greeting you.

I have tried an experiment since I saw you last. I have faced a large audience and spoken a piece without breaking down. I lectured in B—— and in a few western towns. I will do more of it next winter. I have a friend in B—— whom I want you to know,—D—— G—— of the *C.* He is a noble soul—utterly wrong in politics—but a good Democrat and a poet. He admires you as he ought,—gets your short poems by heart, and you, too, in the process. I have given him a line which he will some time present to you. It is not often we can introduce two men who are worth each other's while,—but this time I know I am doing that same.

I hope to see you later in the Spring. I shall pass through New York on my way to Europe. I left some unravelled threads of occupation over there, and must go over once more—my own master now—and pick them up.

HAY TO E. C. STEDMAN.

St. James Hotel, New York.
July 10, 1869.

MY DEAR MR. STEDMAN:

I tried to find you yesterday but failed. I sail to-day.

Might I venture to ask you to withdraw that poem of mine from the *G*——? I do not suppose it is in print,—if it is, never mind,—only suppress the name. I have resumed the padlocked mouth.

I wanted to tell you how much genuine enjoyment I and some other western people have had in your "Blameless Prince." I confess when I heard the subject announced, I was a little afraid of a certain foreign flavor,—but there is not a trace of it. Familiarity with all that has been done before,—assimilation of the best fruits of others,—all this is there, of course; but the poem in manner and sentiment and progress is thoroughly new, and, it seems to me, American. How you can keep your spirit so green and fresh in Wall Street is a marvel to me. I think a month or so of this town would drive me melancholy mad.

Can you use me in any way, in Madrid? I will not be gone long.

DIARY.

Madrid, July 29, 1869.

Drew on Barings for $146.66 for month of transit, June 29 to May 29.

Indolent people imagine they would like to be busy. Industrious people know they would enjoy being idle.

The English servant is a statuesque image of propriety. The French, a sympathizing but respectful friend. The Spaniard and Italian have the familiarity and subordination of children. An American revenges himself on fate by insolence.

Americans in Europe waste time enormously in calculating when the mail will arrive. A mail is like a baby—you can't hurry or retard it by talking about it.

Madrid, October 1, 1869.

The Spanish Cortes resumed their session to-day after a vacation of some months. The Diplomatic Body have a little cage holding fifteen. We have three cards and one I stole.

The seats all vacant in the hall. The President comes in in solemn procession with the Maceros and Secretaries. The Maceros dressed out of Froissart. R—— wears white kids during the whole session. His opening speech. F—— replies. F——, O—— and C—— sitting together, on the top bench of the extreme left. F——, a western Senator sort of man in build and carriage, with a wonderful aptitude of speech and good knowledge of parliamentary practice. O—— the noble factor of the play.

R—— scolds the Deputies like a schoolmaster, knocking them over the knuckles without merci or miséricordia. The Government sits on a bench distinguished from the rest by being in blue velvet instead of crimson. Out of the three hundred and four Deputies, not more than one hundred present. The afternoon sun pouring in through the windows facing the west. Lighting up. The Maceros relieving each other. Not many nobles. Marquis of B——.

October 2. Went with Fabra to see Castelar; found him at his own door coming home with his hands full of documents. Walked up with him—and had a long talk about everything.

He speaks French fluently—learned it in exile in Paris, where he supported himself and many others by writing for South American papers. He has an exquisite face—a soft, sweet tenor voice, a winning, and what the Spaniards call, simpatico manner.

He spoke of Napoleon's sickness and of the humiliating spectacle of a great nation looking for its destiny in the cuvette of an old man. We talked a good deal of art and Italy.

Of Spain he spoke sadly; he seemed to feel that the insurrection in Catalonia was premature and ill-advised. He thought there were evil days coming for the Republicans in Madrid. He said we have just had a hard hour's work to persuade the party of action not to precipitate an insurrection to-night. This would be madness. Madrid is thoroughly monarchical. It is a city of place-holders. The militia is in great majority monarchical. There are 10,000 or 12,000 regular troops here. An insurrection would be smothered in blood. Yet it is hard to keep the fiery young fellows from trying it.

He said he was going to speak in the Cortes to-morrow on the suspension of Guarantees. It is not my subject, he said, mine was the impeachment, but this comes first, and I am to say something on it.

I apologized for having taken up so many of his precious moments; but he insisted on my staying longer.

When I went he said: "After a while, when these troubles are over, if I survive them, we will go to Toledo and the Escurial together."

Fabra and I went to the Theatre Espanol and found the house nearly deserted. An alarm had seized upon the audience early in the evening, and the fear of an insurrection in the city had driven them home. We saw an amusing little farce, stolen from the French, "Les Méprises de Lambinet," which seemed to be highly relished by the well-nourished Madrileñas who sat near me.

October 3, Sunday. The discussion to-day on the Suspension of Guarantees occupied all the afternoon and will be continued to-morrow.

Castelar was superb. His action is something marvellous. He uses more gesticulation than any orator or actor I have ever heard. His voice is, as I suspected, rather rich and musical than strong, and he uses it so remorselessly that it is apt to suffer in an hour or so. But his matter is finer than his manner. I have never imagined the possibility of such fluency of speech. Never for one instant is the wonderful current of declamation checked by the pauses, the hesitations, the deliberations that mark all Anglo-Saxon debate. His whole speech is delivered with precisely the energy and fluency that Forrest exhibits in the most rapid passages of his most muscular plays: and when you consider that not a word of this is written or prepared, but struck off instantly in the very heat and spasm of utterance, it seems little short of miraculous. The most laborious conning and weighing and filing of the most fastidious rhetorician could not produce phrases of more exquisite harmony, antitheses more sharp and brilliant, metaphors more perfectly fitting—all uttered with a feverish rapidity that makes the despair of stenographers. Then his logic is as faultless as his rhetoric. He never says a foolish or careless word. All history is at his fingers' ends. There is no fact too insignificant for his memory—none too stale to do service. They are all presented with such felicity and grace too, that you scarcely see how solid they are.

October 6. Castelar spoke again Monday and

again Tuesday. Sagasta, Minister de la Gubernacion, greatly distinguished himself on Monday. He defended the Government, especially himself, with wonderful vigor and malice. He is the hardest hitter in the Cortes. Everybody calls him a scamp and everybody seems to admire him, nevertheless. He is a sort of Disraeli—little, active, full of energy and hate, tormented by the opposition to the proper point of hot anger, he made a defense offensive that enchanted the Government benches.

Silvela also made a good speech or two—but Silvela is rather too good a fellow for this kind of work. He is very sincere and candid but lacks the devil, which makes Sagasta so audacious and Prim so cool.

Prim's speech Tuesday evening after Castelar had announced the intention of the Republicans to retire, was a masterpiece. He begged them to reconsider—he was frank, open, soldierly; he begged them to stay and threatened them with severe measures if they went—he was not savage and insulting like Sagasta—nor phrasy like Silvela, but he was the perfection of enigma—as always. His speech was powerful and impressive in its deep simplicity—and greatly affected

Castelar and the Republicans. Castelar answered in the same tone of exquisite courtesy, rejecting the advice which was coupled with a threat. The law passed and the Republican Deputies left the Chamber.

To-day the General and I went to the Foreign Office to call on Silvela, to see if we could get any intimation of what the Government thought of the note sent in a week ago.

Silvela was alone and at once received us. He began off-hand by apologizing for not having sent the note before, but the cares of the new and serious situation were a sufficient cause. He said the notes in reply to ours of the third and sixth of September (the last one referring to what he called those "assassinats là-bas"), were written and would be sent to-morrow or next day.

He then spoke of the situation. He said the insurrection had not as yet taken a serious character, there are no armed and organized bodies: no military leaders: little bands of peasants roaming about the provinces: enough of them to be very annoying. He said the last news was favorable: the insurgents, instead of gaining strength, are losing: the insurrection is taking on a socialist character: they have begun to destroy records of property, this has caused a reaction in public opinion against them.

He said that General Prim expected in ten or twelve days to be able to finish the insurrection; the Government had to-day resolved in Council of Ministers to give the Rebels, by proclamation, forty-eight hours' notice to disperse; that failing, martial law will immediately be put in requisition against them. The Government wish to act as rapidly and energetically as possible, so as to end the rebellion and lay down their extraordinary power at the earliest practical day.

He said he was not without hope that a portion of the Republican minority, at least, will remain in their seats. Men like Castelar and Figueras are sensible and cultivated: they are in favor of law and order: we can come to an understanding with such as these. If they could be brought to reconsider their purpose of leaving the Cortes, it would be a great gain, as it would probably result in a division of the Republican party which would eliminate their lawless socialist elements. There exists already this division of the party into Democratic and Socialist Republicans. With the former we can get along: if they remain in the chambers, restricting themselves to a legal and constitutional opposition, acknowledging the authority of the Cortes, we can carry on the Government under this sincere discussion, and if at a given time, the majority of the people desire the Republic, à la bonne heure. He was not without hope that some of the most respectable Republicans will retain their seats. We have no quarrel with men like Figueras and Castelar. Last night after the debate was finished, Castelar and I quitted the Cortes arm in arm. Four of the Republican deputies had a conference with Prim, which was marked throughout by a cordial spirit.

S—— asked about the Deputies from Porto Rico. Silvela said they had taken their seats and voted yesterday. That the Government was ready to begin the initiation of political reform for Porto Rico at once—but that everything had been postponed by the exigencies of this sudden insurrection. The Budget was in abeyance—the question of the Monarch—all waiting for the immediate business of the hour to be accomplished—the crushing out of the Socialists (last time he called them Federalists).

S——, on rising to go, and on Mr. Silvela again repeating his apologies for not having sent his answer sooner, said, that he had fully appreciated the great pressure of business which rested this week on every member of the Government: that he only wished that the Government should understand that the last, like the first note, was dictated by a friendly spirit to Spain, and would wish to be able to inform his Government that Spain so regarded it.

Mr. Silvela said his answer was expressed precisely in that sense.

There is much going to and fro of cavalry and infantry this afternoon, though no disturbance is generally anticipated. The air is full of dust and neigh-calls.

HAY TO NICOLAY.

Legation of the United States.
Madrid, October 7, 1869.

MY DEAR NICOLAY:

I received to-day a letter from C—— H—— in which he tells me you are thinking of returning to your first love of journalism. He mentions your flirtation with the *C—— Republican.* I earnestly hope the surmise is true. I would be glad to see you spared to us, and kept away from the sunset a few years more, and a position of such power and influence as the *Republican*, under your management, would give you, is the best possible reason for your staying. On a large paper like that, with able subordinates, you would not have to do the drudgery which is necessary in a smaller paper—the *Journal*, for instance, where I wrote every day all the editorial matter. I am really grieved to learn that your eyes are not yet in a satisfactory condition, but you could manage in many ways to spare them.

I shall never be done regretting the put-up job by which Fate prevented my seeing you last summer. I had a thousand things to say and to ask which will not keep until next spring.

I still hold to my original plan of coming home next spring. I am glad I committed the folly of coming. I have seen a great deal and learned something. I speak the language—well enough to be understood and not well enough to be taken for a Spaniard—*à Dieu ne plaise!*

The amount of talk we have done since we came here is something portentous. I have been always on hand as a medium of communication, and so have seen more of the *gros bonnets* than usually falls to the lot of Secretaries. We have had a good enough time of it; have done nothing but show our amiable intentions. The Government here is crazy to accept our offered mediation but does not dare. The cession of Cuba to the Cubans—would be a measure too frightfully unpopular for the government to face in its present uncertain tenure. Still if it continues to grow stronger as now seems probable, it may take the bit in its teeth and do something after a while.

Some of the Spaniards are men of sense;—all of them have an astounding facility of expression which is simply incomprehensible to one of our stammering Teutonic race. Castelar, for instance, is an orator such as you read of, and never see. His action is as violent as Forrest. His style as florid as Gibbon. His imagination and his memory equally ready and powerful. He never writes a speech. Yet every sentence even in a running debate when all the government hounds are yelping at him at once, is as finished and as elegantly balanced as if he had pondered all a rainy Sunday over it. I am afraid he will cease to be the Republican idol before long. He has too much sense and integrity to follow the lead of the socialist fanatics.

We are a little blue, just now, we Republicans. The Republican insurrection in Barcelona was premature and silly, and has injured the cause, which looked most promising a month ago. It is by no means hopeless yet, though the propaganda is checked for the moment. . . .

HAY TO WHITELAW REID.

New York Tribune, N. Y.
Monday, Dec., 1870.

MY DEAR MR. REID:

I have read all I could find for three or four years,[1] and don't believe I can do much worse. But why do you talk of columns and halves?—the foregoing ones have not averaged a half. However, I will go to-night—see with what eyes are left me, and write till the time of stereotypers comes and the voice of the devil is heard in the hall.

I am so seedy that I will go home for a nap,

[1] Files of the *New York Tribune* for the period.

and come out this evening so fresh that a daisy would look *blasé* beside me.

Dios le guarde a V. muchos años.

HAY TO NICOLAY.

Legation of the United States.
Madrid, January 30, 1870.

MY DEAR NICOLAY:

. . . . I have no news for you. This Legation has absolutely nothing of importance now on its hands. There is a great deal of tiresome routine work which employs the fingers more than the brain, and, by way of keeping the circulation regular, there is dancing enough to keep the feet from rusting. I am getting rather tired of it, and shall begin to plume my wings for flight some time in the spring. I am sorry S—— has not had a better chance, but nothing was possible with F——'s system of platonic bullying. I am afraid Cuba is gone. This Government wants to sell out but dares not, and has no power to put a stop to the atrocities on the island. The only thing left to our Government is to do nothing and keep its mouth shut; or interfere to stop the horrors in

Cuba on the ground of humanity, or the damage resulting to American interests. . . .

HAY TO MAJOR GENERAL SICKLES.

Legation of the United States of America.
Madrid, May 1, 1870.

MY DEAR GENERAL:

I enclose my resignation of the post of Secretary of Legation in Spain, and beg that you will forward it to the Secretary of State.

I greatly regret that my pecuniary circumstances compel me to sever the official relations which have been rendered so pleasant by your unfailing kindness and consideration. I shall always remember with the liveliest satisfaction my service with you in Madrid and hope that in the future I may find some means of testifying my gratitude and regard.

I am, my dear General,
Your obliged and sincere friend and servant.

HAY TO MISS HARRIET K. LORING.

Madrid, June 30, 1870.

MY DEAR MISS LORING:

I am very glad Mr. Boott and you have not forgotten me, though my poor little verses seem as oddly wedded to his fine music as the beggar-maid to King Cophetua. I am glad he has begun to publish. His original and vigorous melodies cannot but be liked, and will be of positive advantage to the struggling art in our country. I hope you will convey to him my compliments and thanks.

I have a curious year to look back upon,—more entirely out of the world than any since I came into it. There have been almost no Americans in Madrid and I have not been out of the city but once. I went with Mrs. and Miss H—— and Miss Sara S—— to Toledo, and had a few halcyon days favored by fate, weather, and other accessories, in that delicious old town. I have rarely had such larks,—the ladies went crazy sketching adorable doorways, and I sat by, on the shady side, and chaffed the picturesque beggars grouped around in the rags of the period. I felt the coil of cares slipping away from me, and leaving me young and appreciative again as when "I roamed a young Westerner, o'er the green bluff, and climbed thy steep summit, oh Warsaw, of mud."

For the first time since I can remember I have been busy this year, and it does not suit my complexion. There is a good deal to do in the Legation, and I have imposed a good deal of work upon myself beside, having gotten interested in Spanish History. I have a veritable work-shop for the fellows who know things. I cannot conceive how a man like Mr. M—— should have preferred E—— with its pitiful annoyances, to A—— with its quiet and its archives. I should like to read about twenty-years. The first ten would be necessary to reach the proper point of humility, and the last one might hope to gain something substantial.

I expected to return before this, but there has not been a favorable moment yet for me to take leave.

I do not know whether I ever directed a letter to you at W——, or whether W—— is your P. O. or your ancestral towers. I will send this and find out. Towns are sometimes absurdly named. I lived at Spunky Point on the Mississippi. This is a graphic, classic, characteristic designation of a geographical and ethnological significance. But some idiots, just before I was born, who had read Miss P——, thought Warsaw would be much more genteel, and so we are Nicodemussed into nothing for the rest of time. I hope every man who was engaged in the outrage is called Smith in Heaven.

Mrs. E—— and pretty Fanny are in Paris. Mrs. W—— and her daughters, who are growing cleverer every day, are there also. I had a charming sad letter from Mrs. W—— some time ago, keeping his memory green. W—— and F—— and L—— and A—— and I have dined together hundreds of pleasant evenings. I can see them and hear them all to-night,—W——'s fantastic fun, F——'s lambent humor, L——'s crabbed wit, and A——'s gentle culture. I knew so many clever people in Washington that there will be a sort of insipidity about society the rest of my life, I suppose.

Present my regards to your houseful of them, if you please.